THE EIGHT BALL BIBLE

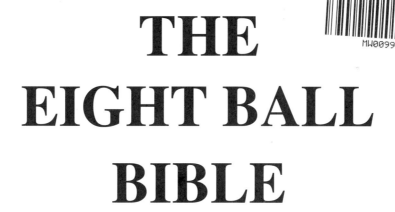

Shot Safety Forever

by **R GIVENS**

A GUIDE TO BAR TABLE PLAY

First Edition
8-BALL EXPRESS
RENO, NV

ISBN 0-9747273-7-7

ACKNOWLEDGEMENTS

Many thanks to Neil Kantor for the unwavering encouragement, sound advice and meaningful support that made this book possible.

Credit must also be given to my old teacher Bud Harris (Three time US 3 Cushion Champion) for the kindly patient instruction that rid me of the myths and erroneous thinking common in the billiard world and taught me a logical, fundamentally sound approach to the cue sports.

The style of play in this book is the direct result of Bud Harris's logical thinking about billiards even though we never played a single game of 8-ball.

CONTENTS

———————— ❽ ————————

♫♪ ♪ "the hours I spend with a cue in my hand are golden" ♪ ♫♪

Professor Harold Hill

The Music Man © 1950 Meredith Willson

———————— ❽ ————————

GLOSSARY

A

ACTION: *1.* The spin and force applied to a ball. *2.* A money game.

ACQUIRED ENGLISH: Collision induced rotation caused by an angular hit on a cushion or an object ball. The amount of english acquired is small, but sometimes significant. Collision induced english is responsible for Throw.

AIR SHOT: A 3 cushion billiard shot where the cue ball hits three or more cushions before striking the first object ball.

AUTOPILOT: The blissful state of dead stroke where no conscious thought is required to play well.

B

BACKER: Someone who finances another player's bets.

BAD HIT: *1.* Failure to hit the appropriate ball. *2.* A foul.

BALK: The space between the head string and the head rail. Sometimes called the "kitchen."

BALKLINE BILLIARDS: The toughest billiard game ever invented.

BALL ACTION: Technically, any movement of a ball. In this book, the term *ball action* applies to the effects of spin, force, and angle on the cue ball and object balls. English, draw, follow, and throw are examples of ball action.

BALL–IN–HAND: The dreadful situation when your opponent is allowed to place the cue ball anywhere on the table and shoot any ball he/she chooses after a foul or a scratch. In some games, players must shoot from within the kitchen after a foul.

BANK: A shot where the cue ball or an object ball rebounds off one or more cushions.

BAR BOX: A coin operated tavern table. Usually 3.5' x 7' (40" x 80").

BARRICADE: A natural (usually) arrangement of balls well suited for hiding the cue ball behind for safety purposes. A valuable asset in eight–ball.

BEHIND THE 8–BALL: *1.* To be literally snookered by the eight–ball. *2.* Figuratively any very bad situation on or off the table.

BIG BERTHA: A 5' x 10' table. Years ago these professional sized tables were known as *Rebel Killers* in the North because Southern players used to 4' x 8' and 4-1/2' x 9' tables were easy pickings on the big boards.

BIG TABLE: A 4.5' x 9' (50" x 100") table.

BILLIARD: *1.* A carom. *2.* A point in a carom game.

BLOCKER: *1.* A snooker ball(s). *2.* A barricade.

BLACK: *1.* A billiard ball marked with a black dot used to identify each player's cue ball. **AKA** The *Spot*. *2.* The seven–ball in snooker.

BODY ENGLISH: An aerobic form of sympathetic magic intended to influence the outcome of one's own or an opponent's shot through bodily gyrations.

BRAGGING RIGHTS: The uncontested superiority of a winner after a clear-cut victory.

BREAK SHOT: *1.* The first shot in a game. *2.* A play to open up a cluster of balls.

BYE: When a player (or a team) has no opponent in a tournament round he/she drew a *bye*. Seeded players get *byes*.

C

CALLED SHOT: The designated ball and pocket where the shooter intends to score.

CANNON: An old term for a carom or billiard.

CAROM: A score in billiards where the cue ball glances from one ball to another. Cushions may also be contacted in making caroms.

CATBIRD SEAT: An invincible position insuring victory.

CENTER SPOT: The exact center of the table. Balls are spotted on the center spot in some games.

CHALK: A friction increasing substance applied to the cue tip to provide non–slip contact between the cue tip and the cue ball.

CHEATING THE POCKET: Driving an object ball into one side or the other of a pocket to create a better carom angle for the cue ball.

THE CHEESE: *1.* The 9–ball. *2.* The money ball. *3.* The cash.

CHIRPING: The insufferable egotism of a bad winner crowing, bragging, ego tripping, and rehashing good shots, tactical successes and opposition errors after a victory. Chirping is outlawed by several international treaties in the interests of global peace.

CHOKE: To develop a paralysis in the shooting arm due to pressure. According to champions there are two kinds of players— those who admit they choke and those who lie.

CLEARANCE: A British term for a table run.

CLUSTER: A group of balls touching or very close to each other.

COATING: An unsavory maneuver perfected by some old-time players to obstruct the referee's or an opponent's view of a shot to prevent detection of a foul or a misplay.

COMBINATION: A shot involving two or more balls.

CONTACT POINT: The spot on an object ball or a cushion that must be hit to score.

CORNER HOOKED: When the side of the pocket blocks a direct shot at the object ball.

COWBOY POOL: *1.* To play with unrestrained aggression like the gunfight at the OK Corral. *2.* Also a pool game.

CRUTCH: A demeaning term for the mechanical bridge.

CUE: The tapered, usually, wooden stick used to strike the cue ball. **AKA** A cue stick.

CUE BALL: The white, unnumbered ball, struck by the cue in the course of play.

CUE BALL MAN: An expert position player.

CUE TIP: *1.* The piece of leather or composite material on the end of the cue that strikes the cue ball. *2.* The amount of english applied to the cue ball is measured in *tips*.

CUSHIONS: The cloth covered rubber bumpers bordering the playing surface of pool and billiard tables.

D

DEAD SHOT: A ball that cannot be missed.

DEAD STROKE: To play at peak efficiency. To "shoot the lights out." To be in the land of "can't miss." To be in the *Zone*.

DEFENSIVE SHOT: Where the shooter attempts to improve the pattern for his/her group in the next inning while leaving the opposition safe. Strong defensive moves can be extremely aggressive in nature and give the lie to the term *safety*.

DETECTIVE: An eyeballer who knows everything worth knowing that goes on in a poolroom. Such as who's in stroke or not, what everybody's best game is, who will bet, and most important, who has the cash. A valuable source of information.

DIAMONDS: The ivory, plastic, or mother of pearl spots on the rails subdividing pool and billiard tables. Diamonds divide the distance between the noses of the cushions. The long rail has eight divisions and the short rail has four divisions.

Diamonds are used as aids for aiming banks and cushion billiard shots. Many diamond systems have been invented based on these spots, but the original purpose of the diamonds was purely decorative. **NOTE—** Diagrams in this book show the zero, four and eight diamond positions on the long rails and the zero and four diamonds on the short rails for the benefit of players using systems.

DOG IT: To miss a shot you would ordinarily make. Pressure or carelessness causes dogging.

DOLLY PARTON: A break shot that's all bust and no balls.

DOUBLE HIT: Hitting the cue ball two or more times on a shot. A foul.

DUCK: *1.* An easy shot. *2.* To play safe.

DRIVE: The distance an object ball travels after being struck with the cue ball or another ball.

E

ENGLISH: *1.* In this book, the term applies to rotation produced by striking the cue ball to the left or right of the vertical axis. *2.* Any angular shift of the axis of rotation from parallel to the bed of the table, including angular rotation acquired from hitting a ball or a cushion. *3.* Draw and follow are not defined as english unless the axis of rotation has an angle to the bed of the table.

EYEBALLER: A *fan*.

F

FAN: *1.* To hit a ball very thin is to *fan* it. *2.* A billiard enthusiast.

FEATHER: To hit an object ball very thin.

FISH: A mark who bets despite the fact he/she has no hope of winning. Sometimes referred to as a tuna, mackerel, mullet, or some other food fish.

FOLLOW: A rolling cue ball caused by striking the ball above center or the roll acquired from the friction of the cloth. Follow can be "lively" or "dead" depending on the rate of rotation relative to the forward speed of the cue ball.

FOOT RAIL: The short rail at the end of the table where the balls are racked.

FOOT SPOT: A spot exactly in the center of a line drawn between the second diamonds at the foot of the table. Balls are spotted on the foot spot after scratches and fouls in some games.

FOOT STRING: A line drawn from the foot spot to the center of the foot rail. Balls are spotted on the foot string when a ball occupies the foot spot.

FORCE: *n.* A good player. *i.e.* A real *force* on the table.

FORCED ERROR: Compelling an opponent to foul, scratch or make some other mistake.

FOUL: An infraction of the rules, such as touching a moving ball, hitting the wrong ball, making an illegal shot or sending the cue ball into a pocket. Fouls are punished by loss of turn, loss of points, spotting balls and/or giving the incoming player *Ball–In–Hand*.

FREE SHOT: See *SHOT–SAFETY*.

FROZEN: When a ball is touching a cushion or another ball.

G

GAME BALL: *1.* The winning shot. *2.* A ball that sets up a game winning sequence.

GATHER SHOT: A play in carom billiards that brings the balls together for easy scoring opportunities. Top old-time balkline players could consistently drive an object ball 20 feet or more around a 5' x 10' billiard table and land the ball within a few of inches of the mark every time. On shorter drives the experts landed the balls on a dime! The goal was to land all three balls under the player's hand at a favorable angle for nursing. (See *Nurse/Nursing*)

GENERAL: *n.* A master tactician who controls the game like a commander marching an army around.

GET A JOB: A derogatory remark suggesting that a player's game is below par and that he/she should seek honest work.

GOOD HIT: A legal shot.

GULLIES: Runways under the table that carry pocketed balls to a compartment under the foot rail.

GUTTERS: Grooves that the balls wear into the cloth one-half ball space away from the cushions on poorly maintained equipment. Experienced players use the gutters to aid in scoring.

H

HANDICAP: A modification of scoring or the rules enabling players of different abilities to compete on more even terms.

HANGER: *1.* A ball on the very edge of the pocket. *2.* A shot so easy Minnie Mouse could make it left–handed.

HEAD RAIL: The short rail with the manufacturer's nameplate on it. **NOTE—** Bar tables seldom have nameplates— the head rail is the end of a bar table where the cue ball returns. Diagrams in this book are marked with a nameplate to help the reader distinguish the head from the foot of the table whenever discussed.

HEAD SPOT: A spot in the center of the head string. Balls are spotted here in some games.

HEAD STRING: A line between the second diamonds on the long rails at the head of the table. This line marks the limits of the kitchen or balk area.

HIGH ROLLER: A player who bets with both hands.

HOOKED: To be snookered.

HOUSE RULES: Local regulations which players are expected to obey. Always check for regional variations of the rules before you begin playing. Getting the rules straight avoids many needless arguments.

HUNGARIAN LOCK: An absolute cinch— like King Kong arm wrestling Tom Thumb.

HUSTLER: *1.* A superior player. *2.* A go-getter.

I

ICE: To freeze a ball on another ball or a cushion.

IN JAIL: A superlative safety where the shooter has no legal shot. An impossible position.

IN ORBIT: To perform at a stellar level.

INNING: Consists of one turn for each player.

INSIDE ENGLISH: Sidespin on the same side of the cue ball as the direction of a cut shot.

INSURANCE BALL: A ball left in position to provide a back up shot to continue a run after breaking a cluster.

INTENTIONAL FOUL: A dangerous tactic that gives an opponent *Ball–In–Hand*.

J

JAM UP: *1.* To be playing at top speed. *2.* Anything exceptionally good.

JAMBOREE: A gathering of top money players for serious action.

JAWS: The playing surface inside the points of a pocket.

K

KEY BALL: *1.* A ball that leads to easy position for the game ball, a break shot or a problem ball. *2.* A critical shot in a run. *3.* An *Insurance Ball*.

KICK SHOT: When the cue ball strikes one or more cushions before hitting an object ball.

KISS SHOT: *1.* A carom of one ball off another. *2.* An uncontrolled shot that *kisses* a ball into or out of scoring— a lucky or an unlucky play.

L

LAGGING: A procedure used to decide the order of play. Players simultaneously bank a ball off the foot cushion. The player landing his/her ball closest to the head cushion has the option of shooting first.

LAMB: A pushover who cannot win even with the best of it.

LEAVE: The position of the balls after a shot.

LIE: The position of the balls on the table.

LION: A top money player who might eat you alive if he gets into your bankroll.

LOCK–ARTIST: A sucker hustler who won't bet that it snows at the North Pole unless he gets odds. Lock–artists pretend to be smart matchmakers, but they never play anyone with half a chance of beating them.

LOCKSMITH: See *LOCK–ARTIST*.

LONG STRING: A line drawn from the foot spot to the center of the foot rail. Balls are spotted on the long string when the foot spot is blocked.

LONG RAILS: The side rails on billiard tables and the rails adjoining the side pockets on pool tables. In earlier days when pool tables only had four corner pockets, the side rails were indeed the long rails.

M

MARK: A poor matchmaker who will bet on his game.

MASSÉ: A shot made by striking down at the cue ball causing it to curve. Some League rules do not allow **massé** shots and "House Rules" in many locations prohibit **massé** shots.

MECHANICAL BRIDGE: A stick with a notched plate on the end used for hard to reach shots. **AKA:** the crutch, granny stick, ladies aid, crow's foot and rake.

MEET MR BRUNSWICK: A needling remark made after a player freezes the cue ball on the head rail near the nameplate a couple of time zones from the nearest playable shot.

MINNIE: A billiard player's term for an easy shot.

MISCUE: A dismal shot where the cue tip slips off the cue ball usually causing a disaster.

MISS: *1.* Failure to accomplish the intended shot. *2.* Failing to contact a ball from the player's group— a foul .

MONEY BALL: A pay ball — the 9–ball or the 8–ball etc.

MONEY PLAYER: A pressure player, regardless of ability, whose skill is not diminished by the necessity to win. A money player who does not need stakehorses or stimulants to win.

MOVE: A strategic play.

MR SNOW: The cue ball.

N

NAMEPLATE: A device on the head rail of the table advertising the name of the table maker. Most bar tables do not have nameplates. On bar tables the head of the table is where the cue ball returns. Instead of nameplates bar tables have the manufacturer's logo is embossed on metal plates surrounding the corner pockets. Nevertheless, nameplates are shown in the diagrams to distinguish the head from the foot of the table for discussion purposes.

NATURAL: An easy shot.

NEST: The large cluster of *eggs* typically left in the rack area after a one-pocket break.

NIP DRAW: A draw shot made when the cue ball and object ball are less than an inch apart.

NIT: A player who won't bet.

NOMINATED BALL: The called ball.

NURSE/NURSING: Techniques used in Straight–Rail and balkline games to keep the balls close to the cushions and close to each other for easy scoring. Master players got so good at nursing the balls that they killed Straight–Rail by running thousands of points.

O

OBJECT BALL: *1.* The ball that must be hit. *2.* The ball you are trying to hit, or any other ball in your group. *3.* Any ball other than the cue ball.

OCEAN TABLE: A 6' x 12' championship size snooker table.

OFF ANGLE: When the cue ball is on the wrong side of a ball to play easy position to the next shot.

OIL: An attempt to score that leaves nothing for the opposition if the shot is missed. See *SHOT–SAFETY*.

ON: Any ball that can be made is on. A combination is on if the ball scores.

ON THE HILL: To be within one victory of winning a match.

ON THE SNAP: To make the money ball on the break.

ON THE SQUARE: The absolute brutal truth.

ONE-BALL-HELL: A dangerous situation where a player misses with one or two balls in their group left. Being restricted to shooting at one or two balls is a tremendous disadvantage that frequently causes a loss.

ONE HOLE: *1.* A player is "in the one hole" when he/she needs one point to win. *2.* A name for one–pocket.

ONE POCKET: A game where each player is limited to scoring in one of the corner pockets at the foot of the table. Considered by many to be the most difficult pool game. Bud Harris called one pocket "the billiard player's pool game" because of the precise ball control necessary to play well.

OPEN SEA: Center area of the table well away from the cushions.

OPEN TABLE: *1.* An eight ball term indicating that the shooter has choice of stripes or solids. *2.* A situation where the balls are well scattered and easy to run.

OUT IN SPACE: When the balls are off the cushions and clear of each other.

OUT OF LINE: *1.* To land at an angle where position for the next shot is difficult or impossible. *2.* A mistake in handling a game, such as spotting a player the seven ball when he/she can beat you even. *3.* Unacceptable behavior.

OUT SHOT: *1.* The winning ball. *2.* A shot that sets up an easy sequence to finish a game.

OUT OF STROKE: To be off your game and play poorly.

OWN THE TABLE: To be in dead stroke. To be in the *Zone*.

P

PACK: The rack or a cluster of balls.

PATTERN PLAY: Planning the simplest sequence of shots to run a rack.

PINBALL SHOT: A reckless or desperate shot that sends balls wildly careening around the table with unforeseen results.

PLAN B: A revision in pattern play resulting from a misplayed shot.

PLAY LIKE MOSCONI: To make an outstanding shot. To play brilliantly.

PLAYER: Technically, any participant in a game, but with the right inflection the word refers to a top shooter — "He/she is a *player*."

POCKET A PIECE: One pocket.

POCKET MAN: An exceptional shotmaker.

POCKET SPEED: When the object ball rolls into the pocket with just enough force to drop in. When the object ball *rolls* into the pocket

POSITION PLAY: An attempt to place the balls favorably for the next shot.

POT: *1.* A British snooker term for pocketing a ball. *2.* An innocent drug plant that drives hypocrites into fits of Reefer Madness.

PRESSURE: A condition that sometimes causes mental debilitation in intense competition. Pressure causes confusion, choking, dogging and unforced errors. Pressure also causes some players to excel. We call them champions.

R

RACE: A contest where the players compete to win a certain number of games. *i.e.* "They played a *race* to seven."

RACK: *1.* The triangle used to position the balls at the beginning of a game. *2.* Also the balls themselves— "He/she ran the *rack*."

RAKE: The mechanical bridge.

RAILBIRD: A spectator.

RAIL SHOT: When the cue ball is frozen or very close to a cushion.

RIDE A BALL: *v.* To forcefully propel a ball [or group of balls] around the table hoping that it will find a pocket. Blasting a ball gives it a *ride*.

ROAD RACK: Bad racking. The infamous *mud rack* or *slug rack* created by leaving spaces between the balls, twisting the rack or any other skullduggery done to unfairly prevent an opponent from making a ball on the break.

ROB: To beat badly.

ROCK: The cue ball.

ROLL: The unforeseen result of a shot, such as "a good roll or a bad roll." A lucky or an unlucky shot depending on the outcome.

ROLL OFF: When an out of level table causes a ball to deviate from the expected path.

ROUGH HUSTLER: A creep who resorts to crude sharking tactics to distract opponents while they are shooting. A person to avoid.

RUN: The number of points made in an inning.

RUN OUT: *1.* Making all of balls from the break to win a game. *2.* To finish a game.

RUN THE RACK: To make all of the balls in your group plus the eight in your first inning.

S

SAFETY: An attempt to leave an opponent with a difficult or impossible shot when a player cannot finish the game. Safety play is often used to solve difficult patterns. The cue ball must hit the correct ball and drive a ball to a rail afterwards. It is not required to call safeties.

SANDBAGGING: The dishonest practice of playing below ability to get an unfair advantage in handicap play.

SCORE: *1.* To make a point. *2.* "Knowing the *score*" means to understand the situation exactly. *3.* To win money— "He *scored* $100."

SCRATCH: *1.* To send the cue ball into a pocket or off the playing surface onto the floor. *2.* Failure to make a legal safety. *3.* An unexpected (*i.e.* lucky) result that causes a shot to score or miss, often due to an unanticipated kiss.

SELL OUT: To make an unforgiving error that insures defeat. **AKA** selling the farm – selling the ranch – selling the plantation – etc.

SEND TO THE RACK: A reference to opponents putting their cues in the cue rack when they admit defeat.

SHAPE: The position of the balls. Getting shape means positioning the cue ball at a good distance and a good angle to score and continue your run.

SHARK: *1. n.* A good player who bets. *2. v.* A disreputable attempt to cause a miss by distracting an opponent.

SHOT–SAFETY: An attempt to pocket a ball and play position to continue the run while leaving an opponent behind the proverbial eight ball.

SHOOT OUT: *1.* To make a maximum effort to score without regard for risks. *2.* To play at top speed.

SHORTEN UP: A reference to shortening the stroke and being more cautious in a tough game. Also, to choke.

SHORTSTOP: A good player who doesn't quite measure up to professional standards. The class just below the rank of *Player*.

SLATE: The playing surface under the cloth.

SLOP: An unintentional lucky play.

SNEAKY PETE: A jointed cue used by gamblers that looks like a house cue.

SNITCH: A low-life double-crosser who betrays friends and strangers alike to gain favor or to escape punishment for his/her own crimes. A spiritual descendant of Judas. **AKA:** Rat.

SNOOKER: When the direct path from the cue ball to the object ball is blocked by another ball.

SPEED: *1.* The friction between the cloth and balls. *i.e.* a table is fast or slow. *2.* The level of play. At top speed, a player is in dead stroke. *3.* A player's skill— "He/she's a mighty fast player." *4.* Stimulant drugs such as cocaine and methamphetamines used to enhance performance.

SPOT: *1.* A handicap given a weaker player. *2.* A cue ball having a black dot on it used in billiard games to distinguish it from the white. *3.* Also known as the black. This term is becoming obsolete now that yellow cue balls are replacing the spot. (Also See: *Foot Spot, Head Spot*)

STACK: The rack.

STAKEHORSE: A financial angel, or devil in some players eyes, who puts up the money for a percentage of the winnings, usually 50%, but more if the player is desperate.

STALLING: *1.* Deliberate delaying tactics designed to upset an opponent. *2.* Playing under speed hoping to increase the bet.

STANCE: A player's form while shooting.

STARTER SHOT: A playable ball left in position to make it easy to resume a run after a safety in eight ball.

STEERING: *1.* An ill advised attempt to get more english by twisting the cue to the side during the delivery. *2.* A fundamental error caused by an instinctive attempt to correct faulty stroke alignment. *3.* When a *Detective* advises on who to play or not play.

STERILE CUCKOO: A deceptive shot that seems playable, but is actually unmakable. A *Stiff*.

STICK: A cue.

STIFF: A shot that may appear to be on, but is unmakable because of a kiss, the angle or some other subtle reason.

STONE: The cue ball.

STRING: *1.* A wire over the table with buttons on it for tallying the score. *2.* A run of points.

STRINGING: An old term for lagging still used in Britain.

SUCKER: A sure loser who always gets in over his head.

SWEET SPOT: The angle and contact point on the rack that makes the most balls.

SWEATER: A fan or spectator who worries over games and contests, usually without any financial interest in the outcome.

T

TABLE ROLL: When a ball rolls off a true line due to an out of level table or a warped slate.

TAPIOCA: The sad state of affairs when a money player has empty pockets.

THROW: *1.* An effect of english that propels the object ball to one side or the other of a no english carom line. Right english *throws* the object ball to the left and vice versa. *2.* When a combination is hit from the side the object ball is *thrown* off the natural line away from the side the cue ball struck. *3.* Maximum *throw* is approximately one inch per foot.

TRAFFIC: Balls that potentially obstruct position routes.

TRICK SHOT: *1.* A fancy shot where the balls are positioned by hand. *2.* A spectacular shot made in game play.

TV POCKETS: Easy pockets used to avoid embarrassing the stars in televised events.

TWO WAY SHOT: See *Shot–Safety*.

U

UNFORCED ERROR: A needless foul, miss, unfavorable position play or some other bad move caused by stupidity, ignorance, pressure or carelessness.

W

WEIGHT: Giving a handicap is taking on weight.

WHO SHOT JOHN: Inane conversation not pertaining to the business at hand.

WHITE: A cue ball used in billiard games to distinguish it from the *Spot*.

WHITEY: The cue ball.

WINDOW: A gap in a barricade that allows a direct shot at an object ball.

WING SHOT: A trick shot where an object ball is rolled down the table and pocketed on the fly. Just to show everyone what real talent is all about Ralph Greenleaf made *combination* wing shots on tough pocket 5' x 10' tables.

WINNER: A player who rarely beats him/herself and is a threat to whack the game out at any moment.

WIRE: Same as string. To get on the wire means to score.

WOODPILE SHOT: A play so good that the opposition uses their cue for firewood and becomes a bingo player or a TV wrestling fan.

Z

THE ZONE: The place where skill, knowledge and execution converge for the highest level of play. To be in the *Zone* is to perform at peak level.

KITCHEN AREA

SHORT RAIL OR HEAD CUSHION

HEAD STRING

HEAD SPOT

LONG OR SIDE RAILS

CENTER SPOT

FOOT SPOT

SHORT RAIL OR FOOT CUSHION

MODERATE HALF BALL HIT

CUE BALL DIAGRAMS SHOW SUGGESTED SPEEDS AND STRIKING POINTS.

ⓒ ① ⊘

BLACK BALLS SHOW ORIGINAL POSITIONS

ⓒ ① ⊘

GREY BALLS SHOW MOVED POSITIONS

DASHED BALLS SHOW CONTACT POINTS ON BALLS AND CUSHIONS

BLACK LINES SHOW FIRST SHOT IN DIAGRAM

GREY LINES SHOW SUBSEQUENT SHOTS IN SERIES

DASHED LINES SHOW OPTIONAL ROUTES

GREY AREAS SHOW POSITION TARGETS

Illustrations represent a 40" x 80" bar table drawn to exact scale.

The Zero – Four and Eight Diamond positions on the long rail and Zero and Four Diamond positions on the short rails are shown in all illustrations.

Diamond markers divide the distance between the noses of the cushions.

Illustrations show a nameplate which rarely appears on real bar tables to denote the head of the table. (The head of the table is where the cue ball returns.)

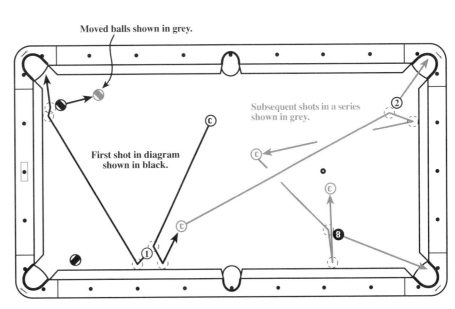

Moved balls shown in grey.

First shot in diagram shown in black.

Subsequent shots in a series shown in grey.

RULES

Here are the rules for bar table 8–ball that *I* prefer. There are a few differences from the rules used in some leagues, like counting an eight on the break as a win, instead of a loss, but these are the basic rules in most 8–Ball Pool Leagues.

The rules below differ in some respects from those used in some leagues. Readers are advised to learn the rules they use in competition well. There's nothing more frustrating than a loss caused by misunderstanding the rules.

The Eight Ball Bible text and diagrams are based on the rules below.

EIGHT BALL BIBLE RULES FOR TAVERN PLAY

Every player is expected to know these Rules.

THE RACK: Head ball on the foot spot with the Eight Ball in the middle and a ball from each group on opposite foot corners. All balls should be frozen to adjacent balls.

OPENING BREAK: The home player flips the coin, the visiting player calls the flip. The winner of the flip has the option to break or rack. Breaking shooter, with cue ball behind the head string, must either 1) pocket a ball, or 2) drive four balls to any rail(s). If the shooter fails to make a legal break, the opposing player may elect to shoot the balls as they lie or have balls re-racked and break them him/herself.

8–Ball pocketed on the break is a win (including on a re-rack). 8–Ball pocketed on break with a scratch is loss of game.

CHOICE OF GROUP: The choice of stripes or solids is not determined on the break shot even if a ball(s) from only one group is pocketed. The table remains open until a player legally pockets an object ball(s) from only one group (stripes or solids) *after* the break shot. Any ball, including the 8–Ball, may be used for a combination shot or a carom shot while the table is still open. If a player scratches or misses while the table is open, the table remains open even if a ball(s) from one group is made. The table remains open until a ball or balls from only one group is made on a legal shot. Players may ask the Captain or Referee if table is open without calling a "time-out".

LEGAL SHOT: On all shots except when the table is open, the shooter must hit one of his/her group of balls first and then 1) pocket any ball except the 8–Ball before its turn, or 2) cause the cue ball or any other ball to contact a rail. If a ball balanced on the lip of a pocket falls into the pocket before the cue ball is struck by the next shooter and assuming the table is not bumped or jostled by the incoming shooter, the first player may continue at the table, subject to the rules regarding the 8–Ball below.

FOULS: The following infractions are fouls

> 1. Failure to execute a legal shot as defined above.

> 2. A scratch shot: cue ball falling into pocket or bouncing off the table.

> 3. Shooting without at least one foot touching the floor, except 1.) where the bar fails to provide a working bridge, 2.) when a bench or a permanent obstacle blocks the reach, it may be sat upon.

> 4. Moving or touching the cue ball by means other than a legal play.

> 5. Jump shots and full massés.

> 6. Causing an object ball to drop into a pocket by intentionally bumping or pushing the table after completion of the stroke.

> 7. Touching or interfering with any ball while it is moving on the table.

> 8. Coaching.

PENALTY: *After all fouls the incoming player may place the cue ball anywhere on the table for position on the next shot.* The cue ball may be positioned by hand, ferrule or shaft (using the tip constitutes a foul) of the stick any number of times until the shot is executed.

ACCIDENTALLY TOUCHING OR MOVING AN OBJECT BALL IS NOT A FOUL UNLESS: 1) the ball was in motion when touched or 2) the moved ball contacts a moving ball. Opponents may have moved balls replaced in their original position(s) or leave them where they are.

OBJECT BALLS ACCIDENTALLY MOVED: Only the shooters involved in the game being played may touch any ball on the table. For example, if a team member other than the shooter handles the cue ball during a "time out" (in a ball–in–hand situation) it is a foul and ends the shooter's inning. If an object ball is touched or accidentally moved during a player's turn (for instance when the cue stick bumps another ball during or after stroking) it is not a foul as long as the moved ball comes to rest without hitting any ball in motion. It is the responsibility of the opposing player to request that the moved ball be addressed. Shooter must allow the moved ball to be returned to its original position or forfeit game.

The opposing player has the option to restore the ball to its original position or leave it where it lies.

DOUBLE HIT RULE: When the cue ball is less than a chalk cube's width from the object ball no foul will be called for a double hit providing the player uses a continuous stroke. This rule is a concession to avoid endless arguments over difficult to call double hits that do not come up all that often, but always cause an argument when they do. However, if a player hits the cue ball a second time after completing the stroke (i.e. the cue ball comes back into the cue) it is a foul. Also if the shooter double hits into a third ball it is a foul.

RULE CLARIFICATIONS: May be requested by a player at any time during his/her game in the presence of both Captains without using a "time out."

INTERFERENCE WITH SHOOTER: It is the Captain's and each player's responsibility to keep bystanders away from the playing area and otherwise protect the shooter from being bumped or jostled while shooting. If a player is bumped during a shot, the shooter has the option of having the balls re-positioned as they were (if possible) and replaying the shot or may accept the position and continue shooting if a ball from his/her group was made.

OBJECT BALLS JUMPED OFF TABLE: If an object ball is jumped off the table, it is a miss and loss of turn, not a foul. Balls jumped off the table from the opponent's group will be pocketed: balls from the shooter's group will be spotted on the foot spot.

SPOTTING BALLS: Balls are spotted on the foot spot or as close behind it on the long string as other balls permit, frozen to any interfacing ball, but not frozen to the cue ball, a small gap must be left between a spotted ball and the cue ball.

FROZEN BALLS: When an object ball is frozen to the rail, the cue ball must contact the frozen ball first and then: 1) pocket the frozen ball or any other object ball, or 2) drive the frozen ball or the cue ball to another rail or drive another object ball to any rail. It is the opposing player's responsibility prior to the shot being taken to call the intended ball frozen, if the opposing player fails to indicate that a ball is frozen, the ball will be deemed not frozen. Rule applies only to the ball the shooter obviously intends to hit first. All other balls on the table are considered not to be frozen.

MARKING SHOTS ILLEGAL: It is not appropriate to use chalk, saliva or other markers to line up a shot. If this occurs, the opponent is free to pick up the chalk or erase any mark and caution the shooter that this constitutes unsportsmanlike conduct. If this action continues after a warning, the opponent may call for forfeiture of the game.

DESIGNATING THE 8–BALL POCKET: The shooter must indicate the intended pocket by placing a marker next to it. The marker does not have to be "moved" if it is already next to the intended pocket from a previous attempt. Caroms, kisses or banks do not need to be called. Pocketing the 8–Ball in an unmarked pocket results in loss of game.

Marking the pocket eliminates arguments and disputes.

OPTION TO SPOT THE 8-BALL: If a player commits a foul and the opponent: is then left with none of his/her group of balls on the table. The opponent has the option of either 1) taking cue ball–in–hand anywhere on the table or 2) spotting the 8–Ball on the foot spot and taking ball–in–hand behind the head string.

LOSS OF GAME:
Any of the following result in loss of game:

1. Pocketing the 8–Ball while committing a foul, or with a cue ball scratch.

2. Pocketing the 8–Ball when it is not the player's legal object ball, or on the same stroke as the player's last ball(s) from his/her group.

3. Jumping the 8–Ball completely off the table. (A ball that bounces onto the rail and lands back on the table is not a foul.)

4. Pocketing the 8–Ball without marking the intended pocket.

5. Pocketing the 8–Ball in a pocket other than one marked.

6. Three consecutive fouls.

7. Captain or team members engaging in coaching when the player is shooting the 8–Ball.

8. Unsportsmanlike conduct such as harassment, intimidation, yelling or abusive language directed toward opposing Captain, referee or players.

WINNING: A player wins the game when the 8–ball is made on a legal shot after clearing all the balls in his/her group.

TIME OUT: Each player is permitted one "time out" per game, not to exceed two minutes, in order to seek advice from team members. Only the 5 players on the match score sheet and the team Captain, even if he/she is a not playing that night, may participate in the "time out." This does not include substitutes not shooting or anyone who is on a different team from the same bar. Only the player at the table, not the Captain nor any other team member may call a "time out."

NO COACHING: When the player's turn commences (and it does so immediately when the opponent's turn ends) team members, Captain and spectators may not talk to, advise, or discuss the shot strategy, or make comments to the shooter. The Captain should warn observers to refrain from making any comments to the shooter at the table. Please note however, that a casual reference to the match by an unaware spectator or bystander, or encouraging words from teammates such as "Drill it" or "Go for it" do not constitute coaching.

REFEREES: Team Captains referee regular season matches. The job of watching the table may be delegated to anyone on that night's team roster, at any time so that no one person need watch all the games. A Captain must let the opposing Captain know who is assigned to watch the table. Only the two players and the designated referees (both teams have a referee watching the game) may call a foul. A foul must be resolved before play resumes. Ignoring a foul call is unsportsmanlike conduct.

SPORTSMANLIKE CONDUCT: All players shall conduct themselves in a sportsmanlike manner. The tavern owner or bartender has the right to remove from the premises any player(s) whose conduct disturbs the peace of the premises. The offending player(s) shall forfeit all games for that evening which are not completed prior to his/her removal from the premises. If a match cannot continue because of a totally unsportsmanlike atmosphere in the tavern, and both teams are at fault, the Captains shall pick a new date to replay the match. If the tavern owner causes or contributes to the unsportsmanlike atmosphere, the **LEAGUE** shall issue a warning to the tavern owner. Disregard for this rule can result in expulsion from the **LEAGUE**.

SCORING: 15 games are played in each match during the regular season. The team winning 8 or more games wins the match. There are 5 players on each team. Each player plays 3 games with *different* members of the opposing team. The same players will not play each other twice in the same match. Team Captains must adjust the order of play to accommodate this rule.

LEAGUE STATISTICS: The **LEAGUE** hires a statistician to provide records of weekly team and individual won–lost percentages, table runs and eight on the break shots.

CATCH–22 — HOUSE RULES

When you play outside a league, always get the rules straight before starting a session. Every bar has house rules players are expected to obey. It is best to get any special rules clear before an infraction costs a game, starts an argument or precipitates a fight.

Asking to play using "league rules" means ***cue–ball–in–hand*** after fouls. The ***ball–in–hand*** rule is the key regulation. Most players in my area know the basic league rules even if they do not play in a league so just saying "league rules" usually gets things straight. If an opponent needs clarification of the rules make sure ***everything*** is clear ***before*** play begins.

When you explain the whole shebang you get to play with the rules ***you*** like.

If you play for money, the last thing you want is a fight or a loud prolonged argument over the rules. So get the rules straight right from the start.

PRACTICE

Pool and billiards are skill games. Just knowing the right moves doesn't help unless you can make the shots.

The old saying "practice makes perfect" only applies when you practice the **right** things. Practicing carelessly or practicing the wrong things actually makes matters worse because the habits developed in practice will be the same ones you take into game play.

Here are a few guidelines to make your practice sessions more profitable.

1. Learn good fundamentals first. Without good basics mastering pool is an impossible task. If you need help with stance, stroke or delivery find a qualified instructor to guide you.

2. Warm up with simple shots until the juices begin to flow. It's a waste of time to rehearse delicate shots before you get a feel for your stroke.

3. Always have a definite goal in mind. Aimlessly banging the balls around or "playing by yourself" does not lead to maximum improvement. Science has proved that people learn faster by sticking to one aspect of a problem at a time. In other words, if you decide to work on banks, spend most of the session on banks. Systematic practice will greatly improve your game.

4. After every miss or misplayed position, determine what the mistake was. Did you aim the shot correctly? Was the stroke right? Did you hit the shot too hard? Was the english wrong?

Finding the cause of a misplay before repeating the shot is much better than just setting a shot up again and again until you make it. Carefully observing the results of your "mistakes" can also be a source of considerable billiard knowledge over a period of time, so pay attention.

5. Keep practice sessions short. An hour or so of *heavy* concentration is plenty. You learn better while the mind is fresh, so avoid grueling drills that leave you exhausted mentally and physically. Ideally, you should practice daily.

6. Practice on full size tables (4-1/2' x 9') to sharpen your shooting eye, but *use an overweight bar cue ball* for maximum benefit. Using an overweight cue ball will expand your range on the bar box. Especially if you play long draws on the big table.[1]

7. Do not try to practice in games. The purpose of practice is correcting weaknesses, learning new techniques and strengthening good habits by repeating shots you want to learn. Since shots cannot be repeated in games it takes ten times longer to learn something new.

This is not to say that you cannot learn from competition. Competing is a very important part of developing your game, but do not confuse the benefits of competition with the advantages of practice. They are somewhat different.

[1] Don't be a jerk by stealing a cue ball. Buy an overweight same size Aramith Red
Dot (Dynamo) bar table cue ball from your local billiard supply shop.

When you play superior players, carefully observe how they manage game situations. You can learn effective ways of handling problems, but you'll have you wait until you get on the table by yourself to develop this newly found knowledge.

Watch tournaments and see how professionals play the game. When you see a shot worth learning take note and practice it later.

———————⑧———————

"When you are learning you need three kinds of action.

You need somebody you can beat, you need somebody that plays real close with you and you need someone better than you to learn from.

You need all three kinds of action."

Howard Vickery touring pro

———————⑧———————

THREE-BALL

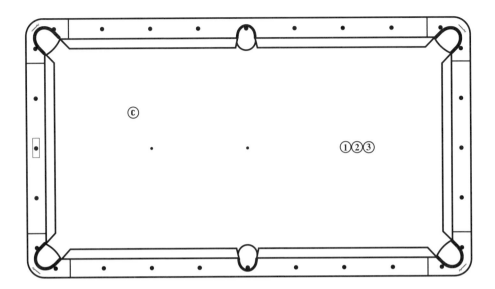

If you've read any basic pool books you already know that pattern play is supposed to be figured in increments of three. This is to say position is played from the first ball for an angle on the second ball that permits easy position on the third ball in the series. As each ball is made another ball is added to the chain.

That's the theory and it's logically correct as far as it goes. But in bar table 8–ball top competitors plan a shot for **every** ball including the eight **before** playing the first ball. Starting off without a good idea of how to finish a rack is the intermediate player's biggest mistake.

Three–ball is an excellent practice game for developing pattern play because three randomly moving balls create situations ranging from sublimely simple to virtually impossible. Figuring the best way to handle these random layouts stimulates the problem solving part of the mind and provides practical experience in handling a wide range of configurations.

Three–ball is an excellent game for teams to warm up for league matches. Usually teams are allowed 30 minutes to prepare for a match which means that each player on a five man team has about 6 minutes to warm–up. Three–ball is a much better use of this limited time than "playing each other" because everybody gets to shoot a few balls off.

THREE-BALL

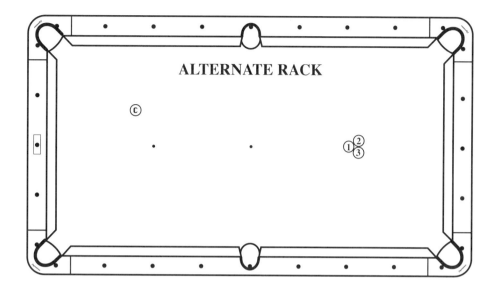

ALTERNATE RACK

RULES

The player sinking all three balls in the fewest shots wins.

A ball must be driven to the head rail on the break. No soft break allowed.

Players are limited to five shots to clear the table. If balls remain after five shots the player does not score.

A scratch or a foul ends a player's turn with no score.

Balls can be played in any order.

Shots do not have to be called.

Low score tie all tie.

COMMENT

Par for three–ball is four shots and there are a lot of threes. Among evenly matched players there are many ties. If money is involved each player antes up a new stake for each tie until one player gets the low score. This can be expensive after five or six ties for one game.

A NEW STYLE EMERGES

This book is about playing high-speed eight ball on **BAR TABLES**. Although some of the same principles apply on big tables this book is *not* a treatise for regulation 4–1/2' x 9' (50" x 100") table play. This instruction is strictly for conditions found on the 3–1/2' x 7' (40" x 80") coin operated tables found in bars, inns and taverns throughout the land.

There is a great divide between bar table play and competing on regulation equipment. The differences in visualizing and executing shots and strokes are so large that big table champions often approach bar competition with trepidation. This book is intended to educate players in the strategies and tactics necessary to compete effectively on coin operated tables.

Although pool is definitely a *skill game* this is not a manual for improving the reader's shooting techniques. Aside from a few pointers on the special conditions created by overweight cue balls, there is no advice here for improving your stroking ability. Those who need help developing executional skills are advised to find a good instructor.

The lessons are intended to help players who already know how to execute shots fairly well to develop some insight into the strategic aspects of eight–ball. The lessons here teach effective game plans for winning in topflight eight ball play, not the physical skills needed to play well.

Players who think high-speed eight ball is purely a sharpshooting duel will be surprised at some of the tactics and strategies recommended. The style of play recommended is similar to modern one pocket where champions *play not to lose* until a winning opportunity arises whereupon they run the game out. Top one-pocket players try to set up game running situations instead of sniping back and forth a ball or two at a time. They are constantly looking for a shot that opens a table run while keeping their opponent paralyzed.

Nine-ball players *play to win* because the game favors aggressive play, but this is not true in 8-ball where many racks are simply too difficult to run right away. In 8-ball risk taking must be considered more carefully because mistakes are more likely to beat you. This does not mean passing up opportunities to win, but more certainty of the outcome is necessary before committing to a run in 8–ball.

In 9–ball it is often possible to play a strong safety with only two of three balls on the table. In 8–ball an effective unplanned safety at the end of a rack is seldom possible. Once a player commits to a run in 8–ball failure to go all the way usually means a loss.

The fencing and parrying that goes on when the balls are tied up is intended to improve the shooter's chances while denying opponents opportunities to win the game. Extreme risk taking is avoided in preference to aggressive safety play. Like modern one pocket everything is predicated on avoiding game losing moves while simultaneously attempting to create game winning opportunities for the next turn at the table.

A NEW WAY OF THINKING

After months of intense training under Bud Harris's[1] watchful eye, I began gunning down players who had beaten me for years. I was playing the best pool of my life. But something was lacking. The execution of shots and position play was no problem. I was pocketing balls better than ever and rarely lost the cue ball. The trouble was that I still didn't know how to plan good patterns and find intelligent responses to difficult eight ball racks.

Despite shooting well enough to regularly run 60-70 balls at straight pool on a big table my 8-ball game on the bar box was seriously flawed. My hell for leather attempts to run the table were good enough to beat average players and shortstops who played the same way but it would never do against really good shooters.

I had seen what top players do to people when who miss after clearing most of their balls— they bury them with sledgehammer run outs and devastating safeties.

BEATING MR GREEN

I decided to do some experiments. Instead of playing to defeat my opponent, I simply played to beat the table. Beating **Mr. Green** means **RUNNING OUT** at all costs *in your first inning at the table after the break*. If you don't get out the table wins.

I began mowing suckers down like a lawn mower, only making note of whether I beat the table or not. I was able to consistently *beat the table* about 20-40% of the time depending on the condition of the equipment. That was the good part— the beautiful part. The bad part, the ugly part, the dismal, disheartening and depressing part was the result when I failed to complete a rack.

When I missed I landed in **One–Ball–Hell**, as I came to call the situation. Having only one or two balls left to shoot made it possible for weak players to unintentionally pick my bones clean by *accidentally* leaving me safe three or four times in the conglomeration of their balls before I lost the game or managed to muddle through because of their ineptitude.

The run outs were exhilarating, but the tours of **One–Ball–Hell** crushed the spirit. It was agonizing being subjected to the brutality of unplayable shots several times in a row at the hands of namby-pamby, lackluster, insipidly anemic players so stupid they didn't even know how to chalk a cue. It was demoralizing knowing that I was beating myself!

The lesson eventually became transparently clear— missing the last couple of balls in your group or missing the eight-ball is tantamount to surrender against a good player.

[1] My teacher, Bud Harris, was a 3 time US 3 Cushion Billiard Champion with the rare ability to play well *and* teach well. Bud's instruction in proper fundamentals and the basics of ball action was instrumental to playing at a professional level for over 20 years.

A GUIDED TOUR OF ONE–BALL–HELL

My experimentation quickly reminded me of an instructive proposition lock–artists used to spring on pigeons that wandered into big city poolrooms.

> "Hey! Kid! Want to play some? Tell you what… I see you don't play so good, so I'll even things up. You break the balls and I'll spot you all the stripes or solids except one and I have to shoot whatever is left in my group. I get to pick which balls go down. If you don't make a ball, I'll pick a group for you and take off six balls. You get first shot after your balls are removed. You only have to make two balls. How can you lose?"

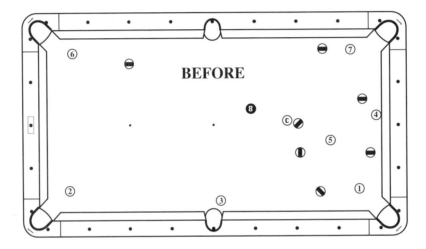

This sucker bet teaches an ornery lesson about the error of thinking that you are ahead in eight ball when you have fewer balls on the table because the exact opposite is almost always the case.

The **AFTER** examples demonstrate how letting any halfway intelligent opponent remove all but one of your balls reduces your chances of winning to practically zero. In fact, the person getting the spot is much worse off after having six of the solids removed than to begin with because solids would have a pretty good chance of running out if they simply accepted the position after the break.

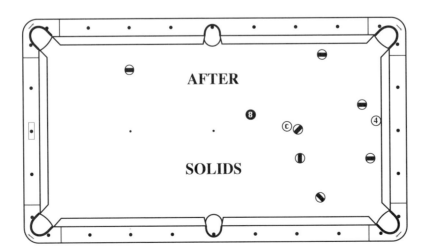

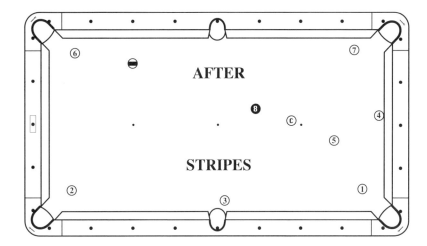

The same fate awaits the chump if the lock–artist decides to leave a stripe to struggle with.

Letting an opponent remove balls from your group is a tremendous disadvantage because no matter how the balls land there's always a snookered ball or a problem ball that can be left for the victim to take a futile stab at. Meanwhile the lock-artist's group is wide open without any balls blocking shots or position routes.

Break a few racks and see how easy it is to ruin an opponent's day by removing all opposing balls but one. Multiple safeties that permit the hustler to solve any problems are easy to arrange with only one ball to worry about and a whole group to hide behind.

Notice how simple it is to run the table with no opposition balls in the way. And most of all recognize the extreme danger of being confined to shooting at one or two object balls while your opponent has soldiers all over the table. That's an important lesson.

It didn't take long to recognize the folly of accepting a six ball spot, but it took years to apply the lesson in game play because I constantly shot myself into **One–Ball–Hell**. In tough competition, I needlessly lost at least 30% of my games because of uncontrolled aggression. Shooting better only made my **One–Ball–Hell** situation worse because I was able to shoot down to the last few balls even more efficiently.

ANOTHER EXPERIMENT
After deciding that gunning down balls like the shoot out at High Noon in Hadleyville is a losing proposition, I did another experiment. This time *allowing two innings after the break shot* to beat the table. That meant that I could miss and then try to finish the rack.

The results were much much better when I could "cheat" by breaking up clusters and moving problem balls without surrendering the table. Playing two-inning games more than doubled my percentage against **Mr. Green**.

I was on to something. The problem was figuring how to use this knowledge in game play where you don't get "free shots" to continue a run.

PREPARING THE BATTLEFIELD

An inspired battle plan quickly blossomed in my mind. A new way of looking at the game. Instead of going all out to run impossible racks, the idea was to find opportunities to break up clusters and take care of problem balls *while shooting safe*. Difficult shots are avoided by *planning* safeties instead of making last ditch stands after a game plan goes off the rails.

In military terms, this strategy is called *preparing the battlefield*. The shelling, strafing and bombardment preceding ground combat are intended to stop opposition assaults, weaken enemy positions and create winning opportunities for your side. Every move is designed to bring about a tour de force when the hammer comes down.

This line of thinking immediately led to the discovery of the *Shot–Safety* — which means attempting a shot and playing position to continue *your* run while leaving your opponent without a playable shot if you miss. (More about the mighty *Shot–Safety* later.)

Meeting up with the *Shot–Safety* quickly acquainted me with its sibling the *Safety–Break*, which is another way of dealing with clusters and problem balls without selling out.

Replacing kamikaze play with tactics that *prepared the battlefield* immediately increased my winning percentage against players at all levels.

When you see a cluster or a ball that cannot be handled because of the lay of the table look for a *Shot–Safety* or a *Safety–Break* that rearranges the scenery.

Safety play becomes absolutely brutal when defensive moves are used to force winning positions. The idea is to make your opponent shoot the most difficult shots possible while positioning your group in front of the pockets for an easy run when you return to the table. Turning safety play into aggressive channels is a double whammy that maximizes your chances of winning.

Risks are weighed according to the possibility of completing a rack and balanced against the chance of leaving the opposition a run out. Safety play in this style is not at all passive because good safety play is designed to prepare easy runs for a later inning.

PLAYING TO WIN
Ordinary players often forget that **winning** should be the **goal**. Game plans should lead to victory, not spectacular shots that look good, but lose games.

Only attempt to run out when you are at least 60% certain of finishing the rack because failing to complete a run after making most of your balls means almost certain defeat against a decent player.

The decision to attempt a run should be carefully weighed against the difficulty of the situation and your ability to cope with the problems. Kidding yourself into futile assaults causes avoidable losses, so you must learn to estimate your chances realistically.

Do not pass up chances to win, but make sure you don't land in **One–Ball–Hell**. Overly aggressive play greatly increases the risk of a loss when you fail to complete a rack.

At the same time don't dally about finishing a game once you see a way to get out because you cannot give good shooters very many chances.

The qualifying factor is being certain your blitzkrieg will succeed most of the time instead of embarking on suicide missions that land you dead in the water. Overextending aggression opens the door for defeat.

Cowboy pool may win against amateurs, but a good eight-baller feeds on unforced errors and becomes ten times harder to beat. Giving away games now and then gives the opposition a tremendous psychological boost.

If an opponent is getting a lot of easy wins, it may be because you are removing the obstacles and leaving road map run outs. When this happens, try deliberately missing with *all* of your balls on the table to see if the opposition can carry their own water.

The obstacles created by 5 to 7 soldiers in the confined area of a bar table often make run outs impossible. If your opponent's game drops off, it's because you have been clearing the road for him/her instead of taking care of your own problems.

Play for two or three inning games when a run out is unlikely — which is a lot of the time on bar tables. The winning percentage with planned safeties is much better than fumbling attempts to overcome positional errors and impossible sequences.

Curtail impulses to demonstrate shot making skills when you know you cannot get out. Once you see that finishing a game is unlikely, you must abandon the run out attempt and find a safety option that solves the problem. Even if you have playable balls, *you must stop scoring* when completing the rack isn't in the cards.

Leaving hangers in front of the pockets makes it difficult for your opponent to get out or to leave you safe so take care of trouble balls before shooting off the ducks. The fewer balls you have the easier it is for an opponent to put you in jail, so get over notions of shoot outs at the OK Corral and play to win.

BEATING YOURSELF
A straight shooter can easily defeat run of the mill players more than four out of five games by deliberately leaving open shots after making one ball to decide group. The odds are more than 20-1 that all an average player will do with an open table is clear some of the obstacles making it easier for a smart competitor to win. Often you can leave weak players several open shots without much risk of loss.

There's no need for Robert E. Lee battle plans against shooters who cannot clear the table with a push broom. In fact, if you are hustling the game, deliberately leaving open shots will speed up the games and keep your victims happy because they are constantly making balls, but rarely finishing a rack.

Among ordinary players most games are lost not won. This is to say, the loser had an opportunity to win, but made errors that gave the game away. By this I mean the shooter chose the wrong shots, left easy shots for their opponent at critical points, repeatedly missed shots, never got good position, played the wrong strategy etc etc etc. Average players beat themselves like a bongo drum in a hail storm.

Learning the propensity of ordinary players for self-defeat is worth 100 times the cost of this book to those who gamble on the bar boxes because people come back for more when they get to make a lot of balls. Even when you win every game they feel like they "had a shot at winning."

You are in the catbird seat when a player misses with all of your balls on the table because you almost always have strong safety or strong aggressive options.

Beating good players requires eliminating as many self-inflicted losses as possible because superior players are going to win games without you making any mistakes at all. Beating yourself very many games makes the difference between winning and losing matches. Eliminating stupid losses, by itself, raises most players winning percentage considerably.

Sometimes two players become so intent on beating themselves that a game refuses to end until the 8-ball winds up in the wrong pocket or some other unforgivable sin occurs.

Pool is a skill game not a raffle or a lotto drawing so it makes me grit my teeth to see losers throwing games back and forth without a clue. One reason I wrote this book is to teach these unfortunates a better way to play the game.

GENERAL PRINCIPLES

Learn to recognize the defensive value of blocking balls and barricades instead of mindlessly removing valuable defensive assets from your group on a trip to **One–Ball–Hell**. Having five to seven balls on the table can be a strong shield for warding off enemy aggression when the balls block pockets and clog up position routes.

Respecting the security provided by your soldiers is essential to playing bar table eight ball at the highest levels because every ball defends certain areas, angles and ball paths.

Removing obstructive balls without completing a rack is sheer suicide in tough competition where opponents don't make many mistakes and never take any prisoners. Stop giving aid and comfort to the enemy by opening up the scoring lanes when you cannot finish the game.

The biggest problem in running out on bar tables is overcoming the congestion of balls on the table which makes clearing paths to the pockets, opening up blocked balls and separating clusters essential for victory. Unless you are reasonably sure you can navigate all the roadblocks, it is unwise to commit to an all out attack.

SHOT–SAFETY

The *Shot–Safety* is an artful blend of aggression and caution that offers a low risk attempt at a difficult ball. The *Shot–Safety* is one of the most valuable concepts in high–speed eight ball. Taking the risk out of tough shots by playing to continue your run if you make the ball while leaving the opposition safe if you miss is a formidable strategy that wins games.

Whenever possible use *Shot–Safeties* or *Safety–Breaks* to open up orphan clusters and to deal with trouble balls when break shots and key position balls are not available. Safety play that creates winning positions is a deadly companion to aggressive shooting. Planned *Shot–Safeties* that open up your group while handcuffing the opposition are lethal.

It is wise to leave at least three or four of your balls on the table when you play safe to avoid having the favor returned. The more balls you have in play the less likely that you can be played safe. Especially if your balls are at both ends of the table. The more widely your balls are scattered the harder it is to play you safe. Particularly when some of your balls are positioned for easy *Starter Shots* in the next inning.

SAFETY–BREAK

The *Safety–Break* is a first cousin of the *Shot–Safety*. The idea is to move clustered balls to makable positions while leaving your opponent behind the proverbial eight–ball. Planned *Safety–Breaks* are deadly when they set your group up for an easy run in the next inning.

When you have orphan clusters look for *Safety–Break* shots to create winning situations.

STARTER SHOTS

Leaving shootable balls in position instead of drilling them in as soon as possible is a hard lesson for many players, but this strategy pays off with countless easy wins. Using defensive and offensive assets effectively is the key to excellence because shooting a difficult pattern when aggressive safeties produce easier and more reliable outcomes is for losers.

Hell for leather shooters who cannot stand leaving a playable ball on the table when they sit down never learn the value of having easy shots to begin the next inning. Learning which balls *not to shoot until the right time* is essential for playing 8–ball at the highest level.

Starter Shots combined with strong safety play is a tough strategy to counter.

PLAY TO WIN

Do not rely over much on safety play. The first priority is finishing the rack as soon as possible. To win you must put your balls into the pockets with deliberate intent because removing your group and sinking the 8-ball is a necessity. As a rule one or two safeties should be sufficient to position your balls for victory when a run isn't initially in the cards. Providing, of course, that you aggressively move your balls to advantageous positions. The goal, when safety play is involved, should be to get out in the next inning.

Merely stopping an opponent from scoring is not effective safety play. Safeties that fail to move problem balls to good positions will not win against strong players. You must make moves that *force* opponents to sell out to win against better players and that means doing more than merely preventing them from making a ball.

When you cannot run out, shot selection should be done with the idea eliminating roadblocks and moving problem balls to better neighborhoods. Sometimes you need to shoot off a ball or two to get the position needed to play a good *Safety–Break*, but don't shoot off too many balls or you'll be on the way to beating yourself.

CONTROL

An all-important concept resulted from my experimentation— the key to winning games is *controlling* the table. Instead of thinking in terms of over–ambitious aggression or fearful safety play, the novel idea occurred that the thing that invariably *wins* eight ball games is *control*.

Control comes in many forms—

Playing a perfect pattern with precise shot making and perfect cue ball position is *control*. Being a good shotmaker and blowing the balls off the table is *control*. Running out is the best *control* of all because you immediately win, but as a practical matter many racks are unrunnable without preparation.

Identifying the appropriate strategy and tactics for each rack is *control*.

Leaving an opponent iced up against the proverbial eight-ball seven time zones from a playable shot is *control*. You have *control* when you keep the opposition muzzled.

A major mistake is thinking that safeties don't work against top shooters. Trust me when I tell you that champions are just as susceptible to force–nine snookers as anyone else. When you jack a good player up behind an impossible shot they do not do much better than an amateur does.

Passing up opportunities to win out of excess caution is a waste of *control*. Once your group is set for a run, finish the game *immediately*. Every time you let an opponent return to the table there's a risk that you'll lose *control* and surrender the game. So don't stall around with needless safeties. After you hook good players too many times they will kick a ball in or return the safety and take *control* of the game. Count on it.

Knowing your limits is *control*. Forcing opposition errors instead of shooting like Superman is *control*. The main thing is learning your limits. Shooting beyond your skill level causes needless losses because when *control* finally goes out the window so few of your balls are left that the opposition has a field day.

The thing that invariably *wins* pool games is *control*. As long as you maintain *perfect control* you cannot lose.

Now for some practical instruction in the *Safety–Blitzkrieg* style of eight ball advocated here.

———————————⑧———————————

OCCAM'S RAZOR

The simplest method that provides reliable results is always best.

———————————⑧———————————

MENTAL IMAGERY
CONQUERING PRESSURE –AIMING – PEAK PERFORMANCE

A reasonable discussion of the concepts involved in using mental imagery is so complex that it requires an entire book to adequately cover the topic.[1] Nevertheless, a few brief comments may be helpful.

Pressure Is Something You Put On Yourself
There is no change of physics or equipment. Your cue is the same, the balls are the same and the table is the same. Everything is the same except the state of your mind.

Pressure comes from desires, ambitions and fears that are allowed to invade the mind during competition. Once you realize that your own mind is the source of the anxiety, discomfort and awkwardness called pressure you are half–way to defeating negative thinking.

It Ain't All Bad
If you ask politely professionals will often tell you that they use the energy created by pressure to raise performance. For them intense competition acts as a stimulant and they count on this nervous energy for peak performance. Learning to channel nervous energy into positive performance is one of the keys to stellar play.

Self–Talk Means Self–Defeat
Players who try to boost performance with inner pep talks, sub–vocal checklists and oral admonishments are on the wrong course because the right–brain that controls execution of the stroke operates in visual and sensory terms and using words is like communicating in an alien language.

The best self–talk for choke situations where you fear a misplay is two words **"STOP IT."**

"STOP IT!" means to end the sub–vocalizing and start communicating with pictures and feelings.

"STOP IT!" means discontinuing negative thoughts and centering on the execution of the shot at hand in a positive way. This is best done using mental imagery, not words!

Telling yourself to **STOP IT!** is merely a reminder to stop putting pressure on yourself.

The right–brain, which controls execution of the stroke, has a very poor grasp of verbal meanings. Instructions such as "do *not* scratch" or "do *not* miss" are easily mistranslated to "*do* scratch" or "*do* miss." More complex verbal communication is apt to be garbled or not understood at all except for the emotional weight it carries.

Players trying to self–talk themselves out of choke situations usually make matters worse with their inner chatter because the right–brain has very poor comprehension of words.

Ideas like "stay down and follow through" are apt to be jumbled into **"fGnl QbJa naQ sbyybJ Guebhtu."** Confusion is especially likely in high voltage pressure situations.

If there's any negative emotional energy hooked up to an encrypted word message the right–brain is likely to think that a miss *IS* the desired result.

Show Me A Picture
The right–brain is the center of feeling, emotion, creative thought, sensation and muscular coordination, but the intuitive mind does not operate well in verbal terms. Consequently players sow the seeds of confusion when they try to use words to boost performance.

[1]The East German and Soviet mental peak performance programs which use mental imagery extensively are supposedly the best training systems for maximum achievement.

Trying to enhance the right–brain delivery program with words is like hooking an AC motor up to DC current—everything goes haywire because the right–brain operates in visual and sensory terms and uses muscle memory to orchestrate a good stroke.

The right–brain intuitively calculates shots from past experience and needs no advice from the analytical mind to execute plays it has already learned. All the right–brain requires is a clear picture of what you want to accomplish and a memory of the muscular effort needed to do it.

Top Players Use Images And Feelings
Interviews with over 50 top professional pool and billiard players conclusively prove that the best players use mental imagery to put their game into hyperdrive, not words. The very best players *visualize* the results they want and *feel* the correct stroke needed to accomplish the shot at hand. Then they shoot the lights out.

Although champions extol positive thinking as an essential ingredient for peak performance, not one top player mentioned using pep talks or self–talk in competition. Learning to think in pictures and feelings is one reason they are champions.

When the right–brain gives them a feeling of certainty that the shot will score as planned top players pull the trigger.

Advice From The Ancients
Old-time Straight–Rail champion Maurice Daly summed up mental imagery with these simple words.

"In playing… [nearly all position shots] one must get into the habit of mentally guiding— for lack of a better term— the balls. Get the mental habit of seeing in your mind's eye the balls moving to certain positions. You see the very spots where you want the balls to stop, and you try to land them there. Mentally see them travel along their course to the fore–intentioned resting places and you'll find this habit of enormous assistance in making the balls do your bidding."
Daly's Billiard Book © 1913 by Maurice Daly p. 178

Taking several no cost mental trial runs before hitting the cue ball eliminates mistakes and puts the shooter on the path to championship play.

Left–brain analysis is good for planning a pattern, but such thinking must stop when you bend over the table to shoot. Using left–brain intellectualizing to deliver a delicate stroke is like trying to thread a needle while skipping rope. There's always a mistake.

Accentuate The Positive
It is important to form positive mental images of what you want to accomplish. This means eliminating negative thinking.

For example, if there's a risk of a scratch on a shot you obviously do not want that to happen. However, instead of forming a mental image based on the idea of **NOT SCRATCHING**, create a picture of the cue ball precisely following the desired path. Replace images of the cue ball falling into the pocket with a picture of the ball traveling the right path. Omit the negative and define shots in positive terms of what you want to accomplish, not what you don't want to happen.

Placing your hand on the table where you want the cue ball to land sends a very direct message to the right–brain about the outcome you want. No words are required. Just put your bridge hand down where you want to shoot the next shot from and then go back and execute the play at hand.

Stroking Machines

The stroking machines used to test cues for deflection etc are a good example of the complexity of delivering an accurate stoke. These machines create a mechanically accurate stroke that is humanly impossible to duplicate—like making off angle combinations with the balls 3 feet apart and the last ball two feet from the pocket twenty out of twenty times.

So far as I know none of these pool-shooting machines can actually calculate a shot. An operator must line the shot up with a few test runs before the machine begins doing what machines do best— repeating an activity with robotic precision.

A human player faces a much more complicated task. Instead of stroking from a platform that can be locked in place, hundreds of muscles throughout the body must be controlled. Instead of shooting the balls a few times to get the range, a human player must estimate the force and angle needed based on past experience and get it right the first time.

The optical and muscular calculations necessary to execute a precise stroke are so complex that it would take hundreds of pages of computer code to instruct the muscles to purposely make a simple shot. The speed and timing of the stroke must be controlled... the grip hand must be coordinated... the stance must be properly aligned… the cue must follow–through ... the eye–hand timing must be right… etc etc etc.

Once the true complexity of executing a reliable stroke is understood, it is readily seen how woefully inadequate sub-vocal check lists and worded descriptions are for the task at hand.

Delivering a billiard cue in a precise path at a precise speed is not a simple activity that can be defined with a few words. The analytical left–brain is simply not capable of communicating or even understanding all of the information necessary to make pool and billiard shots. The left–brain is very good at figuring logical sequences and the like, but the actual delivery of the cue can only be done well by the intuitive right–brain which is hardwired for muscular control.

When the logical mind gets involved in muscular activity things immediately begin going wrong. The player feels uncomfortable and uncertain of the shot at hand— even figuring ridiculously simple shots is a tough proposition for the rational side of the mind which lacks any concept of what muscular force means in the terms necessary to play a fine game.

Muscular coordination is so complicated that it must be done intuitively and that's the right–brain's strong suit. When the right–brain takes over phenomenal precision is the order of the day.

Think Long Think Wrong

Overcoming pressure means eliminating inner chitchat about the game and concentrating on the *feel* and *mental image* of the shot you are trying to accomplish.

Taking an excessive amount of time to execute a shot tends to shut down right–brain thinking because the intuitive mind sees a shot almost instantly. After the right–brain is ready it is a mistake to spend more time than it takes to get set solidly in the stance and to do a few mental rehearsals of the play at hand before shooting.

It is stupidity personified to let yourself become so disoriented by irrational thinking that you cannot execute a simple pattern.

When you cannot *see* a shot, stand up and go through the aiming process again. Walk around the table and sight the shot from different angles. Try to get a *feel* for the shot.

Tap Into The Right–Brain and Win

Because pool and billiards are skill games involving graphic and sensory input players will profit from setting up the illustrations in this book and moving the balls around by hand to educate the right–brain about what you want to happen.

Seeing a graphic image of the shot helps the right–brain calculate what is needed to accomplish a play better than ten thousand words. After imprinting the mental image of how you want to play the shot, set the balls up again and actually make the shot. Use clear mental pictures of the desired result to guide your delivery.

Remembering the *feel*, form and shape of previous successful attempts enables the right–brain to repeat a shot again and again so it is vital to focus on muscle memory to get the intuitive right–brain involved in your practice sessions. If the right–brain knows how to make a shot, the stroke will be delivered with micrometer precision to accomplish the desired result.

Talking A Player Out Of Dead Stroke

A sure-fire way to lower a player's performance is to get them talking. An argument does the job. The more intellectually complicated the debate the better. The more left–brain the discussion becomes the farther from peak performance the player moves.

A less abrasive way of distracting an opponent is to praise a good shot and innocently ask "How do you do that???" Most players cannot resist showing off their knowledge and willingly get their left–brain involved in explaining things.

A diversionary question is "Exactly how hard did you hit it?" Because the left–brain has no verbal concept of speed and force the player will have a hard time answering. The right–brain knows, but has no words to explain.

Don't make the mistake of talking during tough competition. Very few players can talk at the table and play well at the same time because the right–brain doesn't know how to carry on a conversation and shuts down while you blather away.

Players who can talk and play at the same time have learned to shut off the left–brain the instant they bend over the table to shoot. The playing and talking are distinctly separate activities although they may not seem so to observers.

Minnesota Fats was a good example of how an intelligent player keeps his mouth shut while he actually shoots. Fats would talk and talk and talk while he was moving from one shot to the next, but when he lined up to shoot all the chatter ended for a few seconds while Fatty's right–brain delivered a great stroke. Once the shot was finished Fats began jabbering again.

Players who entered into a verbal joust with Fats made a serious mistake on two counts— first off no one ever outtalked the Fatman. Even Mohammed Ali took a back seat when Fats got the floor.

Second and more important the player had to put the left–brain in charge to fight a word battle and most people cannot quickly switch back and forth from left–brain to right–brain thinking so their play suffers when they get to talking during a contest. All Fats needed was a little edge to whack a top player out.

The Fatman's victims seldom realized that their own words played a big part in beating them.

OBSTACLES

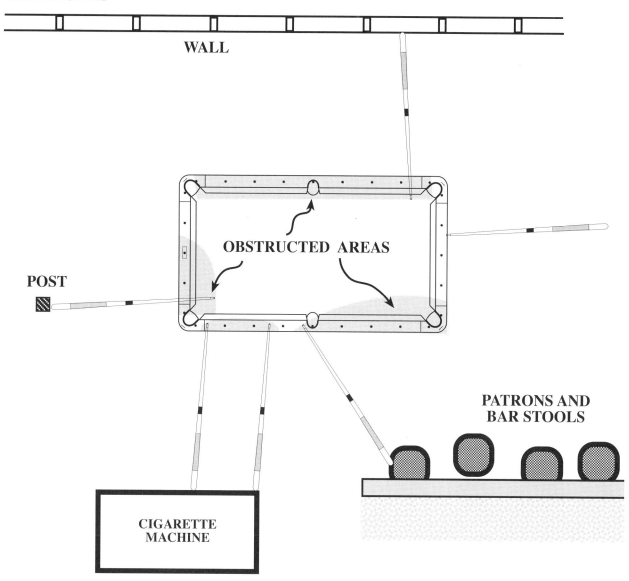

WALL

OBSTRUCTED AREAS

POST

PATRONS AND
BAR STOOLS

CIGARETTE
MACHINE

When you get on an unfamiliar bar table the first thing to do is to check for barriers. Obstructions abound in taverns because walls, posts, booths, bar stools and customers get in the way. Size up which angles are blocked by each impediment so you do not shoot key shots jacked up at a 70-degree angle.

Plan patterns to avoid human and inanimate stumbling blocks whenever possible by playing positions where you can deliver a clean stroke without some drunk elbowing you on the backswing.

Use these roadblocks when playing safe. Forcing opponents to shoot tough shots without a backswing or using a short cue takes the wind out of enemy sails.

Establishments where league play is taken seriously make bar stools that interfere with the pool table off limits during matches.

THE MADDENING CROWD

Ball concentration is 156% greater on a bar table

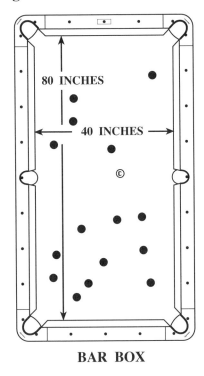

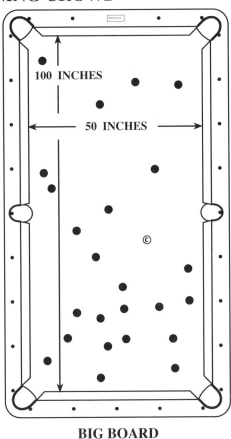

100 INCHES

50 INCHES

80 INCHES

40 INCHES

BAR BOX

BIG BOARD

40" x 80" = 3,200 SQUARE INCHES   **50" x 100" = 5,000 SQUARE INCHES**

The first thing big table players notice about 3–1/2 x 7 foot (40" x 80") bar tables is that the smaller size generally makes shots easier to execute. What never seems to dawn on casual observers is that to get the same concentration of balls that you have on a bar box you need 25 balls on a regulation table.

Playing with 25 balls on a regulation table provides a good idea of the conglomeration you must cope with in every bar table game. Clusters, multiple problem balls and blocked position routes nip run outs in their pre–embryonic stage. It only takes one little slip amid the intense accumulation of balls to convert a sure thing into an impossible dream that leaves you sputtering with mud on your face as you try to figure out what went wrong.

Shotmaking *is* easier on bar tables, so the area problem balances out somewhat. Nevertheless, the effects of a smaller surface area must be included in game planning. In many respects bar table play is actually tougher than regulation table play, so don't fall into the trap of thinking that smaller automatically means easier. It simply isn't so. Coping with blocked scoring lanes and obstructed position routes are challenges that must be dealt with in almost every game.

The high concentration of balls on bar tables also lends itself to power safety strategies that would be very difficult to duplicate on a full sized table.

As Dorothy said to Toto "We're not in Kansas anymore."

Because you have room to move around on a nine-foot table, it's actually an easier game on the big table.

On seven-foot tables you're a lot more restricted. It's obviously a tougher game.

Your cue ball control has to be better on a bar table.

"Southside Louie" Lemke — Five Time National Bar Table Champion

RICHIE FLORENCE HAS A HEAD-ON COLLISION WITH BAR TABLE REALITY

Back in the early 1970s Richie Florence encountered the devastation that even professional big table players can fall prey to when they trespass onto bar tables. At the time Richie Florence was the hottest regulation table player in the country. Florence had busted every big money player he met for months.

Richie was playing so well that he entered the US Open straight pool tournament and made a 100 ball run in a match that year. This was remarkable since Florence spent most of his time playing 9-ball and one pocket. Florence was without doubt the best money player in the country at that moment in time.

Richie's downfall came when he heard about a bar table player called "Mexican Joe" Salazar who was taking on all comers so long as they were willing to make sizable bets. In his heart Richie Florence *knew* that no bar table player could possibly defeat him because he was absolutely in dead stroke. His victories over the top gamblers proved it. His performance against the best straight pool players in the US Open proved it.

When Mexican Joe suggested playing 8-ball for $500 a game, Richie thought that was just fine with him. He'd bust this yokel in a hurry. Except for Joe and his backers everyone in the joint thought Florence would pound Salazar into a side pocket with dispatch.

Only it didn't work that way. Mexican Joe immediately took control of the game and began bashing Richie with shots that Florence didn't even know existed. Richie kept trying to make the cue ball behave the way it does on big tables which was an enormous mistake with Mexican Joe using every nuance of the overweight cue ball to his advantage.

Remembering Mexican Joe's masterly speed control and visualization of the overweight bar table cue ball path still makes me drool.

Richie Florence lost his entire bankroll within an hour and a half winning only a game or two in the whole session. The difference in results was striking. Florence kept fighting the overweight cue ball and the heavy ball beat him flat. Joe used the extra weight to his advantage making shots big table players do not understand.

Richie left the Sunset Bar that morning screaming, "I'm going to practice up on bar tables for a couple of weeks and then come back and beat Joe's brains out.... Then I'm going to go all over the country telling stories about him." However, Richie never came back.

The difference between Mexican Joe's play and Florence's style was awesome to behold. Florence did everything the hard way and the results were terrible. Joe played according to the reality of the equipment and won every exchange. Joe administered a royal beating to the hottest big table player in the country without even breaking a sweat.

Richie Florence isn't the only big table champion to go down in flames on a bar box. Many others have met the same fate. Mexican Joe proved that top bar table players can have a huge edge over regulation table players unfamiliar with small table play.

Competition on small tables can be just as ferocious as professional play so keep your guard up. The guy challenging the table could be a future world champion.

Richie Florence was a premier money player in the 1960s and 70s.

Florence kept his word about learning to play on bar tables by winning the Lite Beer's World Series of Tavern Pool in 1983.

No less a player than Buddy "The Rifleman" Hall admits to losing a session to "Mexican Joe" Salazar on a bar box so don't think this is an exaggeration.

Incidentally, before Buddy Hall became a world-beater on the big boards, he was a champion bar table player.

Johnny Archer is another current professional who began his career on bar tables.

WHAT'S THE PROBLEM?

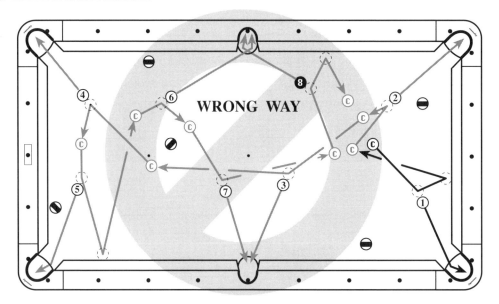

What's wrong with this pattern? Maybe nothing— *if* you are playing on a 4–1/2 x 9 foot table with 5-5/8" side pockets. But planning so many side pocket shots into a run on a bar table is almost suicidal.

Read on to see why.

SIZE MATTERS

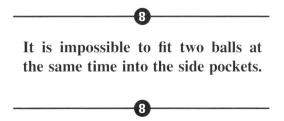

REGULATION TABLE

MOUTH
5-3/8" to 5-5/8"

THROAT
4-1/2" to 4-7/8"

BAR TABLE

MOUTH
3–3/4" to 4–5/8"

THROAT
3-1/4"to 3-5/8"

Big table players are slow to pick up on the fact that side pocket shots on bar tables are pure poison. According to the BCA Rule Book the side pockets on regulation tables must have a minimum width of 5–3/8" to a maximum of 5–5/8". On bar tables the side pockets measure from 3-3/4" to 4-5/8" wide at the mouth and the throat quickly narrows down to 3–5/8" or even little as 3–1/4".

⑧

It is impossible to fit two balls at the same time into the side pockets.

⑧

The side pockets on big tables are wider at the **back** than the sides on a bar table are at the mouth. The sides on a bar table are actually much tougher than snooker table side pockets! In fact, the side pockets on bar tables are tighter than **anything** found on **any** other pocket table because the balls are still the regulation 2.25 inch size.

The miserly size of side pockets on bar tables is one very good reason to avoid them.

CORNERS

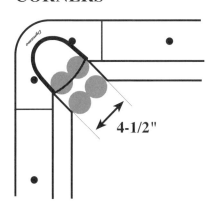

4-1/2"

Measuring 4–1/2 inches front to back the corner pockets on bar tables are a much better bargain than the stingy sides. Although the 4–1/2 inch corners are smaller than those often found on full sized equipment, the corner pockets on bar tables are usually somewhat more forgiving than those on big tables because they allow a *cheat* of about an extra half ball space for scoring.

MINIMUM SIDE POCKET ANGLE

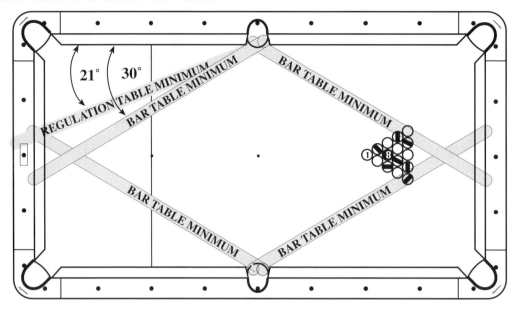

On regulation tables balls can be made in the sides at a 21° angle to the long rail. On a bar table 30° is the minimum cut angle into the sides. And a ball doesn't have to go even if it hits dead on target at the minimum angle because the ball is going straight into the face of the pocket. On some bar tables the minimum cut angle is even larger because of the miniature size of the side pockets. Even at the best angle there's very little room for error on a side pocket shot on a bar table.

You can quickly determine the minimum cut angle for the sides on a bar table by directly shooting the cue ball into the sides a few times and noting where the line of the shot crosses the end rail. If you cannot shoot the cue ball straight in, you know there's no chance of making an object ball from that angle.

After you go below the minimum cut angle for the sides, a ball can hit the face of the pocket giving the illusion that the ball *almost* scored even though the shot can *never* go. Many players never realize that these *near misses* are actually off the mark by the proverbial 1.609 kilometers and could never ever score on a level table. Onlookers often applaud these futile shots as "great tries."

Do some experiments and remember that if you cannot make the cue ball there isn't a prayer of pocketing an object ball at the same angle. Mentally mark where the minimum cut line crosses the end rail and bank balls that are below the minimum cut angle, shoot them into the corners or the opposite sides.

Selecting side pocket shots when corner options are available is bad pattern play on bar tables because the sides have all the worst of it. Position play must be very precise to land the cue ball in the pygmy sized position zones required for side pocket sequences and *any* mistake is apt to beat you.

Players who fail to recognize the perils of side pocket shooting on bar tables are relegated to the rank of pigeon, no matter how well they play on the big box. It's impossible to give up this kind of handicap and win against skilled competition because shooting side pocket shots courts disaster on every play and taking unnecessary chances is sure to lose a lot of games.

Observing how a competitor uses the side pockets provides an instant read on how well a player understands the bar table game. When I see a shooter *avoiding* side pocket shots, I bear down because I know I've got a tough customer to deal with.

THE CORNERS

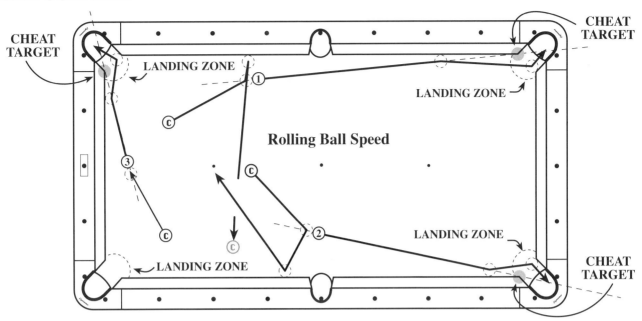

The corner pockets are a better bargain than the sides because on most bar tables you can *cheat* a corner pocket by about 1/2 ball space on the cushion side of the pocket and still score providing the ball is not hit too hard. In other words, if you aim at an imaginary ball with its center positioned on the cushion side point of the pocket and shoot with rolling ball speed, the shot will probably score if the angle into the cushion is not extreme.

All other things being equal this extra half–ball–space leeway makes corner shots the choice whenever decisions must be made between sides and corners.

Do a few experiments to see how far into the cushion the imaginary target can be placed and still score. Knowing exactly how much leeway a corner has is valuable knowledge when you must shoot into a partially blocked pocket or need to create an angle for position play. Favoring the cushion side on corner shots is smart pool.

Notice the small **Landing Zone** planned for these shots. Leaving the object ball hanging in the pocket if you miss obstructs an opponent's progress and provides a *Starter Shot* for the next inning. That means hitting the shot with just enough speed to *drop* the ball into the pocket.

When you make these shots with the proper speed the object ball never hits the back of the pocket.

CORNERS (Continued)

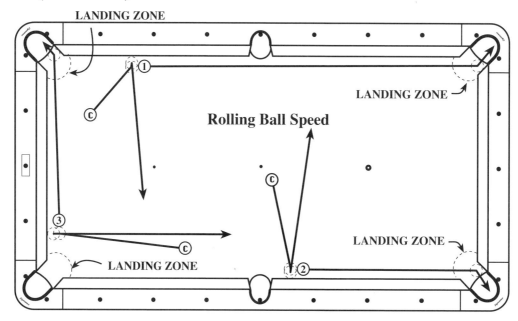

Because of the forgiving nature of the corner pockets on bar tables I fearlessly shoot the shots above any time they fit into a pattern. As long as the cue ball is close enough to guarantee an accurate cut (within two or three diamonds [30"] of the object ball), I go for these shots.

Because of the smaller size of bar tables I make a lot of these cuts and when I miss the object ball usually blocks the pocket. If you do not overpower thin cuts the leeway on corner shots makes these plays worthwhile.

Of course, on very thin cuts where the object ball is almost frozen to the cushion there isn't much room for error. For balls close to the rail aim to cut the object ball parallel to the cushion and do not deliberately play for any *cheat*.

Using no english or inside english helps the object ball score by applying a small amount of cushion–side english to the object ball, which tends to spin the ball *into* the pocket if it hits the point. You must slightly overcut the ball to compensate for the *throw* toward the cushion, but not very much.

When using outside english allow for the throw and aim to hit the pocket opening very slightly toward the cushion side.

Keep the speed down so the ball is *rolling* when it gets to the pocket. A *rolling* ball has the best chance of scoring on a marginal hit.

I remember watching Luther Lassiter making razor thin cuts. Lassiter rolled the ball so slowly that I was sure the ball wouldn't get to the pocket. But Wimpy made every one of them— ker plunk — ker plunk — ker plunk.

Landing the object ball in front of the pocket where it blocks your opponent's balls when you miss takes some of the risk out of these shots.

Visualize the ball *dropping* into the pocket.

TAKING A SHORTCUT

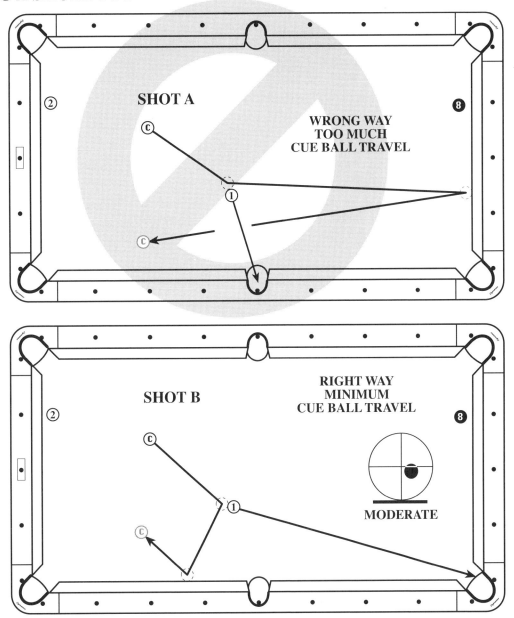

Opting for side pocket shots in situations like this puts players in the loser's bracket in bar table play. Even though there are no balls blocking the position route this time, the side pocket shot should be rejected in the interest of the better cue ball control afforded by a shorter position route and out of respect for the small size of the side pockets on bar tables.

On regulation tables it *might* be better to play some of these shots in the sides, but on a bar box a side pocket habit is fatal.

Sooner rather than later the side pocket shooter will make an unforgiving mistake and you simply cannot afford needless errors on bar tables.

RATING THE SIDES

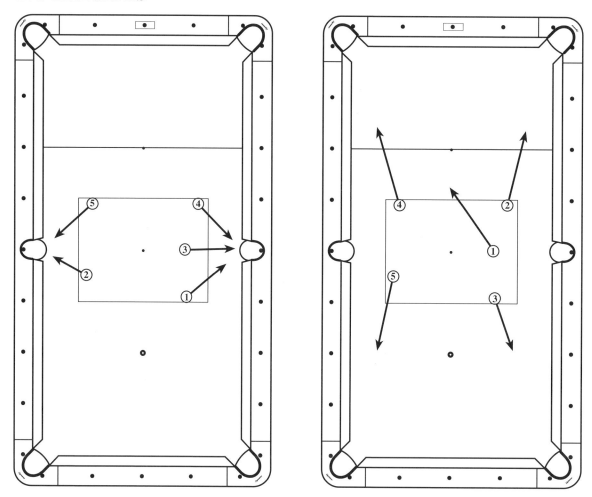

If there are still any skeptics here's an educational experiment that should prove that planning side pocket shots into patterns on bar tables is a losing proposition. Scatter four or five balls between the side pockets in the rectangle area and **mark** their positions. Starting with **Ball-In-Hand** figure a pattern shooting all the balls in the two sides and see how you do. Then try shooting all of the balls into the corners.

A few experiments should convince you that the small size of the side pockets makes them a genuine hazard to navigation even when you have good position to begin with. The corners are much more forgiving and far more useful in making runs. Especially when position errors force a change in plans.

Recovering from a position error going from one corner shot to another corner shot is much easier than doing the same thing with a side pocket shot even when the balls are easy to make. This is due to the fact that there are two cushions near the corners to play position from while the sides only have the long rail nearby and a half–table trip to an end rail for recovery. Redemption from a corner pocket error generally requires much less cue ball travel.

Sending the cue ball to the end rail and back to regain position— *if* a recovery is possible is problematic. The corners offer better options, so wise up and begin playing the percentages by eliminating as many side pocket shots as possible from your battle plans.

Reducing the number of side pocket shots you play will improve your runout percentage because the four corners support each other far better than the two sides do.

WHAT'S THE PROBLEM REVISITED

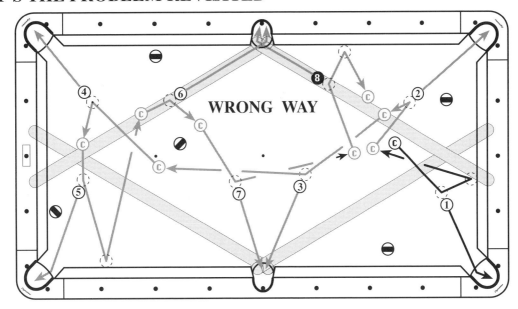

Now that you know that side pocket shots are laced with arsenic and cyanide, the hazards of side pocket patterns should be more conspicuous.

Let's return to the game where we began this discussion of the side pockets. With the minimum cut angles laid out it is clear that the 6-ball and the 8–ball are right on the minimum cut line. On many bar tables making these balls in the side is impossible.

Even if the balls can be made in the sides the shooter is asking for trouble because the effective pocket width is almost exactly the same size as the ball leaving zero margin for error.

The 3–ball and 7–ball shots in the side are also poor choices because the player has to get a good angle for the passing position and then control the speed very well to avoid screwing up the sequence.

Planning four side pocket shots into a run on a bar table is a sign of delusional thinking. I would bet that most players couldn't finish this side pocket run as planned one time in 20 on a small table.

Especially when the last two balls before the eight and the eight–ball itself are side pocket shots. Shooting the last three balls into the sides from the open table is not a game winning strategy. Shooting a ball from the open sea into a side pocket for a critical position shot into another side is a dangerous task that can go horribly wrong. If the cue ball lands a few inches on the wrong side of the angle to continue the run even a top professional may be finished.

Let's see a better plan.

SQUARING THE BOX

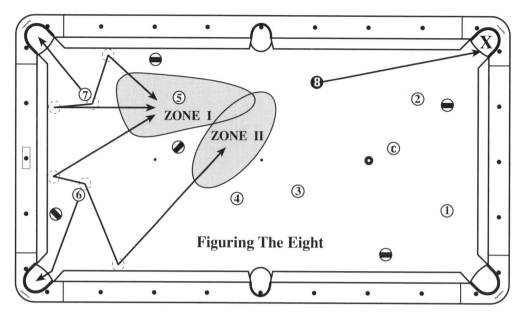

Figuring The Eight

The first decision in planning an open run is figuring where to shoot the eight ball and how to get there. Unless the eight was *hanging* in a side the last place I'd plan to shoot the game ball is in a side pocket.

The verdict here is to play the 8–ball into corner **X** shooting from where the 5–ball is located (the 5–ball will be gone by then). The 6 or 7–ball will be the last shot before the eight depending on exactly how the 5–ball is played. I feel very comfortable about making the 8–ball from **ZONE I** or **ZONE II** and there are several easy options for getting these positions from the 6 or 7–ball. The main factor is the transition from the 5–ball to the 6 or 7–ball. The last ball before the eight will be decided by the exact angle for the 5–ball shot.

Now that the end game has been planned, let's figure the rest of the shots to get there.

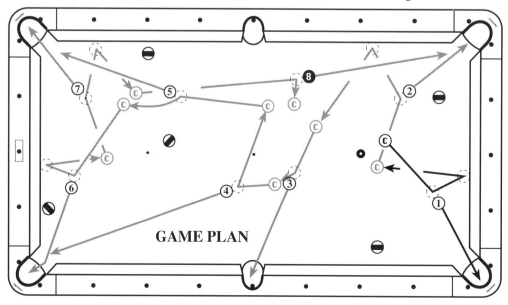

GAME PLAN

SQUARING THE BOX 2

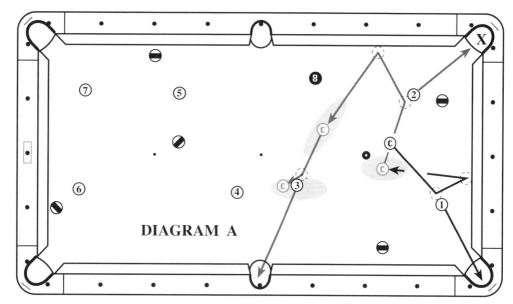

DIAGRAM A: Since there are no clusters or problem balls to cope with, begin the run by shooting off the balls at the foot of the table because the cue ball is already there.

The 3–ball shot is a critical play because good position is needed to go from the 4–ball to the 5–ball with proper alignment for the 6–7–8 sequence. Because this is a side pocket shot extra care is taken for the preliminary shots leading to this play. The leave on the 2-ball is as perfect as possible to provide a maximum opportunity to continue the run as planned. The plan is to land the cue ball right on top of the 3–ball position for the shot on the 4–ball. (The diagram shows the cue ball to the side of the 3-ball to avoid confusion.)

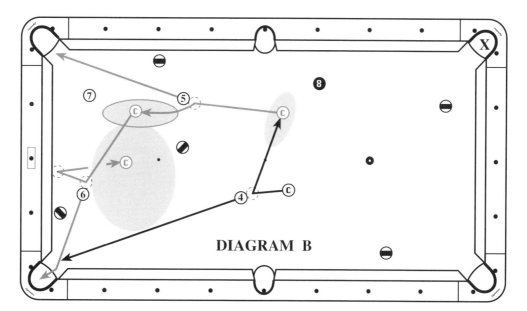

DIAGRAM B: The transition from the 4–ball to the 5–ball must accurate, so I put extra energy into getting dead perfect position on the 3–ball shot. If the leave for the 4–ball is good the passage to the 5–ball will not be difficult.

Before shooting a single ball I walk around the table and sight each shot in the planned sequence. I place my hand on the table where I want the cue ball to land and make sure that the angle is right to continue the run without undue difficulty. Stalking the table eliminates a lot of simpleminded errors.

SQUARING THE BOX 3

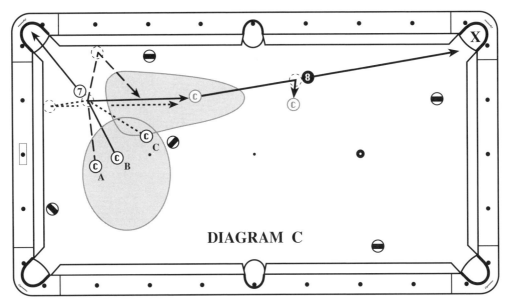

DIAGRAM C

If the play from the 6–ball to the 7–ball is successful the game is over because of the huge area for the 7–ball to 8–ball transition and the large position zone for the 8–ball shot.

Finishing the game is a simple matter once the shooter gets a good 6–7–8–ball sequence lined up.

The important thing is developing the ability to see these easy outs.

The value of getting there a little ahead of an opponent outweighs either skill or the finest calculations.
SUN TZU   THE ART OF WAR

A MELBA TWIST

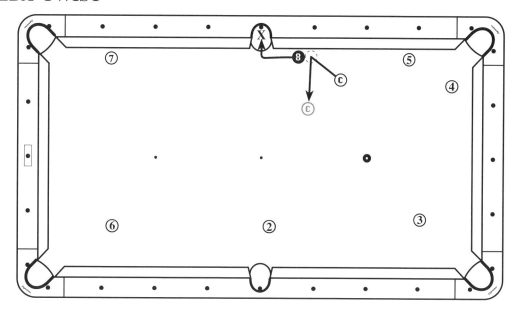

Just to show that you can never take anything for granted here's a trick shot a wise guy put on me at Melba's Bar one night.

My opponent appeared to be headed for a sojourn in **One–Ball–Hell** because there was no open pocket for the 8–ball.

Surprisingly my foe called the eight in side **X**. I thought he probably meant to lag the ball in front of the side hoping for a good shot in case I didn't run out because there was no possible way to score in the side from this position. At least that's what I thought.

I watched in stunned silence as the shooter very lightly tapped the eight parallel to the cushion and the slow moving ball caught a table roll and dropped right into the side. I was flabbergasted because I had checked the table for roll–offs during the warm up session and didn't find anything at all.

Checking the table *very* carefully after the game revealed no roll–offs *except* in front of this one errant side pocket.

I got revenge by playing the same shot in a later game, but I prefer tables without tricky rolls.

SLIDE–THRU

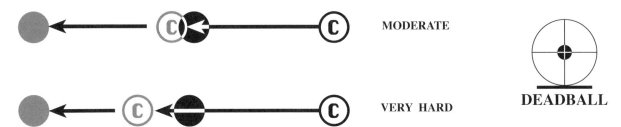

MODERATE

VERY HARD

DEADBALL

STOP SHOT ACTION WITH OVERWEIGHT CUE BALL

Now let's consider the *Slide–Thru* effect an overweight Aramath Red Dot Cue Ball (a standard bar table cue ball) has on stop shots, draw action and follow shots.

STOP SHOT: Careful observers notice that stop shots do not really stop on bar tables. Unless some draw is applied the cue ball *falls* forward a half a ball space or so when a sliding cue ball hits an object ball dead on as shown above. When more force is used the cue ball may *fall* forward a ball space or two past the contact point with the object ball. I use the term *fall* to describe this ball action because the cue ball seems to *stagger* forward a bit after the collision and *slouches* down flat on its face.

When I first noticed this phenomena I thought I had inadvertently hit the cue ball with a touch of deadball follow. However, careful experimentation proved that no rotation whatsoever is needed to propel the cue ball forward a bit after the collision.

Slide–Thru is caused by the fact that the Red Dot Cue Ball weighs 6.8 ounces compared to 5.7 ounces for the object balls.[1] The increased weight is only needed to separate the bar cue ball from the object balls in the ball returns, but the effects of this extra mass–energy are felt on every shot.

A same weight cue ball that is sliding with zero rotation stops dead when it hits an object ball full in the face. But the extra ounce of mass–energy in the Red Dot Cue Ball makes it impossible for the object ball to absorb all of the forward energy of an overweight cue ball even with a full ball hit— thus you get some *Slide–Thru* when deadball action is used. The harder the shot is hit the farther the cue ball moves beyond the normal deadball resting spot.

Gaining an understanding of the way things really work enables players to conform game plans to the physical realities of the game. Studying the *Slide–Thru* phenomena a bit will help to avoid attempting the impossible and will teach you ways to use *Slide–Thru* to your advantage.

---

[1] **NOTE:** The exact weight difference between the cue ball and object balls varies from table to table. The greater the weight difference the more pronounced the *Slide–Thru* effect will be. Some of the newest coin operated tables use same weight cue balls.

SLIDE–THRU: DEADBALL DRAW

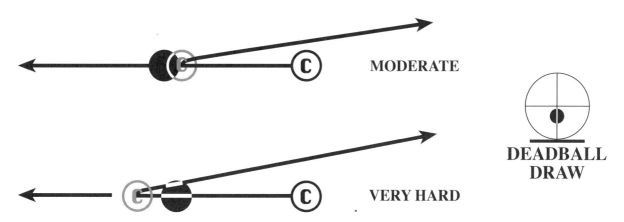

MODERATE

VERY HARD

DEADBALL DRAW

DEADBALL DRAW: The *Slide–Thru* phenomena is easily seen by using deadball draw and applying enough force to send the cue ball well past the object ball before the draw action takes effect. The amount *Slide–Thru* is determined by the friction between the ball and the cloth and the force you use relative to the amount of draw. The greater the difference in weight between the balls the farther the cue ball slides past the object ball.

The main thing is to experiment until you see the *Slide–Thru* in action and learn how to create this effect. If the cue ball does not *Slide–Thru*, use **less** draw and **more** force. It takes a pretty good lick and very little backspin to drive the cue ball past the object ball before it draws back.

As we will see in a bit using very little backspin and a lot of force can create some mind–bending shots by smashing an overweight cue ball well past the normal carom angle.

Please note that the cue ball remains in contact with the surface of the table throughout these *Slide–Thru* shots. No jump is needed to send the cue ball across the normal carom line. The extra mass-energy of the cue ball cannot be absorbed by the object ball permitting the cue ball to continue moving past the normal carom line without any bounce.

PROOF POSITIVE

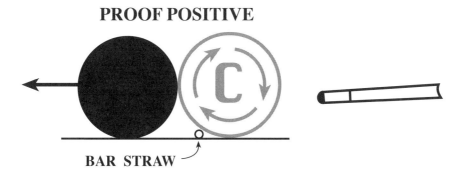

BAR STRAW

Place the cue ball in contact with the object ball and set a bar straw on the cloth where the cue ball will hit it after the cue ball passes the impact point. With a same weight cue ball it is impossible to cross the carom line using draw without leaving the table. However, this is absolutely not the case when the cue ball weighs one–ounce more than the object ball.

Purists are probably thinking "He's bouncing or jumping the cue ball to get this *Slide–Thru* action." However, this is definitely not the case. If you perform the experiment above, you can prove it to yourself. The idea is to *Slide–Thru* the object ball and draw back while driving the straw down table proving the cue ball was touching the table at the instant of contact.

Without getting into the physics involved it is adequate to say that there is an extra ounce of mass–energy left in the Red Dot cue ball after a full ball hit. This unspent energy forces the cue ball forward after the collision. The harder the cue ball is hit the more unabsorbed mass–energy there is left and the farther the cue ball slides past the object ball.

When I first tried this test it only took a couple of attempts to create an undeniable *Slide–Thru* draw shot that sent the bar straw skittering down the table like an errant Frisbee.

FAST DRAW

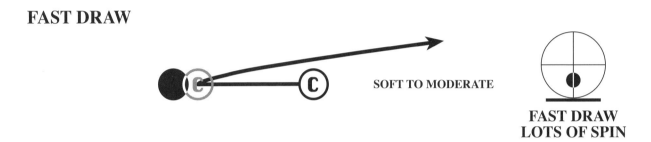

SOFT TO MODERATE

**FAST DRAW
LOTS OF SPIN**

Now we come to the fast draw— the shot that makes big table players cry for mercy when they have to use an overweight cue ball.

Let me preface these remarks by stating the fact that draw shots pose no special difficulty with an overweight cue ball **at close range**. When the cue ball is no more than two or maybe three diamond spaces away from the object ball draw shots can be made almost as easily as with a regulation weight cue ball. You do have to shoot a little harder and/or hit the cue ball lower, but there's no special difficulty involved.

When a fast draw is applied without excessive speed, the cue ball does not *Slide–Thru* very far. Instead some of the backspin is burned up stopping the forward motion of the cue ball during the collision and getting it started back again. Overcoming the *Slide–Thru* effect greatly reduces the strength of draw shots when any force is needed to get enough backspin.

Avoiding Miscues

The cue tip must be properly shaped, properly conditioned and properly chalked. If the tip is glassy and devoid of chalk or badly shaped, you can miscue at any time. So the first step is to make sure the tip is properly prepared and well chalked.

Look at the tip while you *brush* the chalk on with light strokes until the tip is evenly coated with a thin layer of chalk.

Grinding the chalk onto the tip sometimes misses a spot causing a miscue. It only takes a second to observe the chalking process to be sure the tip is well covered .

DRAW SHOT SECRET

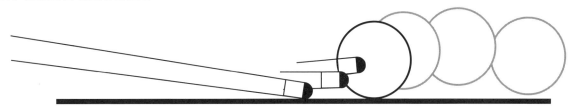

HITTING THE CLOTH FIRST CAUSES MOST MISCUES ON DRAW SHOTS

The secret to eliminating miscues on draw shots is to avoid hitting the cloth before the cue tip strikes the cue ball. If the cue tip is well chalked and properly shaped it is virtually impossible to miscue on a draw shot unless you hit the cloth first. The cause of 99% of all failed draw shots is hitting the cloth before hitting the cue ball.

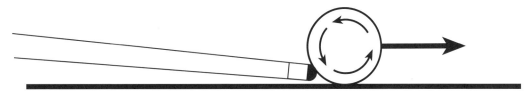

NO MISCUE WHEN CUE BALL IS HIT FIRST

If you watch the cue tip go through the cue ball, it will be seen that no miscue occurs so long as the cue tip strikes the cue ball first, no matter how low you hit.

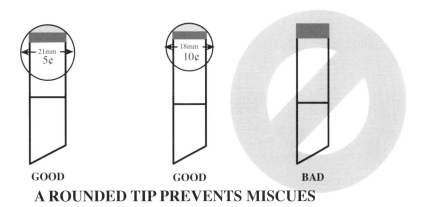

A ROUNDED TIP PREVENTS MISCUES

Another factor for eliminating miscues is a properly prepared cue tip. The shape of the tip should match the curve of a nickel (5¢) or a dime (10¢). A flat tip causes miscues when the cue ball is hit off center.

When the tip is well chalked and properly shaped and you do not hit the cloth first, the cue ball can be hit as low as possible without miscuing. Needless to say, if the tip is glossy and as hard a marble a miscue is still possible.

Keep your eyes on the cue tip as it goes through the cue ball to be sure that the cue tip does not hit the cloth until *after* contacting the cue ball.

SPIN TEST

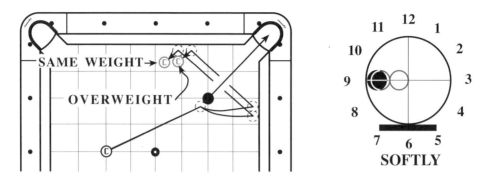

When the overweight and same weight cue ball paths are superimposed it becomes clear that the heavy bar cue ball listens to its own drummer and plows through the object ball following a path separated by more than a whole ball space from a same weight cue ball route.

An infinite number of diagrams showing how overweight carom angles diverge from a same weight ball path could be provided. But as a practical matter the best way to learn to use a heavy cue ball is by getting on a table and carefully observing ball action by using a *systematic approach* to explore the effects of different contact points and speeds.

If you want to see same weight cue ball action on any particular shot use an object ball in place of the overweight cue ball.

It is important to develop accurate mental imagery of heavy cue ball action to avoid unwanted collisions and misplayed positions on over crowded bar tables. Failing to realize that a bar cue ball path is *always* somewhat different from a same weight cue ball is one reason big table players often go down like the Titanic on bar tables.

The illustrations in this book show the precise contact points used and the exact cue ball routes produced on bar tables in reasonably good playing condition. Although some equipment plays differently these diagrams provide a good starting point for duplicating the shots on most tables.

The important thing is to pay some attention to exactly where you hit the cue ball on every shot. Missing the intended contact point on the cue ball is a very common fundamental error that causes erratic results.

There's a big difference between 1/2 tip of english and a full tip of english so learn to pay attention. Watching exactly where you strike the cue ball and remembering the results is the price of excellence. Learn to *measure* the amount of english you use in precise terms. One reason pool players have so much trouble with english is that they do not practice spinning the cue ball and they do not pay enough attention if they do.

When you ask a pool player what english to use for a shot, he/she is apt to say "left" or "right" as the case may be. Ask a billiard player the same question and you will be told how many "tips" of english to use and where to hit the cue ball according to a clock dial. For example, the shot above calls for maximum english at 9 o'clock.

Unless you learn to think about english in terms that you can *remember*, it will be impossible to repeat shots with certainty. Winners want to *know* the path the cue ball will follow and where it will land instead of guessing in critical situations. Winners make a point of hitting the cue ball exactly where they intend.

OVERWEIGHT CUE BALL ACTION

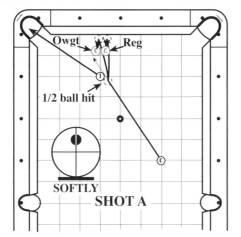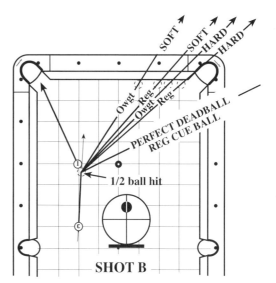

Owgt = Overweight Red Dot Bar Cue Ball   Reg = Standard Same Weight Cue Ball

It may seem irrelevant to compare heavy cue ball action with a same weight cue ball that is never (under the rules) used in bar competition, but the plain truth is that most players intuitively calculate shots based on the unconscious notion that a heavy cue ball reacts the same way a same weight cue ball does on a big table.

As we will see an overweight bar cue ball and a regulation weight cue ball *always* take a somewhat different path when the same speed and ball action are applied. Faulty mental images of heavy cue ball paths must be corrected if you hope to develop a high level of skill on the bar box.

SHOT A: On soft follow shots unobservant players seldom notice that an overweight cue ball immediately diverges a whole ball space from the regulation cue ball path. This divergence in carom angle begins immediately at even the slowest speeds grows larger the farther the cue ball travels after the carom.

Here the heavy cue ball lands **one full ball space** to the left of where a same weight cue ball comes to rest. In a game where millimeters mean the difference between victory and defeat a ball space (2.25") is nothing to sneeze at. Especially when we realize the divergence only gets bigger with more cue ball travel.

In the confined area of a bar table you are not going to get very far unless you develop an accurate mental image of how an overweight cue ball reacts.

SHOT B: More cue ball travel with differing speeds readily illustrates a 4-10° difference in carom angle between same weight and overweight cue ball paths.

Failing to notice the unsubtle differences in carom angles caused by an overweight cue ball is one reason big table players make so many positional errors on bar tables. Neglecting the effects of the extra mass of a bar cue ball causes game losing mistakes because *small* errors on *every* shot quickly accumulate into an unsolvable situation. Within four or five shots *little* mistakes can convert a runout pattern into an unplayable trap.

Going against the natural tendency of an overweight cue ball to *follow* the object ball is asking for trouble and you'll get plenty of it if you try to duplicate same weight cue ball action with an overweight bar cue ball.

GREAT ESCAPES — AVOIDING SIDE POCKET SCRATCHES

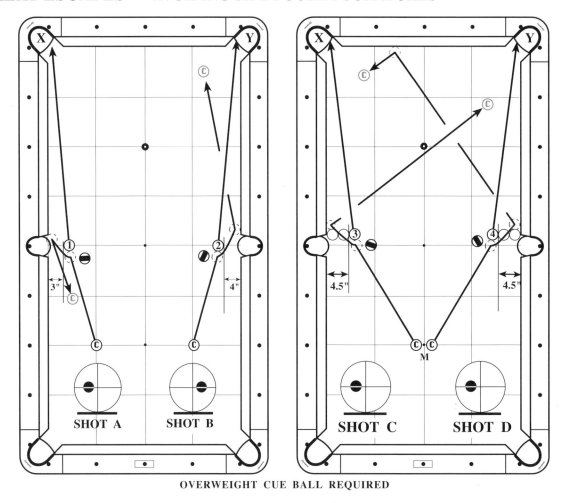

OVERWEIGHT CUE BALL REQUIRED

Now for a practical application of the overweight cue ball's propensity to *SMASH–THRU* the object ball.

SHOT A: This is a last ditch shot. Even though the object ball is ***only*** three inches out from the center of the side pocket, on many tables you can hit the point of the side pocket and avoid a scratch or even go on past the pocket entirely from this angle.

SHOT B: Moving the object ball out four inches from the edge of the pocket changes the shot angle enough to allow the cue ball to safely pass the nose of the side pocket from this angle.

SHOT C: Placing the object ball so the center is even with the edge of the pocket and two ball spaces from the cushion completely removes the chance of scratching at this angle (unless you draw the ball). When left english (reverse) is used the cue ball heads toward pocket **Y**.

SHOT D: When running english is used the cue ball hits the cushion well away from pocket **X** and can be driven back up the table for position if necessary.

Shots C and **D** can be made from position **M** without scratching on most tables so long as you avoid using draw or excessive force. Experiment to see how close to the pocket the object ball can be and still score without a scratch.

Players who do not understand overweight cue ball action actually think it is safe to leave shots like these.

RING AROUND THE ROSY

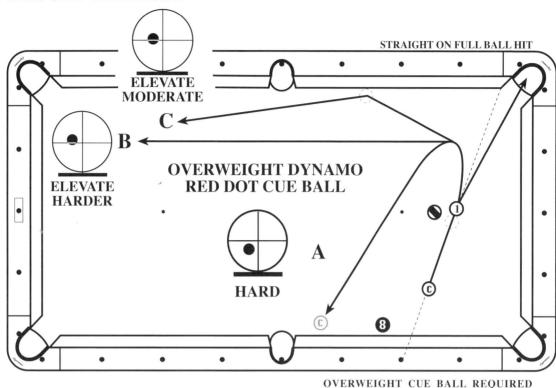

When **_Slide–Thru_** is deliberately put to work some spectacular position plays are possible.

These are not traditional bounce-draw shots. Although a small bounce helps the action, the extra mass–energy of a bar cue ball by itself can **_drive_** the cue ball through the object ball while the cue ball remains in contact with the cloth.

Deadball draw swings the cue ball around and brings it back.

Aiming the object ball straight into the point of the corner pocket and firing with considerable force makes all three shots. The english **_throws_** the object ball into the pocket and the force and deadball draw action create the fireworks. The amount of **_Slide–Thru_** obtained depends on the friction of the cloth, the force of the stroke and the amount of draw used. The harder you hit the cue ball the farther past the impact point it slides before the deadball draw action takes effect. Very little draw should be used because too much retrograde spin will kill the **_Slide–Thru_**.

A small bounce helps these shots but **_do not use a jump ball stroke_**. Merely elevating a bit and stroking hard provides all the hop you need. The secret to these shots is **stroking very hard** and **using very little draw**.

On brand new cloth **_Slide–Thru_** can be so exaggerated that cue ball control is extremely difficult.

> **NOTE:** There must be at least a one ounce weight difference between the cue ball and object balls to make these shots. It takes a **_very hard_** stroke to drive the cue ball so far **_Thru_** the normal carom line. Use three-quarter break speed and hit the cue ball **_very_** close to center with a **_touch_** of draw.

BUMP AND SMASH SHOTS

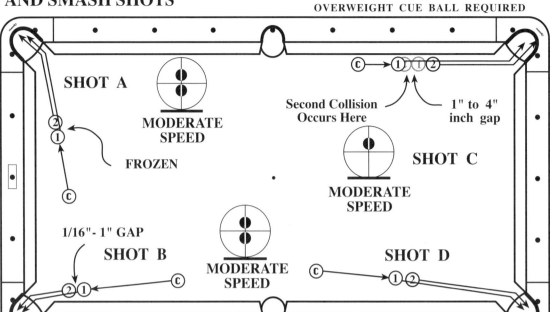

SHOT A: The extra weight of a bar table cue ball makes it easy to pocket *both* balls when they are frozen straight in and a foot or more from the pocket. With a regulation ball this shot is far more difficult. The heavy cue ball's the extra weight *Smashes–thru* through giving the 1-ball an authoritative shove toward the corner.

Instead of waiting for the cue ball to acquire forward motion from the follow action the heavy cue ball *Smashes–thru* and catches up with the 1-ball immediately and rudely pushes the 1–ball forward right into the pocket. Surprisingly little force is needed.

When the balls are close together this shot is a piece of cake— so long as you have a dead straight line up. Experiment to see how softly you can play these shots and still make both balls.

SHOT B: A gap of as much as an inch between the balls is irrelevant because you can still make both balls using draw or follow. It does not take much force to get the second impact that drives the 1-ball forward into the pocket. The overweight cue ball surges forward giving the 1-ball an extra bump that sends it rolling right into the pocket. Experiment with the gap and see what you can do on your equipment.

When the balls are up to an inch or so apart *Smash–thru* shots can be made using deadball draw or stop shot action.

Shots A and **B** can be easily made using either draw or follow action. When you miss the 1–ball usually blocks the target pocket making this a good *Shot–safety* in many situations.

SHOT C: As the gap gets larger the draw and deadball options become more and more difficult to execute. However, *Follow and Bump action* works like a charm with a gap of several inches between the balls.

If the 2–ball is near the pocket a *Follow and Bump* shot is very playable with a couple of feet between the 1 and 2–balls providing the balls are lined up well.

SHOT D: Distance from the pocket is secondary if you have perfect alignment and the balls are close to each other. A soft follow stroke does the trick with arbitrary authority.

FOLLOW, ROLL AND BUMP

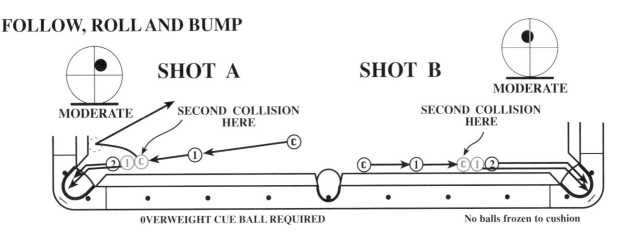

SHOT A   SHOT B

MODERATE   MODERATE

SECOND COLLISION HERE   SECOND COLLISION HERE

OVERWEIGHT CUE BALL REQUIRED   No balls frozen to cushion

SHOT A: Here's a **Follow, Roll and Bump** shot with more distance between the balls. When the 2-ball is close to the pocket, play the combination softly so the 1-ball **lands in front of the pocket where the cue ball catches up and bumps it in.**

You can often make the 1–ball with the help of a cushion. Finessing these shots a little bit by sending the cue ball into the cushion slightly before the second impact can provide an extra half-ball space margin of billiard error so pay attention to the carom possibilities when these shots come up.

If you develop a knack for **Bump** shots you can send the cue ball back up the table after the second collision for position on the next shot. Making both balls is a snap when everything is lined up good, but playing position to continue the run in style puts the frosting on the cake.

The biggest danger in these shots is having the 1-ball follow the 2–ball into the pocket leaving nothing to stop the cue ball resulting in a scratch that probably defeats you.

When you *want* to roll the 1–ball in after the 2–ball without any second collision set your mind on that shot and forget about bumping the 1–ball in.

It's a good idea to carom the 1–ball off the 2–ball slightly toward the cushion side whenever it won't spoil the shot. Doing this prevents the 1–ball from following the 2–ball it into the pocket before the cue ball arrives. There is very little leeway for cheating on these shots.

SHOT B: The follow and bump shot can be made when the 1–ball and 2–ball are up to a foot apart with 2–ball a foot or so from the pocket *if you are very careful and the shot is lined up perfectly.*

If you don't make the 1–ball there's very a good chance of hanging it in the pocket which is a good move in many situations.

SMASH THRU A GAP USING DRAW

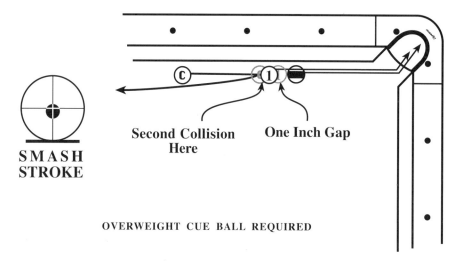

SMASH STROKE

Second Collision Here   **One Inch Gap**

OVERWEIGHT CUE BALL REQUIRED

When the balls are an inch or less apart, the second ball can also be made using deadball draw with a smash stroke.

Using very little draw and a lot of force allows the cue ball to slide through the collision giving the first object ball a second impact that sends it into the pocket.

Using lively draw creates so much retrograde spin that the cue ball cannot slide forward to bump the 1-ball in, so pay attention to where you hit the cue ball. *Very little draw* and a *powerful stroke* does the trick. A little experimentation quickly shows how the *Smash–thru Draw* works.

A *Smash–thru Draw* can be a lifesaver, but the extreme force required puts a premium on accuracy and precise setup, so take extra care.

Unless draw position is critical, *Follow and Bump* action is preferable because it is much more reliable for making both balls. A *Follow and Bump Shot* is a virtual certainty when the angle is right while a *Smash–thru Draw* is considerably more difficult because the cue ball must be *forced* through to where the first ball stops for the second impact with the 1–ball.

That requires perfect position and very good execution. So when you plan these shots into a run be triple sure you can land the cue ball on a dime for the exacting position necessary to make the second ball.

I hope the drawing isn't too confusing. The grey cue ball and the grey 1–ball show where the second collision occurs.

This is a fairly difficult shot and should be approached with caution.

NOTE: The friction between the balls and the cloth is the critical factor in determining the amount of *Smash–thru* you get on a table. The more friction there is the less *Slide–Thru* there will be. On slick new cloth *Smash–thru* and *Slide–thru* action can become so extreme that incredible position play becomes the norm.

GETTING THE SHOT

OVERWEIGHT CUE BALL REQUIRED

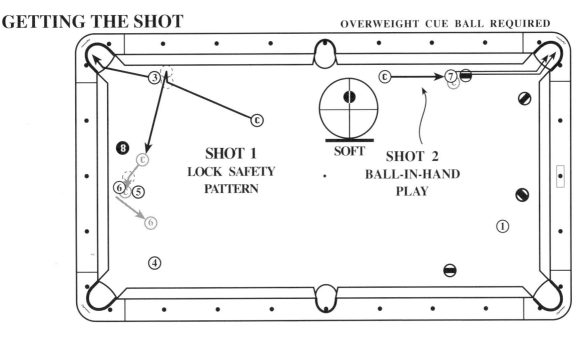

This game shows how put a *Smash–Thru* shot into play using a lock safety.

Smash–Thru Shots require *perfect* cue ball placement so look for an iron–clad–life–without–parole safety to get **Ball–In–Hand** for the pinpoint position needed to make these shots.

Solids could easily make all of their group except for the 7–ball, which is far from any help. But by now we know the penalty for shooting yourself into **One–Ball–Hell**, so a different plan is called for.

SHOT 1: LOCK SAFETY If solids can get **Ball–In–Hand** the 7–ball can be made with little difficulty, so a maximum–security leave is required. The 5–6–ball congregation offers an opportunity to freeze the cue ball against the 5–ball leaving stripes an extremely difficult shot just to hit a ball.

Make a maximum effort to leave the opposition *frozen* to the 5–ball to get **Ball–In–Hand**. That means **getting good position to make** the safety, instead of hoping for a lucky leave or playing a superhuman cue ball move.

Good safeties require as much planning and position play as using key balls, breaking clusters and other critical aspects of pattern play.

A take–no–prisoners safety can win the day when uncompromising position is needed and no key shot is available.

Getting **Ball-In-Hand** is a Godzilla move that resolves ornery situations and brings champions to their knees.

SHOT 2: BALL–IN–HAND SHOT The importance of getting dead straight in on a *Smash–Thru* shot cannot be overemphasized. There's very little margin for position error on these shots. In other words, *Smash–Thrus* are either very easy to make or virtually impossible.

THREE BALL BUMPS

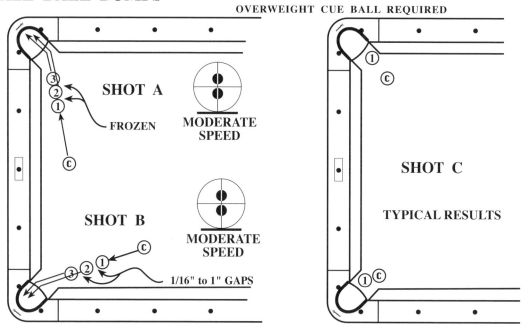

OVERWEIGHT CUE BALL REQUIRED

SHOT A

FROZEN

MODERATE SPEED

SHOT B

MODERATE SPEED

1/16" to 1" GAPS

SHOT C

TYPICAL RESULTS

Following Grady Matthews's advice to expand principles as far as possible, I tried some three-ball line-ups to see what an overweight cue ball could do. The likelihood of three balls lining up dead straight on a pocket is pretty remote, but I was curious to see what could be done with a third object ball in the mix.

SHOT A: It quickly became apparent that sinking the 2-ball and 3-ball in the chain is a piece of cake. The overweight cue ball herds the balls forward with multiple collisions *forcing* the 2 and 3-balls into the corner.

Occasionally I made all three balls during my experiments (using follow), but I cannot do it reliably. However, making the last two balls in the chain is *very reliable* providing the cue ball is dead straight into the shot.

SHOT B: Next I tried the same configuration with 1/16" to 1" gaps between the balls. It was a very simple matter to make the 2–ball and 3-ball almost every time.

SHOT C: The Leave
These are typical results of three–ball *Bumps*. Very often the 1-ball is left right in the jaws of the pocket with the cue ball near at hand. Despite the close proximity the leave is usually easily playable for position down table.

I've made two–ball bumps in games quite a few times. The *Bump* shot has a devastating effect on enemy morale when they are counting on the blocking ball to prevent a run.

A three–ball *Bump* may not come up for ten thousand games, but I took a **CPR** course to revive my opponents when it does.

SMASH–THRU AT AN ANGLE

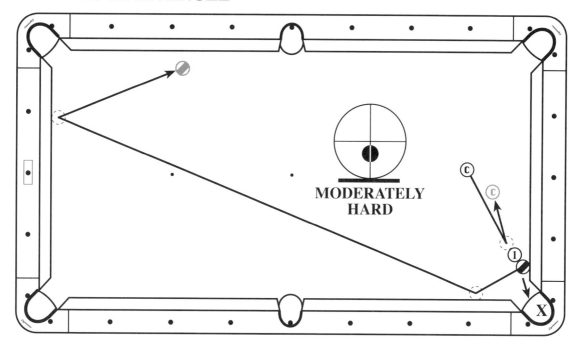

MODERATELY HARD

An overweight cue ball makes a **Smash-Thru** on the 1–ball an easy proposition when the balls are frozen at a good angle like this. Hitting the 1–ball very slightly off center away from the cushion side of the ball with a solid draw stroke drives the 1–ball through the stripe into corner **X**.

This shot can be made with a regulation cue ball, but an overweight cue ball makes it much easier to *smash* the 1–ball through the stripe.

SMASH–THRU FOR POSITION

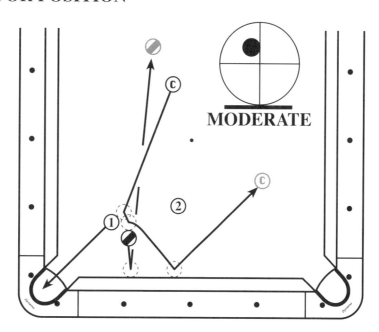

MODERATE

Here's a good shot that players unfamiliar with overweight cue ball action often pass up. Firm follow combined with the extra weight *drives* the Red Dot Cue Ball through the stripe at an unexpectedly sharp angle and comes back for position on the 2–ball. These shots come up frequently on bar tables and it only takes a little work to get a feel for this type of shot, so practice, practice, practice.

SMASH-THRU KISS SHOTS

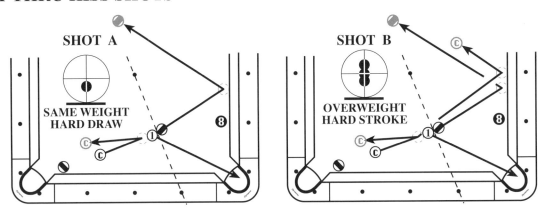

After seeing an object ball smashed clear through an interposing ball, it shouldn't come as a surprise that kiss shots using an overweight cue ball can send an object ball across the normal carom line.

SHOT A: This shot can be made using a same weight cue ball by applying forceful draw. Backspin puts a small amount of follow action on the solid sending it across the normal right angle carom line (dashed line). However, the shot is much easier using an overweight cue ball to **force** the 1–ball over the normal carom line.

SHOT B shows what can be done with an overweight bar table cue ball. Smashing the 1–ball enables you to drive the 1–ball through the stripe into the corner with draw, deadball or follow. With a same weight cue ball it is very difficult to make the 1–ball using follow or deadball action. With a heavy cue ball all it takes is a powerful stroke. The extra mass of the overweight cue ball easily *forces* the 1–ball through the intervening stripe regardless of ball action.

With an overweight bar cue table ball you can make the 1-ball and play position up table to make the 8–ball on the next shot, a play that is impossible with a regulation cue ball (for me and everyone I know).

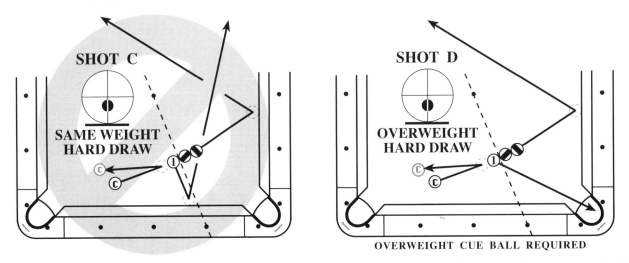

OVERWEIGHT CUE BALL REQUIRED

SHOT C: With a same weight cue ball no matter how much draw and no matter how much force was applied it was impossible to generate enough thrust on the 1–ball to drive it through two balls. In fact, the 1-ball follows the right angle carom line very precisely.

SHOT D: With an overweight cue ball the 1–ball can be made, but only by using a *very* forceful draw shot. The combination of draw, speed and extra mass drives the 1–ball through two balls demonstrating the unique physics when different weight balls collide.

TICKIES

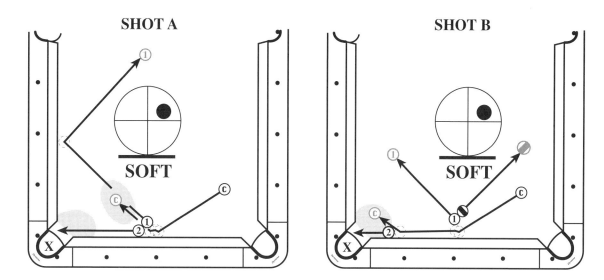

SHOT A   SHOT B

SOFT   SOFT

SHOT A: This shot is harder to explain than it is to make. Just bank into the 1-ball cushion first with running english and a relatively soft stroke and the 2-ball scores a surprising amount of the time.

If you miss, the 2-ball lands in the gray area blocking pocket **X** most of the time. It takes very little practice to learn this move.

The main drawback to these shots is that the cue ball is bound to land near the foot rail.

SHOT B: Another easy tickie. When the 2-ball is sitting near the rail anywhere between the 1–ball and the pocket there's a good chance of making the ball.

If you miss, the 2-ball blocks pocket **X** most of the time making this a good *Shot–Safety* in many situations.

KISSY KISS

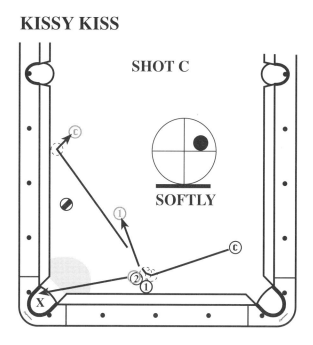

SHOT C

SOFTLY

SHOT C: Here's a nifty *Shot-Safety* time shot that can be made with some regularity.

The 1 and 2–balls are touching each other and frozen to the cushion. The idea is to hit the 1–ball thin *springing* the 2–ball out a bit to where the cue ball catches it on the fly and sends it into pocket **X**.

I like these shots because when I miss them, which happens a lot, the 2–ball usually blocks pocket **X** making this an advantageous *Shot–Safety* in many layouts.

When the 2–ball goes, act like the shot was a piece of cake and run the game out.

POSITION ROUTE 1

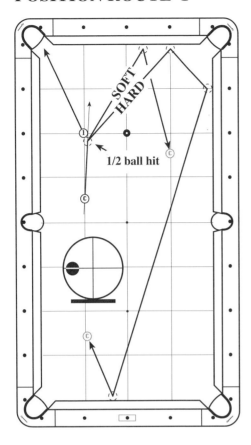

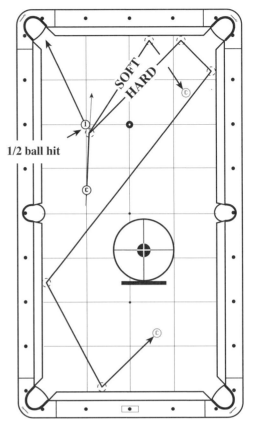

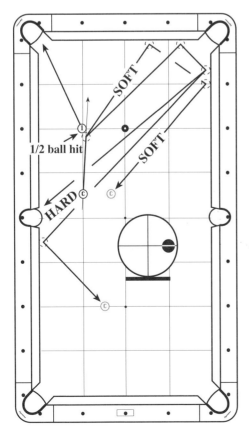

Experimenting with english and speed systematically teaches control of the bar cue ball in a practical manner.

Learning the effects of spin and force on fairly common shots should enable players to extrapolate the effects of ball action and speed on many similar shots.

Pay attention to position routes that provide safe, reliable, no scratch paths to the next shot.

NOTE: All of the illustrations in this book unless otherwise stated were made using an overweight Aramith Red Dot cue ball that outweighs the object balls 6.8oz to 5.7oz.

Many modern tables use lighter cue balls closer to the same weight as the object balls that react differently. Readers should practice with the same kind of cue ball used on their tables. The important thing is learning cue ball control.

POSITION ROUTE 2

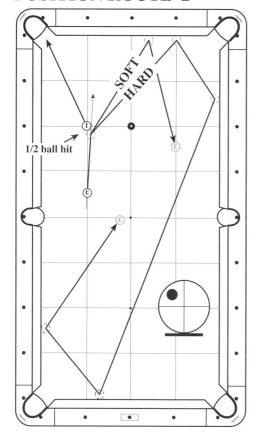

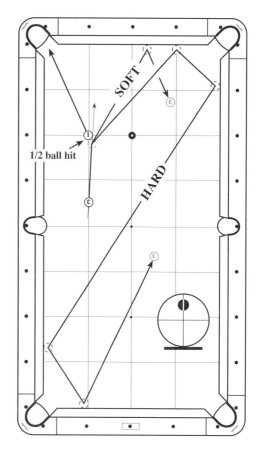

This time we'll see what happens using follow with and without sidespin on soft and hard strokes.

Position routes vary according to the condition of the cloth and cushions. The important thing is to experiment with cue ball control under game conditions.

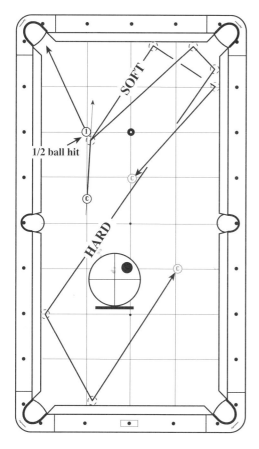

POSITION ROUTE 3

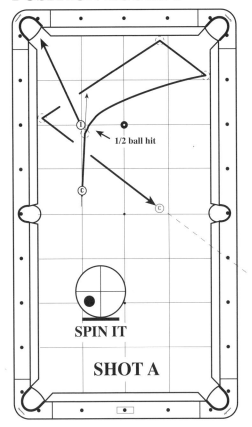

SPIN IT

SHOT A

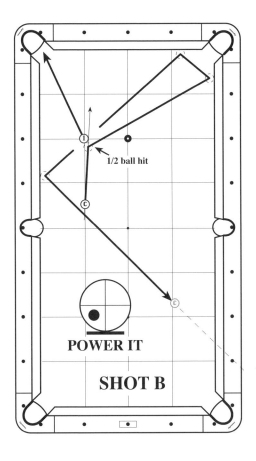

POWER IT

SHOT B

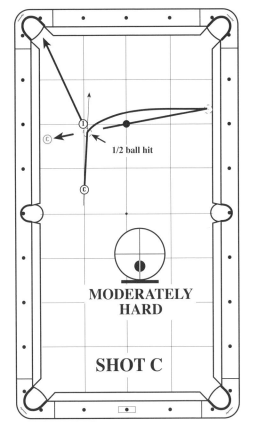

MODERATELY HARD

SHOT C

Now we'll use draw with and without sidespin.

SHOTS A and **B** show two distinct position routes created with almost the same contact point on the cue ball.

Shot A: Draw pulls the cue ball over near the first diamond and then the spin propels it back to the middle of the table. When you get the action right the cue ball accelerates a bit coming off the first cushion. You need to *spin* the cue ball for this one.

Shot B: Hitting harder reduces the effect of the draw driving the cue ball back up table on a different route.

Shot C shows what happens with a power draw and no english. If the cue ball still has some back spin when it hits the cushion the draw acts like english causing the cue ball to rebound toward the head of the table a bit.

Less draw sends the cue ball almost straight across the table on the rebound.

POSITION ROUTE 4

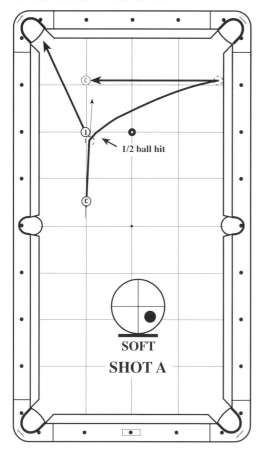

SOFT

SHOT A

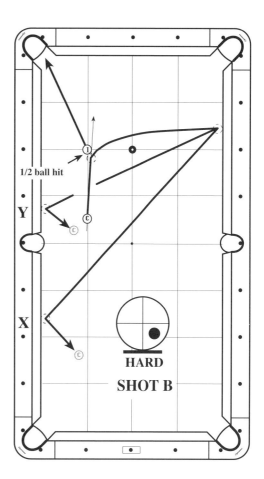

HARD

SHOT B

This time outside draw is used.

SHOT A: When played softly right draw hits near diamond 1 and brings the cue ball straight across the table.

SHOT B: On many tables it is possible to hit the cushion between **Y** and **X** with reasonable control. Exactly how far up table you can swing the cue ball depends on an accurate stroke and the condition of the cloth and cushions. Bringing the cue ball back to **X** is possible on many tables.

A forceful stroke is required, but spin does the work.

POSITION ROUTE 5

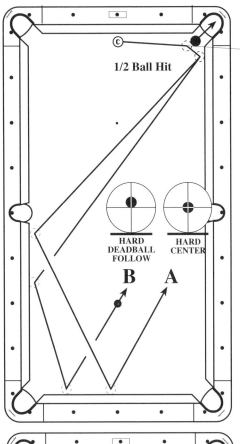

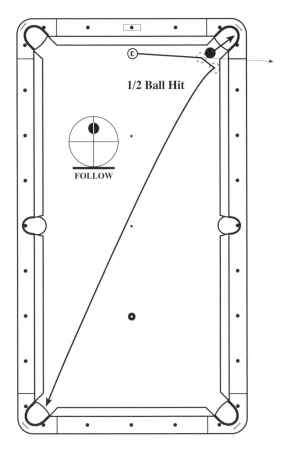

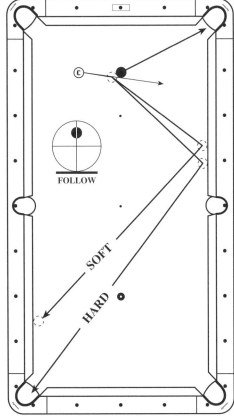

Notice how small changes in ball action and force change rebound angles.

Small nuances of speed and contact point can be used for precision cue ball control.

Of course, you have to practice and pay attention.

POSITION ROUTE 6

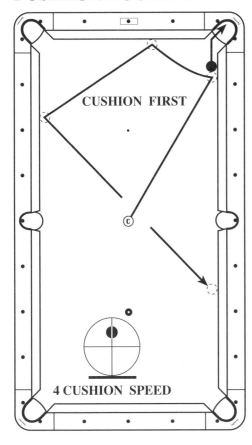

Object Ball Frozen 3 Inches From Facing of Pocket

CUE BALL ON CENTER SPOT

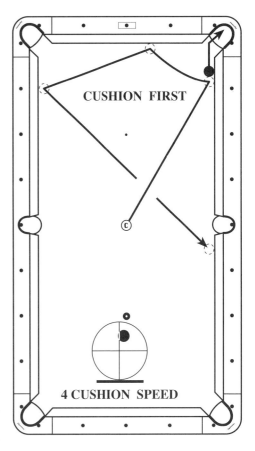

Two things pool players fear are follow shots around the table and using reverse english on a cushion shot.

Nevertheless, many important position plays call for driving the cue ball back up table using reverse english.

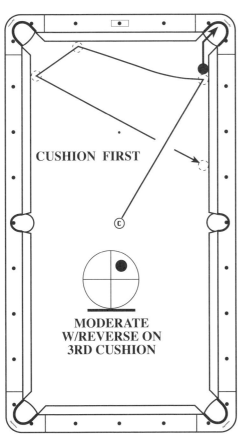

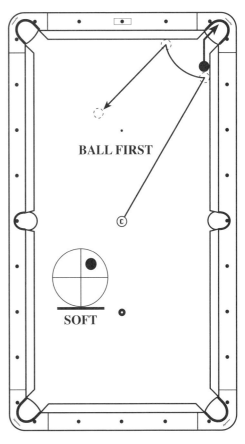

POSITION ROUTE 7

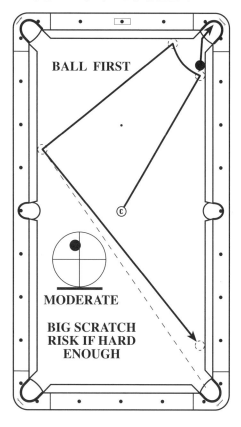

BALL FIRST

MODERATE

BIG SCRATCH
RISK IF HARD
ENOUGH

Object Ball Frozen
3 Inches From
Facing
of Pocket

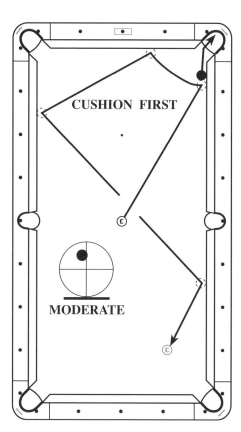

CUSHION FIRST

MODERATE

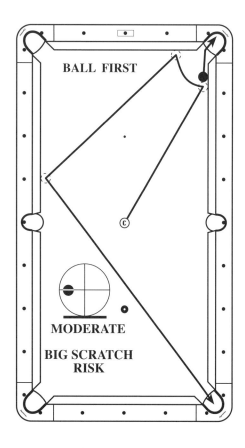

BALL FIRST

MODERATE

BIG SCRATCH
RISK

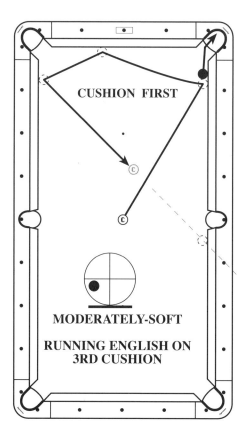

CUSHION FIRST

MODERATELY-SOFT

RUNNING ENGLISH ON
3RD CUSHION

POSITION ROUTE 8

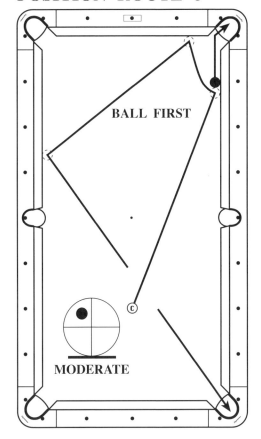

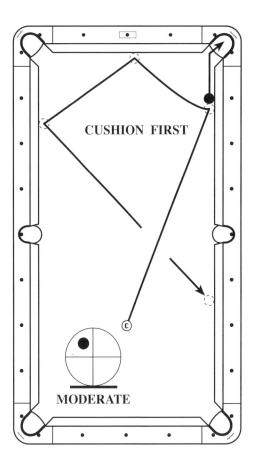

These diagrams show the difference between hitting **ball first** and **cushion first** on rail shots. The general rule is that hitting cushion first results in a **shorter** landing distance down the fourth rail.

In the example above, there's more than a two diamond difference in the fourth cushion destination between ball first and cushion first shots using the same english and speed.

Players seeking to master the cue ball must study the rebound angles caused by cushion first and ball first shots because knowing the destination of the cue ball eliminates the risk of scratching and adds new dimensions to position play, cluster play and safety play.

The secret to making cushion shots is to play the object ball as though there was no cushion there. Allow for throw as if the ball were clear of the cushion. This is especially important when using cushion–side english.

Hitting cushion first or ball first is decided according to the cue ball route you want to follow. A competent shooter can play both options.

Practicing systematically will program these shots into your game plans.

POSITION ROUTE 9

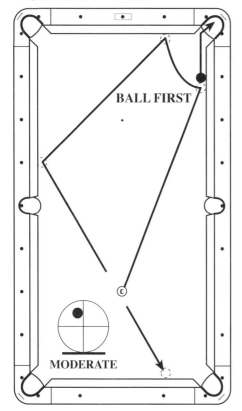

BALL FIRST

OBJECT BALL
FROZEN

MODERATE

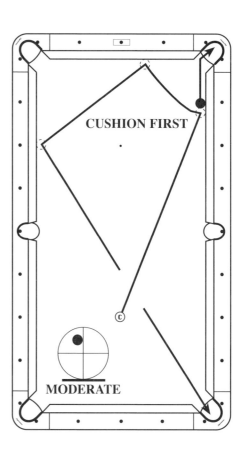

CUSHION FIRST

MODERATE

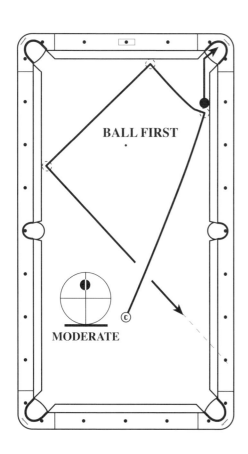

BALL FIRST

MODERATE

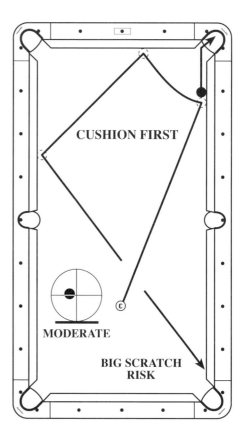

CUSHION FIRST

MODERATE

BIG SCRATCH
RISK

POSITION ROUTE 10

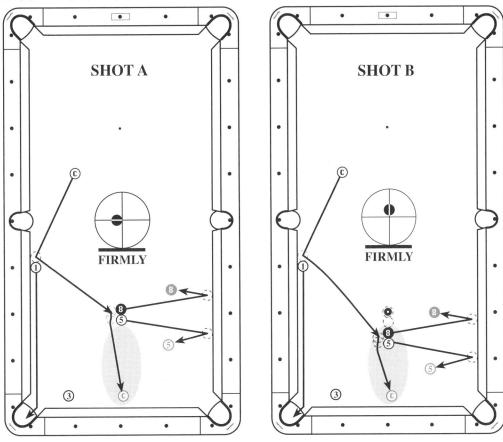

Small changes in english make a considerable difference in carom angle.

SHOT A: Making the carom requires using 1/2 tip running english (left–hand). Any *follow* at all sends the cue ball too far forward to hit the cluster as shown in **SHOT B**.

SHOT B: If the cluster is just a couple of ball spaces closer to the foot rail all that is needed is a touch of follow to break the group apart. Using follow changes the rebound angle by 10 degrees, which results in a considerably different destination for the cue ball.

Paying attention to small differences in ball action is the price that must be paid to master the cue ball.

POSITION ROUTE 11

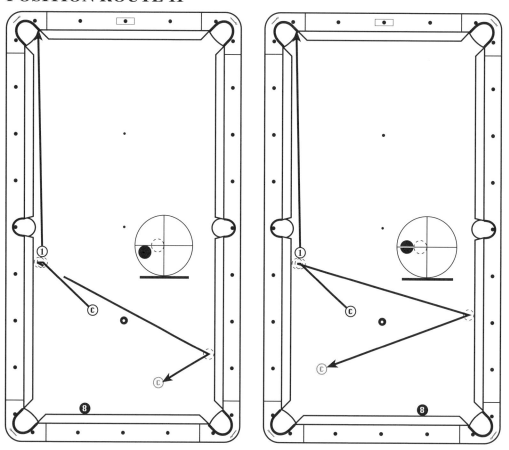

Here are a couple of *1–2–3–System* shots. If you practice using english systematically position plays like these are relatively easy.

Watch the cue tip go through the cue ball when you practice to make sure you are applying the amount of english you think you are. A lot of intermediate players never hit the cue ball where they think they do. The amount of error in their stroke is revealed by position plays gone wild.

See *1–2–3–System*.

POSITION ROUTE 12

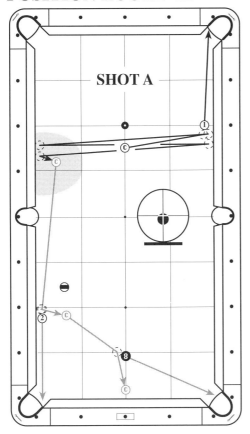

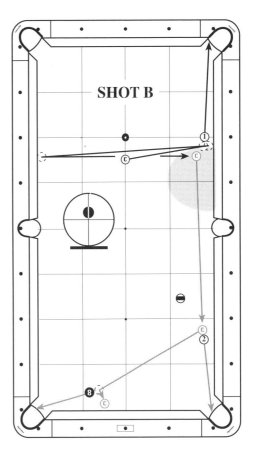

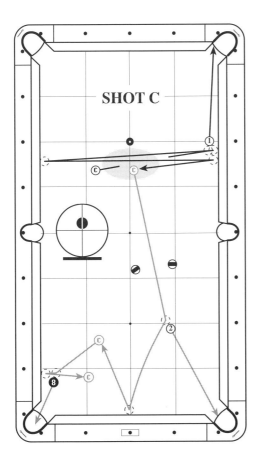

On thin cut shots most players focus so much on making the object ball that they forget all about where the cue ball will land.

The secret to success on these shots is concentrating on driving the cue ball the right distance instead of only thinking about making the 1–ball. The *first* thing to figure is the speed needed to play the planned position. Deflection, throw, carom angle and ball travel are all affected by speed. The cut shot must be aimed according to the speed needed to drive the cue ball into the desired position zone.

When you get plays that *might* be possible going one rail, forego the temptation and play a safer three or four cushion route to the position zone.

The number of times the cue ball must cross the table to land in the position zone depends on how fast the cloth is. The idea is to choose the position route that seems most certain even if it means hitting the shot considerably harder than just cutting the object ball requires because you won't get far shooting from the wrong side of the table after every thin cut.

POSITION ROUTE 13

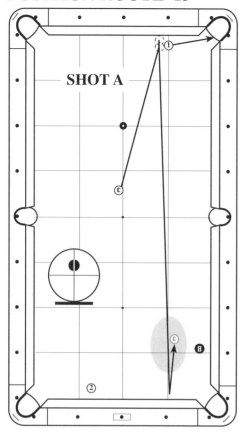

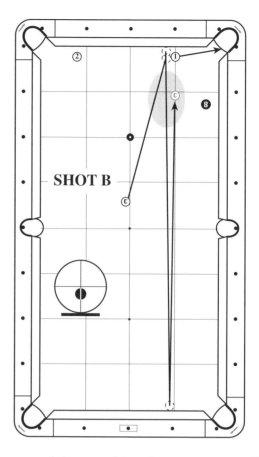

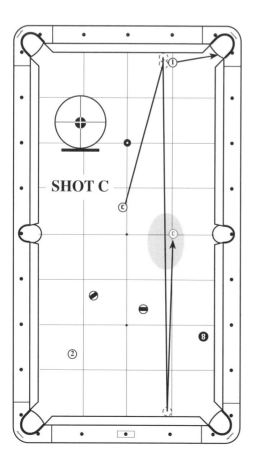

Long up and down position plays are no more difficult to control than their cross table cousins. It's just a matter of fixing the speed in your mind *before* you bend over to shoot.

Trying to adjust the force of your stroke while in the stance is a good way to wind up on the wrong end of the table or to miss the cut shot entirely. Figuring the speed accurately from the beginning is vital for making the object ball since force affects the cut angle.

The fact that a ball loses around 50% of its velocity with a square rebound off a cushion means that the speed for two or three cushion routes is considerably greater than a 1–cushion roll.

The idea is to *visualize the whole shot*. This means *pre–seeing* the speed as well as the cut angle.

As your control of the drive improves zero in on smaller and smaller target areas.

POSITION ROUTE 14

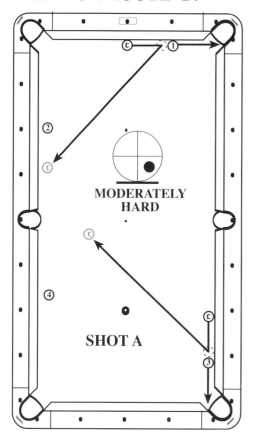

MODERATELY
HARD

SHOT A

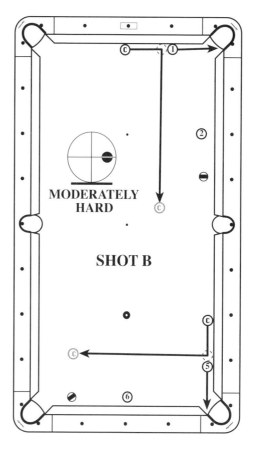

MODERATELY
HARD

SHOT B

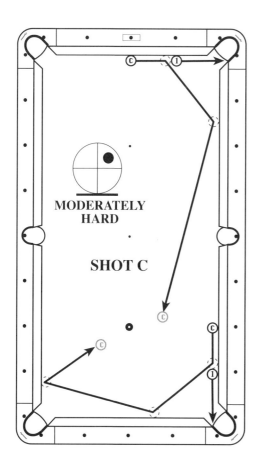

MODERATELY
HARD

SHOT C

Knowing how to play position when both the cue ball and object ball are frozen to a cushion is a valuable asset.

The secret to these shots is using outside english (away from the rail) and hitting with a moderately hard stroke. Focusing your attention on making the 1–ball and delivering a straight–through stroke with outside english gets the job done. Varying the english enables a player to create almost any exit angle on these shots.

When the balls are not too far from the pocket the position routes shown are possible.

SHOT A: Using right–hand draw english sends the cue ball along the paths shown.

SHOT B: Deadball with outside english propels the cue ball off the cushion at a right angle. Landing the cue ball in the center of the table is not too difficult on most cloth. The spin *walks* the cue ball it up to the middle of the table. The more spin the farther the cue ball travels.

SHOT C: Follow with right–hand english produces these useful position routes. When the spinning cue ball hits the second cushion the rotation sends the cue ball 3/4 of the way down table.

REVERSE REBOUNDS

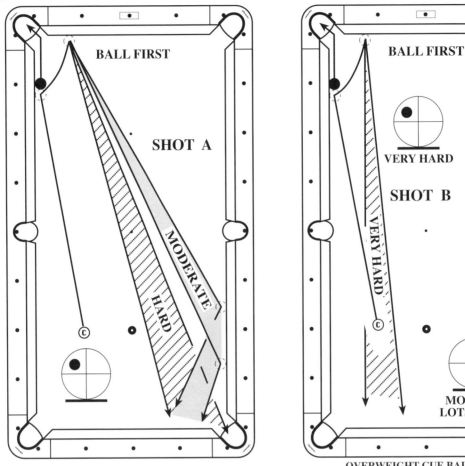

SHOT A: Using reverse english with an *overweight cue ball* adds a new dimension to position play because the extra weight *drives* the cue ball through the object ball to the second cushion with enough speed and english remaining to radically alter the cue ball path off the end rail.

SHOT B: Players go into shock when they see the cue ball coming back down table like this because the shot is *extremely difficult* using a same weight cue ball due to the fact that adding spin increases resistance to following the path shown. The unexpended inertia of the *overweight cue ball* overcomes the *braking* effects of the reverse english making these shots possible

An overweight cue ball makes this a sure thing if you practice it a bit. Just add another tip of reverse english, hit harder and the mass of the bar table cue ball plows through the shot with plenty of reverse english and sufficient speed to come back down the same side of the table the cue ball started on.

It is important to allow for *throw* on these shots as though the cushion was not there

This shot puts good players on notice that they have battle on their hands.

SHOT C: This is a trick shot requiring a special touch that I lack. I only make the shot one or two times in ten which puts it in the sheer desperation category. This shot is *not* on my menu for game play when anything else is available. It merely illustrates the range possible using reverse english with an *overweight cue ball*.

REVERSE REBOUNDS

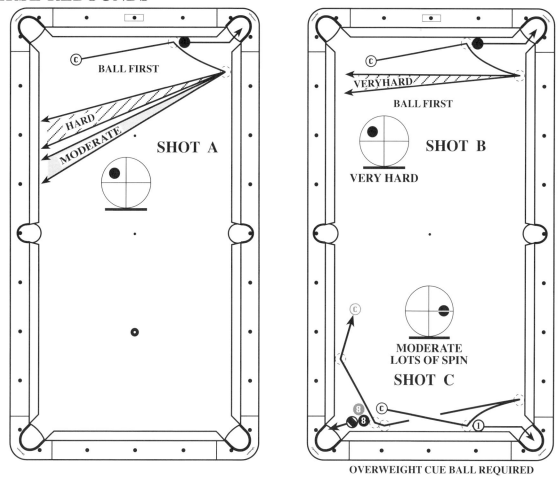

Following Grady Matthews's advice to expand a principle as far as possible provides additional position routes using reverse english.

SHOT A, B, C: Work the same way going cross table.

As mentioned before **SHOT C** borders on the fantastic, but if nothing else is available give it a try.

These routes are barely possible with a regular weight cue ball, because it takes a very delicate touch to send a same weight cue ball through to the end rail with enough reverse english and enough speed to bring the ball back down table. My friend Laz Janoska, who happens to be a Hungarian acrobat, is the only guy I know who *likes* the shot with a regulation cue ball.

Making one of these shots puts players on notice that they have battle on their hands.

> **WARNING: Reverse Rebound position routes are extremely difficult if not impossible without the extra weight of a Dynamo Red Dot cue ball. How far back the cue ball can be driven depends on table conditions, but the results shown here are often possible.**

Movies and TV liquor ads constantly show glamorous people setting drinks on the rails of pool tables, but doing this in many bars results in one warning and then ejection from the establishment.

Spilling liquid on a billiard cloth is a major disaster that renders a table unplayable until the cloth dries out. Indeed, the playing characteristics of the cloth can be permanently changed for the worse by an alcohol bath.

Dousing a table with beer, wine or whisky will almost certainly cause the person responsible to be thrown out of the bar, perhaps permanently, but any fool who spills a drink on a table gets no sympathy here because it is just plain stupid to wreck a table this way.

Onlookers should intervene instantly when some drunkass sets a drink on the table by immediately warning them of the risk they are taking. If a boozewit dismisses the warning (as drunks sometimes do) get the bartender involved and have him/her thrown out.

Nobody will be able to play any pool after some idiot soaks the table with firewater.

SAFETY PLAY

Players who think safety play is dirty pool, unsportsmanlike, anti-American or just plain chicken will find no sympathy in this book. Nowadays, league matches are fought with the same intensity as professional play and sometimes with equal skill.

Needless to say, if your opponent cannot clear the table with a push broom, safety play is irrelevant. However, taking needless chances against formidable opponents means defeat, so good defensive play is essential in high-speed competition.

Good safety play does more than simply stop the opposition from scoring. Strong defensive moves relocate problem balls, scatter clusters and solve tactical problems. Good safety play *improves* the shooter's group without surrendering control of the table. That's strategy.

Strong defensive play stifles opposition plans by shattering favorable positions before they can be used. That's strategy.

Strong safety play changes apparently defeated positions into almost certain victories by forcing game losing errors and setting up road map runouts. That's strategy.

Unfortunately, average players seldom know how to use safeties to convert bad positions into winners. Hopefully, the information here will resolve some of these mysteries and improve the reader's winning percentage. Strong safety play is the cornerstone of the *Safety–Blitzkrieg* style of play.

WHAT IS A SAFETY?
A safety is any leave that increases opposition difficulty in winning the game. The more so the better.

The most effective safety is the snooker, which is discussed at some length, but some very strong safeties deliberately give an opponent a playable shot at one of their balls. That's strategy.

A good safety also makes the player's group easier to make. That's strategy.

BALL–IN–HAND
The **Ball–In–Hand** rule is critical to this style of play because it prevents deliberate fouls, illegal safeties and unfair stalling tactics.

Ball–In–Hand is a tremendous asset for converting difficult situations into easy victories. Indeed, getting **Ball–In–Hand** tilts the battlefield so far that it usually wins the game. **Ball–In–Hand** blurs the boundaries between aggressive and defensive play by converting strong safety play into a lethally belligerent channels.

Getting **Ball–In–Hand** always provides the optimum position for the situation at hand so you have everything to gain if a lock safety succeeds.

Ball–In–Hand means defeat against players who use safety play to move problem balls, break up clusters and maneuver their group into winning positions.

The **Ball–In–Hand** penalty makes reckless shooting expensive because giving up **Ball–In–Hand** usually means a quick loss against a good player. The **Ball–In–Hand** penalty should curtail impulses to let the cue ball run loose because a scratch costs you the game.

Getting **Ball–In–Hand** is a worthy goal at any point in a game providing you do not take a big risk doing it.

The **Ball–In–Hand** rule is the single most important aspect of league play.

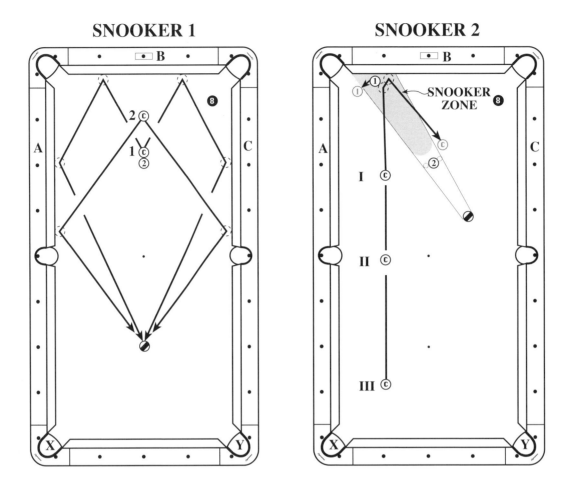

SNOOKERS— The Superlative Safeties

Snookers are the workhorses of effective safety play because forcing a player to kick, jump or massé to hit a ball sets the stage for misses, miscues, fouls and game losing forced errors. Strategic snookers win games even when an opponent hits the target ball.

Needless to say, some snookers are better than others. Let's see what makes one leave a sell out while another safety is a trip to solitary confinement.

SNOOKER 1: Freezing the cue ball against a snooker ball (position **1**) is clearly superior to leaving the cue ball farther away (position **2**) where the shooter can use cushions **A** and **C** for bank routes to the stripe. Freezing the cue ball or leaving it very close to the blocking ball forces an opponent to shoot much more difficult two–cushion banks to hit the stripe. A **Ball–In–Hand** foul often results, so this is a very desirable leave.

SNOOKER 2: Actually freezing the cue ball on an object ball is easier said than done when there's much cue ball travel involved. A freeze on the 2–ball *might* be possible from position **I**, but from positions **II** and **III** most players are more likely to lose the snooker altogether.

SNOOKER 3   **SNOOKER 4**

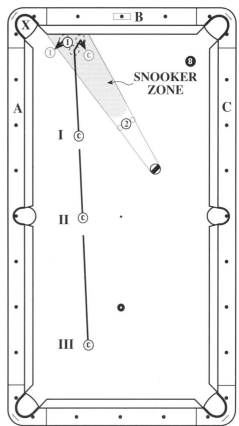

SNOOKER 3: Here's another aspect of snooker play to consider. The closer the cue ball lands to the snooker ball the weaker the safety becomes right up until the balls freeze up. Until the cue ball gets into the tiny area where cushions **A** and **C** are blocked the kick to hit the stripe actually becomes easier.

It's an observable fact that players do better kicking balls as the angle of incidence comes closer to 90 degrees. The more acute the bank angle becomes, the more accurate and consistent the kicks become.

In the example above the kick is measurably more difficult from position **1** than from position **5**. From position **1** even a good banker will have trouble making the stripe, but from position **5** mediocre bankers will hit the ball almost every time and are apt to *make* the ball from time to time. A good banker will frequently pocket balls from position **5,** but from position **1** just hitting the ball requires some skill and *making* the ball is a professional challenge.

A risk–benefit analysis shows that trying for a freeze up is a difficult proposition that will most likely help the opposition more than going for a simpler snooker that leaves a longer wider angle bank.

SNOOKER 4: An effective safety that can be made from any distance is to shoot softly landing the cue ball in the snooker zone near cushion **B** while bumping the 1–ball in front of pocket **X** for a *Starter Shot* in the next inning. The opposition may hit the stripe, but the chance of making the ball is remote.

Only *making* the stripe or lucking into a safety can save stripes from here.

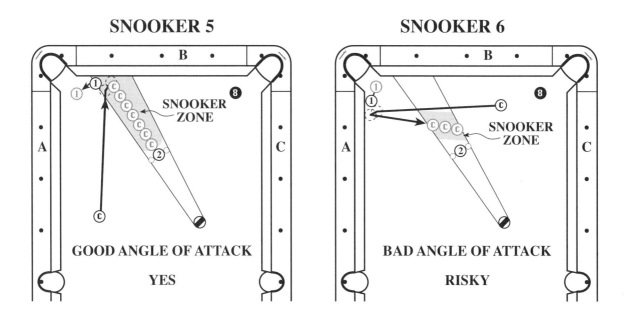

ANGLE OF ATTACK

Notice that the *Snooker Zone* shrinks considerably when the angle of approach is perpendicular to the shadow area.

SNOOKER 5: With a natural carom angle heading right at the blocking ball, the effective *Snooker Zone* could be several feet long. With a good angle like this you should get the snooker most of the time.

SNOOKER 6: When the angle of approach is *across* the neck of the *Snooker Zone* the area for a good safety dwindles to a few easy to miss square inches making a snooker attempt far more risky. Unless you are in good stroke avoid approaching *Snooker Zones* from lateral angles.

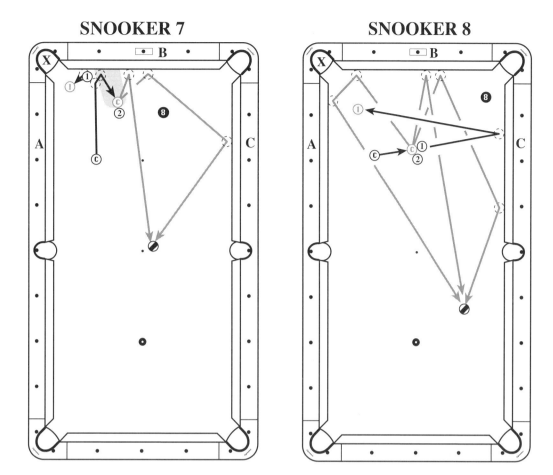

SNOOKER 7   **SNOOKER 8**

SNOOKER 7: Getting a freeze up is easy when the cue ball is close to the 1–ball and the distance to the 2–ball is short. Even mediocre players can make this lock safety.

If solids freezes the cue ball stripes has do some good banking just to hit the target ball. Even if stripes hits the ball, the 1–ball is waiting to cinch the game for solids if stripes fails to pocket a ball or get safe.

SNOOKER 8: Here's a good opportunity for a freeze–up because a simple stop shot does the trick.

Aim to miss the 1–ball. If you make the 1–ball you will become a victim of your own safety play.

The idea is to leave the 1–ball parked in front of corner **X** for a devastating *Starter Shot* in the next inning. Landing the 1–ball in easy position makes stripes a loser.

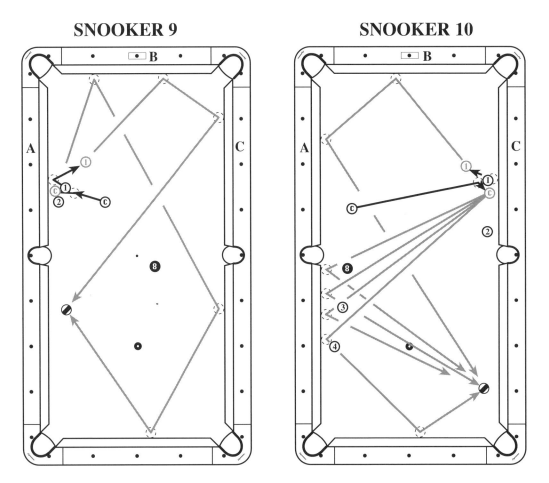

SNOOKER 9: Clusters near the rails often offer opportunities to put opponents in very bad spots. Especially when you play really good position to shoot the safety from.

Deliberately cutting off the two–cushion route by landing the 1–ball right on the two–cushion bank track puts the finishing touch on a spicy play like this. If the shot succeeds in blocking cushion **C**, stripes will be forced to shoot a very difficult 3 or 4 cushion kick shot that even professionals miss.

SNOOKER 10: Getting lock safeties where *all* bank routes are eliminated is mostly a matter of recognizing the opportunity because it is rarely possible to control enough balls to create one of these monster leaves. Nevertheless, these situations occur frequently in the confines of a bar table.

SNOOKER 11

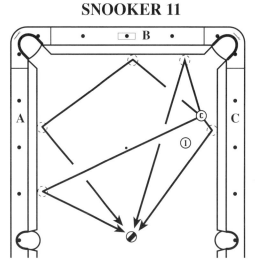

SNOOKER 11: This is a loose snooker that leaves four bank paths to the stripe. Your opponent will probably hit the stripe, but making it is not likely. When you only need a no foul miss leaves like this will suffice.

SNOOKER 12

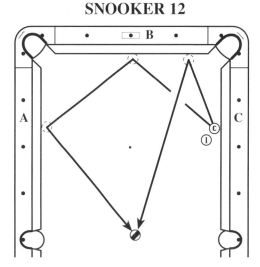

SNOOKER 12: When pool players are forced to kick off the end rail they get in trouble.

SNOOKER 13

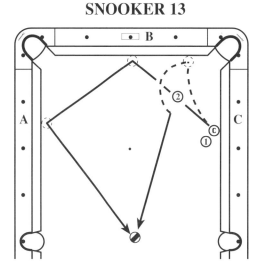

SNOOKER 13: With the 2–ball blocking both the one and two-rail bank paths only a jump shot off the nose of the cushion offers any hope. Very few players recognize the cushion jump and even fewer can make it in open play. Figure on getting **Ball–In–Hand** most of the time.

SNOOKER 14

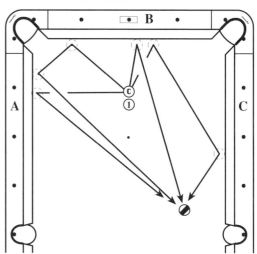

SNOOKER 14: Average players will fail to hit the stripe 9 out of 10 tries and there isn't much hope for a good outcome even if the ball is hit.

SNOOKER 15

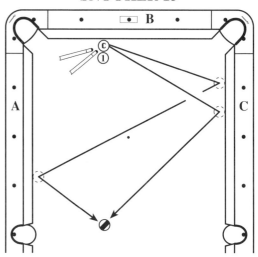

SNOOKER 15: This safety is so lethal that it is outlawed in 18 states. The victim of this deadly leave has the choice between two extremely difficult banks off Cushion B. Not many players make a good hit from here.

Whenever a player is forced to kick off a cushion from a very short distance, it is tough to visualize the bank angle correctly. Small errors are greatly magnified at close range so look for the opportunity to pin the cue ball to a cushion.

SNOOKER 16

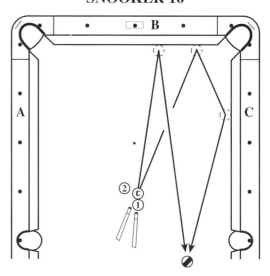

SNOOKER 16: When an opponent is forced to stretch out across the table and shoot jacked up over a ball you have the best of it.

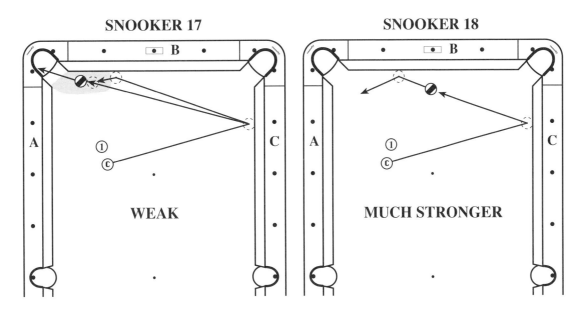

SNOOKER 17   SNOOKER 18

WEAK   MUCH STRONGER

SNOOKER 17: Whenever the target ball is less than a diamond space away from the pocket, near the cushion and the bank angle is natural, you can count on better players sinking the ball a good deal of the time. Any ball in the gray area is likely to be made. Weak safeties like this will beat you.

Balls near a cushion offer the extra aiming reference of the rail which makes accurate visualization much easier than for a mid–table shot. Balls within a diamond space of the pockets and near cushions, but not frozen, are especially vulnerable. Never think you are safe when an opponent's ball is close to a pocket and the angle of approach is simple.

SNOOKER 18: A good player will hit the stripe every time, but making it requires maximum accuracy because of the distance to the pocket. When you only need to force your opponent to fail to score, snookers like this will do the job.

SWINDLES, EMBEZZLEMENTS and DEAD–END SHOTS

CAROM LINE
for BREAK SHOT

SHOT A

SHOT B

SHOT C

Swindles are subtle safeties that create orphaned enemy clusters or leave impossible position plays for the next shot.

SHOT A shows how swindles work. As long as stripes lands the cue ball in the shaded area on the *wrong* side of the carom line, solids cannot break up the 2–3–ball cluster.

Making the 1–ball without breaking the clusters in positions like these is a huge strategic error that always bites you in the ass before very long.

Any other shot is preferable to gunning down a prospective break ball without opening the cluster. Shooting swindle shots is one reason players end up in **One–Ball–Hell.** Average players constantly shoot their way into dead-end streets without a second thought. Especially early in the rack when the possibilities seem endless.

Gunslinger types never seem to think twice before shooting a swindle— *IF the embezzlement is the simplest shot they have.* When setting up a swindle try to leave the 1–ball shot as short and sweet as possible. Try to snooker other balls in the opposing group to *force* the dead-end shot whenever possible.

Duping adversaries out of break shots cripples offensive capability by forcing difficult or impossible shots down the road. Leaving swindles for opponents and avoiding shooting into them will win dozens of games.

When *you* are faced with a fraudulent shot the best move may be to shoot directly into the cluster leaving your group open for the next inning. If you can do this and get safe so much the better, but leaving isolated coveys is suicidal so do not shoot your own foot off by playing into a swindle.

ROBBERIES, PRE–EMPTIVE STRIKES and ORPHAN CLUSTERS

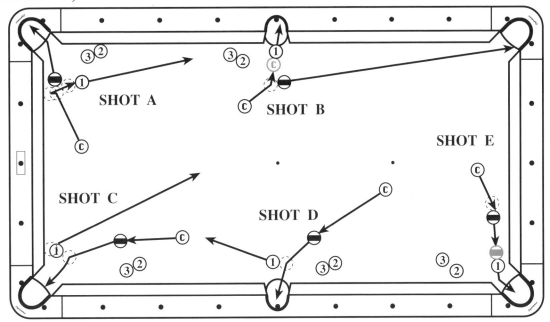

Robberies are plays where you relocate or remove hostile break balls leaving orphan clusters and impossible problem balls for your opponent to deal with.

Whenever a runout is not in the offing try to erase enemy capability by moving possible break balls a couple of zip codes away from the action.

Plan these shots and play position to get the best angle to give the 1-ball a ride into a different time zone. Figure the drive of the 1–ball so it does not tie up your group.

You know you are playing an idiot when an opponent *thanks* you for making their balls with moves like **SHOT B** and **SHOT E** because it almost always weakens your group when an opponent makes balls for you. If the pocketed balls were hanging in pockets, poised for break shots or were situated for key moves, eliminating them will beat you.

Isolating rival coveys provides the breathing space needed to rearrange *your* orphan cluster balls on a subsequent shot where you cannot hide the cue ball. The forsaken flock will stop a competitor's run.

BARRICADE 1 — Using Natural Defenses

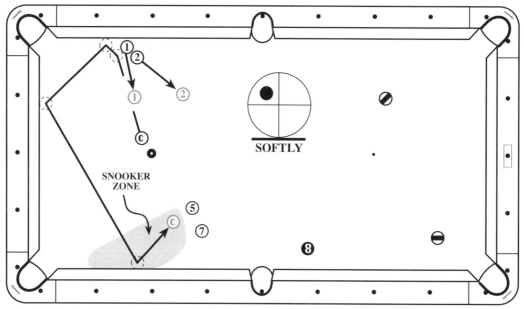

SNOOKER ZONE

SOFTLY

Effective Safety Play Requires Planning and Good Position

When ordinary players see arrangements like the 5–7–ball formation, they gun these balls down without a second thought. It escapes their attention that these balls might have great strategic value for opening up clusters while maintaining iron *control* of the game.

If you are a shooter who only thinks about playing safe after you end up seven time zones from a playable shot, examining a few barricade shots should quickly prove the advantage of *planned safeties* that leave easy *Starter Shots* for the next inning. Playing safe *after* you get in trouble is for losers. Winners realistically assess their chances and *plan* a safety beforehand when a runout is not within their grasp.

In the situation above you can open up the 1–2–ball cluster and bury the cue ball behind the 5–7–ball barricade. There's a chance of getting **Ball–In–Hand** with this safety, but stripes has to do more than just make a legal hit to escape this trap.

These moves demonstrate the brutally aggressive nature of strong safety play. Merely preventing the opposition from scoring is for chumps. Putting your group into winning positions while paralyzing your foe with lethal safeties is what wins on bar tables.

The preparatory shots for safety plays are not always shown, but it should be clearly understood that planning, position play and cue ball control are essential for effective defensive play. Without good position many of the moves in this book are very difficult if not impossible to make. The point being that a strong safety requires the same planning and careful preparation as any other shot.

Planned safeties are absolutely devastating.

Now for some practical examples of barricade shots in action.

BARRICADE 2 — SAFETY BREAK

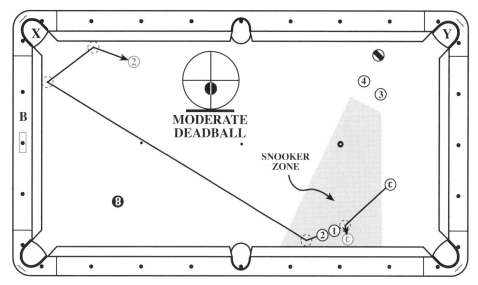

The 3-, 4-ball blockade takes care of this troublesome cluster. Prevent a kick off of cushion B which might make the stripe by landing the cue ball behind the 1-ball, which should not move very much. Snookering the bank cushion for a kick into pocket **Y** puts the icing on the cake by virtually eliminating any chance the opposition will score from this leave.

Landing the 2-ball in front of pocket **X** will provide another *Starter Shot* further improving your chance of finishing the game in the next inning. Leaving four open balls in front of three pockets puts your opponent in a real bind because there is no place for stripes to hide.

No matter what your opponent does you have greatly improved your likelihood of winning while making victory as difficult as possible for the opposition.

Barricade shots demonstrate the extreme vulnerability of shooting down to the last couple of balls in your group and missing. Snookers are very easy to come by when a foe only has one or two balls to shoot at and you still have 5 or 6 balls to hide behind. When an opponent puts him/herself at such a disadvantage, do your best to keep them in hot water until you lock up a victory.

Preventing this kind of abuse from being inflicted on yourself requires developing the discipline to *stop making balls* when you see that you *cannot* finish a rack. Playing all the makeable balls and leaving problems unsolved is a good way to beat yourself.

Learning to leave *Starter Shots* in position for your next turn is one of the hardest lessons for intermediate players, but the difference in results is clear. Shooting off every open ball when you cannot get out guarantees defeat against good eightballers because smart pool wins almost every one of these exchanges.

When you cannot get out, you must **stop** making balls and zero in on removing the obstacles in your way. Focussing on the real problems in a rack eliminates the frustration of a trip into **One–Ball–Hell.** This means opening up clusters with effective safety play that paralyzes enemy aggression.

Control is the key to victory in eight ball, not unrestrained aggression.

BARRICADE 3—SAFETY-BREAK

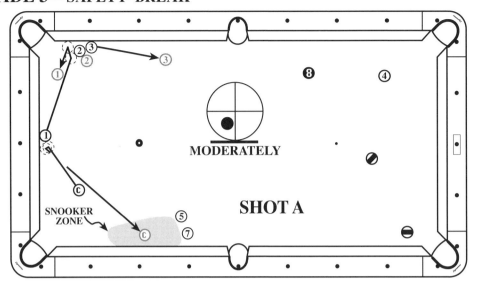

SHOT A: Using your imagination expands opportunities to use barricades to your advantage. Notice that the 4–ball has been left for a *Starter Shot* in the next inning. The value of leaving playable shots when a runout is too risky cannot be overstated. Having easy shots waiting for your next turn puts great stress on opponents because they see defeat staring them in the face when you put strong moves on them.

BARRICADE 4— SAFETY BREAK

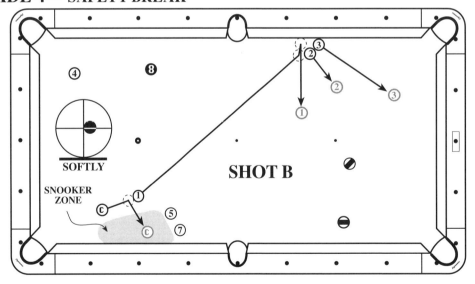

SHOT B: Getting **Ball–In–Hand** should cinch the game, but even if stripes hits a ball they are not out of the woods because it's going to be very difficult not to sell out with six open solids awaiting your return to the table. Setting up an easy run out sequence for your next inning greatly outweighs the small risk that stripes will kick a ball in and win the game.

BARRICADE 5— SAFETY BREAK

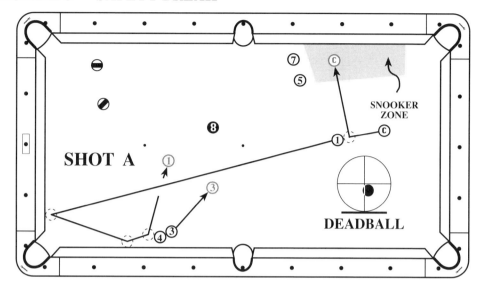

SHOT A: If you cannot hit a cluster straight on and get behind the barricade, bank the 1–ball into the 3–, 4–ball bundle to get the carom angle for a snooker.

BARRICADE 6— SAFETY BREAK

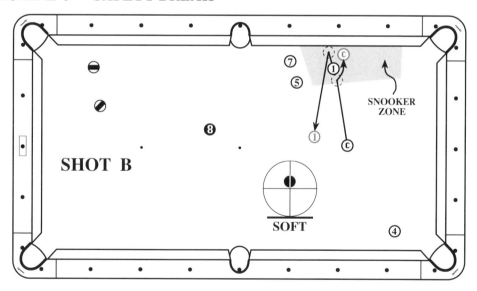

SHOT B: Eliminating a pesky cluster with a virtually risk free safety like this is smart pool. Just tap the 1-ball back to the middle of the table and watch your opponent squirm. Note that the 4-ball has been left for a *Starter Shot*.

Getting **Ball–In–Hand** wins the game, but even if stripes makes a legal hit opening up the 5–ball and 7-ball makes it tough to leave you safe.

BARRICADE 7— 3 CUSHION KICK

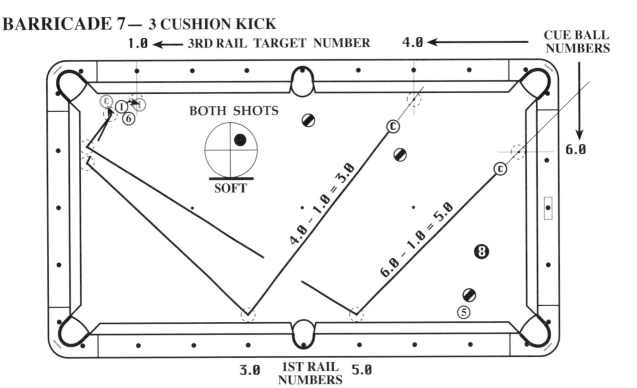

The 3 Cushion System can be used to calculate mind-blowing safeties like the ones above.

Figure the shot to hit Diamond 1 and shoot softly. Subtracting Target Diamond 1.0 from Diamond 4.0 (4 – 1 = 3) shows that hitting **opposite** Diamond 3 is the correct 1st Rail aiming point for this bank path. Subtracting 1 from Diamond 6 (6 – 1 = 5) indicates that shooting **opposite** Diamond 5 will send the cue ball to Diamond 1.

If you calculate 3 cushion shots **opposite** the diamond numbers, the cue ball **will hit opposite** the 3rd rail target diamond on **most** bar tables. The 3 Cushion System works very well on pool tables so far as figuring the two-cushion path to hit a specific point on the 3rd rail.

It takes some practice to get the calculations right, but the satisfaction of escaping from desperate situations makes the effort of learning the basic 3 Cushion System worthwhile.

See **THREE CUSHION SYSTEM**

BARRICADE 8— SAFETY BREAK

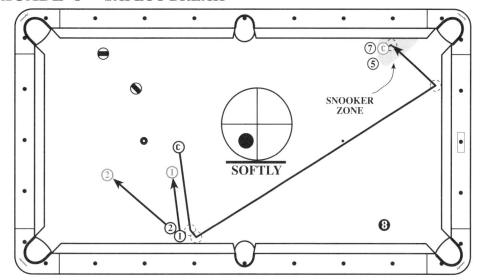

Three cushion safeties make opposing players sit up and take notice once they realize the leaves are deliberate.

This shot should be played very softly. Pay attention to the force applied to the 1-ball when it's pinned to a cushion on shots like this because the ball can easily rebound clear across the table causing a secondary problem.

Good safeties are **planned shots** where you *control* the balls in play.

"It's the birth of pool. More people play in bars than anywhere else. Out of 700,000 licensees, 200-300,000 of them have one or more pool tables."

STEVE MIZERAK commenting on bar table play

BARRICADE 9 — SAFETY BREAK

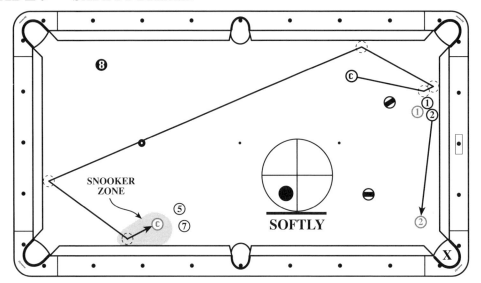

Billiard players will recognize this standard three or four cushion shot. Notice the excellent position played to make this devastating snooker. The cue ball is less than two feet away from the 1-ball and sitting at a perfect angle to make an accurate carom to land behind the barricade.

Make an effort to leave the 2-ball parked squarely in front of pocket **X** to further add to your opponent's distress. Leaving the 2–ball for a *Starter Shot* in the next inning greatly decreases the chance of the opposition getting a lucky safety. If you *block* the stripe in front of pocket **X**, the game should be yours.

An iron rule of good safety play is to *always improve the position of your balls if at all possible*. That means planning a destination for *any* balls that you move. It means taking *control* of the game.

The secret to good safety play is finding the worst possible positions to leave your opponent *before* the need arises. Finding shots that put enemy plans into limbo is an important aspect of picking a group and planning a pattern.

Locating positions where you can bury the opposition behind the proverbial eight–ball is valuable data that wins games.

More than anything else effective safety play depends on an alert mental attitude.

BARRICADE 10 — CRISS-CROSS

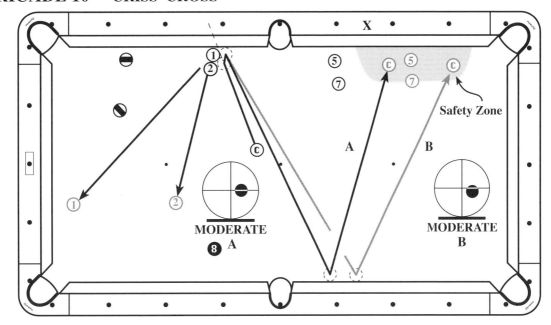

Using a half–ball hit to control the angle on these shots makes it possible to land the cue ball along cushion **X** with considerable accuracy.

Being familiar with the half–ball rebound angle and using the *1–2–3 System* provides consistent results for this type of shot.

Practicing *1–2–3 System* shots will enable you to land the cue ball in the *Safety Zone* almost every time.

"A good safety is one in which your opponent can't pocket a ball or even hit a return safety. A very good safety is one in which your opponent can't even hit the ball that he or she has to hit. Shoot a very good safety, and you receive ball in hand. That's a huge advantage, especially among better players."

Ewa Laurance, Former WPA World 9–Ball Champion & Player of the Year
from **Pool & Billiard Magazine January 2003**

WRONG WAY

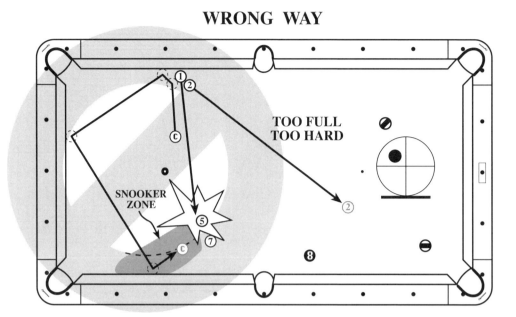

WRONG WAY: Driving a cluster ball into the barricade spells disaster, so concentrate on where the 1– and 2-balls land when you practice these situations. Letting cluster balls run wild causes needless disasters, so *pay attention*.

RIGHT WAY

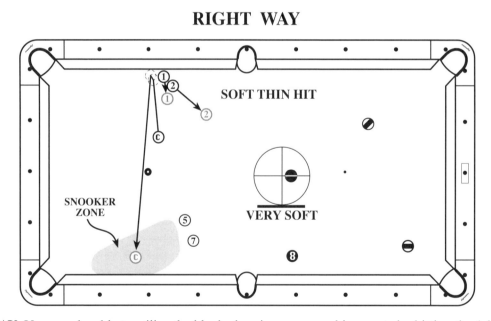

RIGHT WAY: You may be able to utilize the blockade using a one-cushion route by hitting the 1-ball thin with very little force.

A very soft tap scatters the 1 and 2-balls a few inches to playable positions and sends the cue ball into the snooker zone.

Practice safety play with the goal of leaving *all* of the balls you move positioned for an easy run in the next inning whenever you can.

CHEAP SHOTS, SMALL MOVES AND DOWN RIGHT DIRTY TRICKS

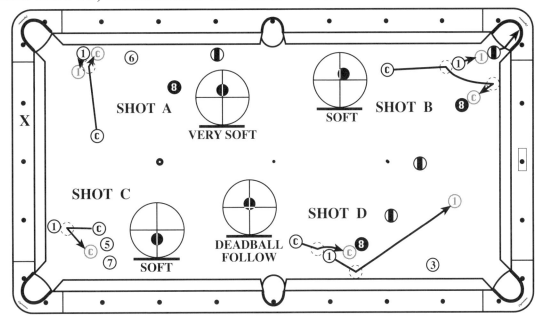

SHOT A: The idea is to carom softly off the 1–ball pinning stripes behind the 6–ball. You can make this simple move more deadly by driving the 1–ball out just far enough to clear a path for the 6-ball.

This may block kick routes off cushion **X** and averts the possibility of stripes leaving a nasty off–angle 6–1–ball combination in the next inning. Putting thought into safety play eliminates problems before they happen minimizing the **work** you have to do.

SHOT B: This easy move comes up frequently in the clutter immediately after the break. Simply drive the 1–ball into the stripe clearing the pocket and land behind the proverbial eight ball to handcuff the opposition. Simple shots like this break up log jams and win games in the next inning.

Practice *freezing* the cue ball on the intervening ball because this makes it even tougher for the opposition to make a legitimate hit on their ball. Use a very soft stroke and be sure to chalk up.

(See: ***Bump and Follow Shots***)

SHOT C: If the 1–ball is very close but **not** frozen to the rail, you can drive an opponent crazy by kissing the cue ball back behind the 5–7–ball barricade. Try to *freeze* the cue ball against the five or seven ball. This move frequently causes a **Ball–In–Hand** foul.

Note: If the 1–ball ***is frozen to the cushion*** you must drive a ball to a different rail for a legal shot. Your opponent must call the ball frozen **before** you shoot for this rule to apply.

SHOT D: Deadball follow reduces the risk of overhitting the shot and driving the snooker ball away. Practice *freezing* on the snooker ball because this greatly magnifies the difficulty of stripes making a legal shot.

Cheap safeties are easy to play, but they are not so easy to counteract.

MIGHTY MOUSE MOVES

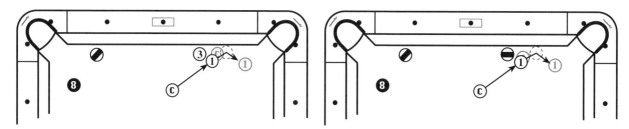

There's no difficulty executing these safeties, but the opposition will have a hard time finding a suitable reply.

Whether you hide the cue ball behind the 3-ball or merely leave the cue ball next to a stripe at a bad angle, the enemy has no shot.

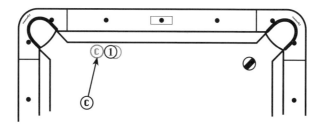

This killer safety is very easy to execute when the cue ball is within 18" or so of the 1-ball. Just graze the glisten on the 1-ball leaving it in place and land the cue ball behind it with a very gentle touch. This is a tap shot using a *very* short delivery (less than 1/2" stroke) to keep the speed to a minimum.

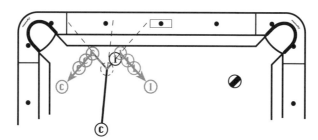

Here's a situation where a billiard trick can help insure a snooker. When the cue ball hits an object ball *half–full* the cue ball transmits about 50% of its velocity to the 1–ball and both balls travel approximately the same distance if there's no english and no obstacles involved.

When the cue ball and 1–ball are aligned at more or less a right angle to the cushion, you can use a *half–ball hit* to keep the balls aligned after the rebound because both balls hit the cushion with almost the same speed and angle.

The *half–ball hit* method works like a charm when you only move the balls a short distance after the hit.

Developing some insight into how the fullness of the hit affects the travel of the cue ball and the first object ball enables players to make simple snookers with considerable skill.

GYROMATIC

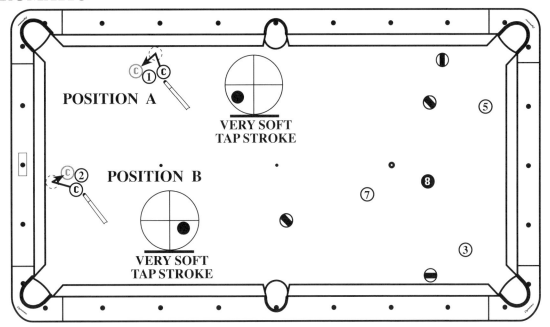

An ornery opponent left solids safe by almost freezing the cue ball to the 1–ball. But this time solids has a devastating come back.

There is a small gap (1/8" or *less*) between the cue ball and the 1–ball. Using inside–draw english avoids a foul and spins the cue ball behind the 1–ball for a strong safety. Sometimes it is possible to freeze the cue ball to the 1–ball at a very nasty angle making a **Ball–In–Hand** reward possible.

POSITION A: The 1–ball scarcely moves as the cue ball rebounds into a snooker position. This is a *tap shot* where the tip of the cue does not penetrate into the cue ball. Inside draw deflects the cue ball to the right avoiding a foul. This is a *very* light stroke.

It is essential to *pre–see* the speed needed for these shots. If you try to adjust the force in the stance a mistake is likely. Visualize a *very short stroke* that just *taps* the cue ball into a gyroscopic spin.

The slowly moving cue ball has a rate of spin faster than its forward speed. Picture the cue ball dancing around behind the 1–ball to hide the foot of the table. The spin does all of the work.

POSITION B: This time you only want to go half–way around the snooker ball.

Anytime the cue ball and a ball from your group are close to each other, badly aligned to make the ball and near a cushion, there may be a good chance of playing a deadly snooker.

When your opponent doesn't have any balls on the snooker side of the blocking ball, these can be lethal **Ball–In–Hand** safeties.

Unless stripes gets lucky and makes a ball or falls into a safety, solids figures to win after a spin safety like this.

When playing snookers form a mental image of the exact configuration you want to leave. Mentally rehearse the shot until you are confident of putting the cue ball in the deep freeze. Getting the right–brain involved in the shooting process improves results exponentially.

DAVE LE BLANC'S CHEAP SAFETY

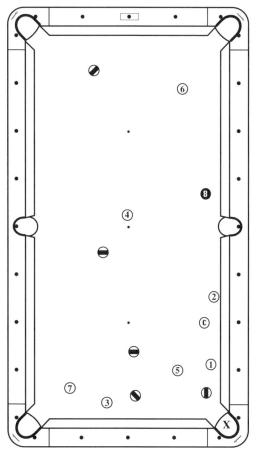

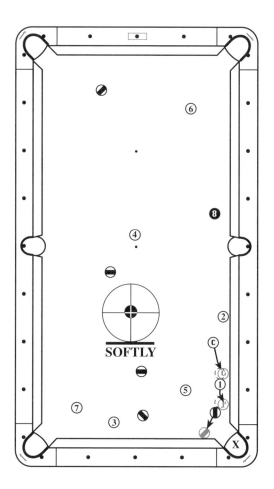

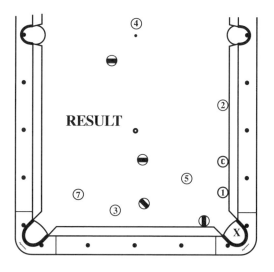

A reckless attempt to clear the table would probably leave solids in a very bad situation. Instead of chasing wild rabbits Dave LeBlanc used this cheap, but deadly safety to open up the game for solids.

This simple move immediately put the 1–, 2– and 5–balls into play for corner **X** as well as denying stripes critical shots at the foot of the table that could win the game.

With pocket **X** under *control* solids is sitting in the catbird seat and stripes cannot afford to miss.

Stripes made the side pocket shot and the ball at the head of the table, but found it impossible to navigate the balls at the foot of the table because the 3–, 5– and 7–balls block pockets and position lanes.

LeBlanc then ran the solids showing how strong this bargain basement safety really is. The important thing is recognizing the opportunity.

TOO MUCH WORK— A Passive Safety

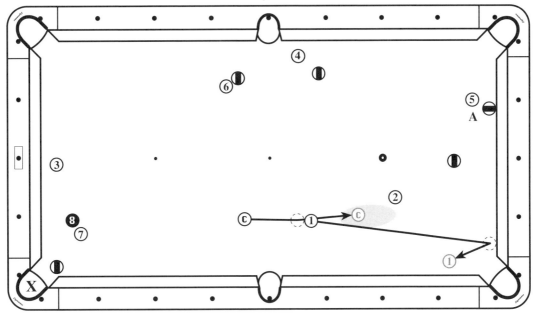

Shooting safe when you can make several open balls shocks opponents so much that I often pretend to misplay shots like this. But in this situation solids has very little chance of running out. There's too much work to do and too few break balls to do it.

One goal is to swindle the opposition into clearing pocket **X** for the 7 and 8–balls. There's very little chance that stripes will run out because an *Orphan Cluster* will stop the march to the 8–ball. Needless to say, these isolated coveys also put the brakes on any run out notions solids may have.

The idea is to break the stalemate by offering the opposition a shot that improves your situation a lot more than the opponent can help him/herself. With that thought in mind be sure to snooker stripe **A** because leaving a shot at that ball might leave a game winning break shot on the 6–ball–stripe cluster. On the other hand forcing stripes to shoot at any of the other balls could help solids a great deal.

If stripes refuses the swindle, solids could lose ground in this exchange, but in game play average players seldom pass up the easy shot on the stripe blocking corner **X**. Of course, better players won't move the stripe in front of the 7– and 8–balls until they open the game up even if you put a gun to their heads.

Solids next move will be determined by stripes response, but unless stripes does something really good or really lucky solids will be better off.

If a shooter runs the stripes out from a leave like this, I sit right up and take notice that I'm playing a *very* lucky stiff or a *very* dangerous player.

Learning to forego futile assaults that fizzle into sellouts is an important step toward becoming a strong 8-ball player.

THE TRUTH ABOUT SAFETIES
No Refunds — No Returns — No Exchanges

Examining a safety duel fought with ***Ronco Ron — the thinnest slicer in the West*** should improve understanding of the risks and skill involved in topflight safety play.

Ronco Ron is an outstanding bar table player who has defeated almost every top bar table player in the Bay Area for the cash. When women's professional champion Vivian Villarreal dropped by to hustle the local shortstops between tournament games she had the misfortune to match up with ***Ronco Ron*** on a bar table and had her head handed to her on a platter. Crushing such an accomplished player should give you an idea of what you might be up against when you cross cues with a good bar table player.

A SAFETY DUEL WITH RONCO RON

Ronco Ron is an extremely aggressive shooter who prefers ***Shot–Safeties*** to just going for a leave, so these moves demonstrate what happens when you ***force*** a safety exchange on a good player.

SOLIDS SHOOTING

SHOT 1: Solids has shots at the 7–ball and 1–ball. The 1–ball shot is selected because it offers a ***Shot–Safety*** with position on the 2-ball, which is the only other problem ball solids has.

This move will not leave ***Ronco Ron*** an out sequence providing the cue ball lands behind the 3–ball.

The 1–ball missed, but ***all*** of the stripes are snookered.

SHOT 2: ***Ronco Ron*** plays a devastating return safety by double kissing the cue ball off his stripe near the rail almost freezing the cue ball against another stripe.

This is a move that every serious player should master. Place an object ball an inch or less from a rail, and practice kicking dead full into the rail ball. The closer to the rail the ball is the easier the shot is to make. It only takes a little practice to begin getting good results from this type of shot.

The object ball must ***not*** be frozen against the cushion. If the ball is frozen you must drive the object ball to another rail or drive the cue ball or another ball to a cushion after contacting the object ball to make a legal shot.

The opposing player must call the ball frozen ***before*** you shoot.

SHOT 3: I try to nestle the cue ball between the 4–ball and 5–ball, but fall short.

(CONTINUED)

RONCO RON BREAKS JAIL

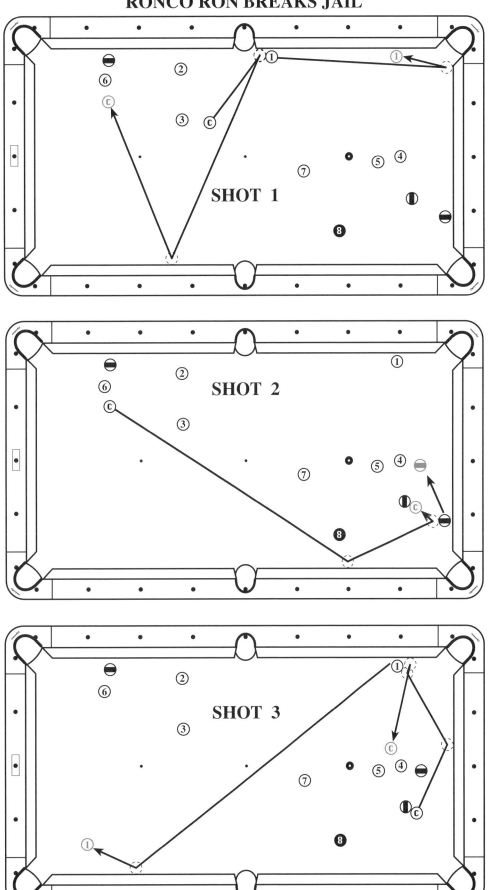

SHOT 4: Regrettably the cue ball landed a tad short leaving *Ronco Ron* a *very* thin hit on the stripe next to the 4–ball. Fortunately, *Ronco Ron* could only hit a glimmer of the ball and could not pocket it.

Ronco Ron proceeds to feather the stripe and almost freezes the cue ball behind it.

SHOT 5: A 2–cushion kick into the 1–ball leaves *Ronco Ron* a very difficult shot.

Besides facing a fairly tough cut, *Ron* must negotiate a perilous journey for position to continue a run.

SHOT 6: I was in trouble the instant *Ronco Ron's* dice–o–matic eyes locked onto a stripe at the foot of the table. After briefly sighting the shot *Ronco Ron* showed the nerve of a second story man and whacked the ball in with authority while playing perfect up and down position to make stripe **A** in the same pocket. He ran the game from there.

Note the scratches *Ronco Ron* risked if he made a little slip. Also notice that *Ronco Ron* would have left a tough *Safety* if the stripe blocked corner **X**.

Critique: The *Shot–Safety* on the 1–ball was a calculated risk. If the 1–ball fell, there was a shot at the 2–ball and a good chance of finishing the game. Even though the game was eventually lost, I'd play the same shot again.

Safety play is never a sure thing. Especially against players who cut balls like a gigawatt Argon laser. There's no way of predicting how a safety exchange will end, so do not put faith in defensive plans that require more than one or two moves at most.

There's no disgrace in being out moved by an excellent player like *Ronco Ron*, but I've had players with strokes like Arkansas woodchoppers beat my best moves by sheer accident. A good safety *usually* works, but you are always playing a percentage shot any time you shoot safe.

RONCO RON SHOOTS THE LIGHTS OUT

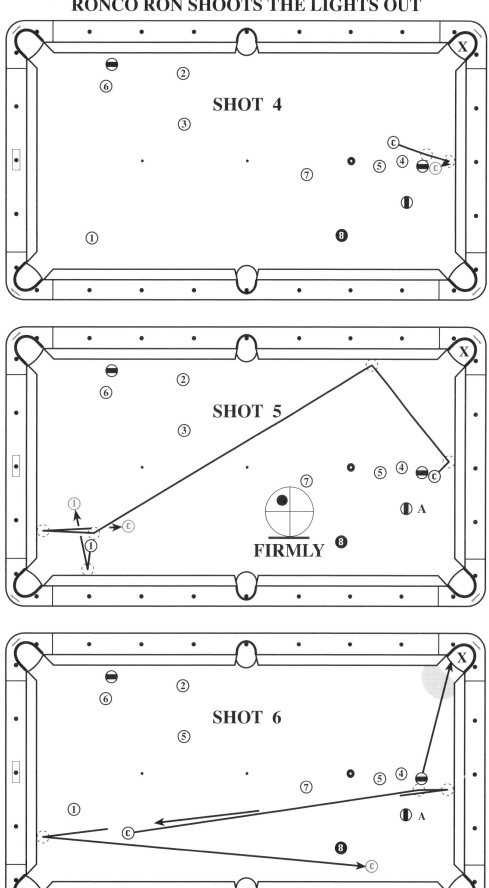

MOVING DAY

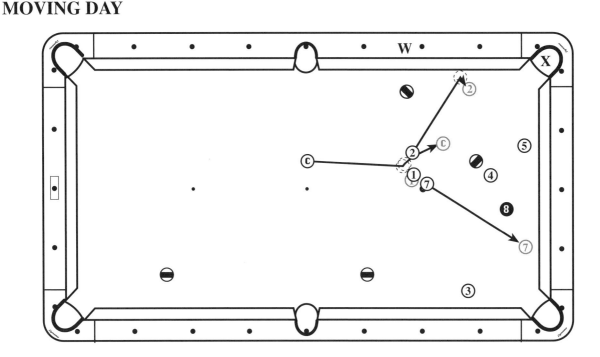

If I'm in stroke making the 2–ball in pocket **X** presents no problem, but experience warns me that attempting a run after a break shot like this is fraught with peril. Getting a good second shot is a real problem in this congestion where tie–ups and blocked balls can go wrong. Very often solids loses control after this kind of shot and subsequently surrenders the game.

With these thoughts in mind I decide on a safety move that solves all of solids problems and creates a nightmare snarl for stripes to contend with. At the same time solids are positioned for an easy run with all six balls supporting each other in the next inning.

If solids lands the 2-ball in a blocking position for the stripe near cushion **W** and at the same time obstructs the 8–ball, stripes will have their work cut out for them. Solids will control the foot of the table with multiple ways of finishing the rack in the next inning.

Stripes needs a championship move to prevent a loss in the next inning.

THE ICEMAN COMETH

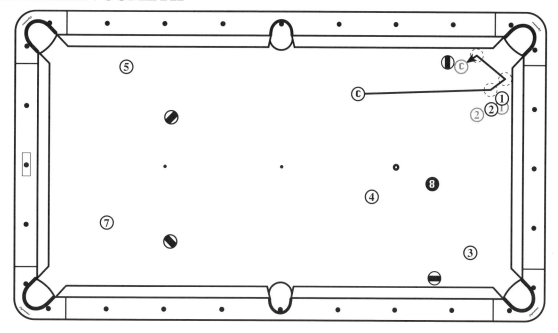

The move here is to *bump* the 1–, 2–ball cluster apart and leave stripes safe against their own ball.

Anybody who has played for a while knows how frustrating it is to get "snookered" by one of your own balls. Just touching the side of a ball with the cue ball is enough to spoil your dreams.

Oddly enough very few players use snookers with opposition balls tactically. Needless to say there's a chance of leaving a dead shot on the "snooker" ball, but often the situation justifies the risk.

Opportunities to put an opponent in the deep freeze by welding the cue ball to one of their own balls are so delicious that I seldom pass up such a play. The mental impact can be devastating.

If the safety appears to be *accidental*, so much the better. Then your foe may begin muttering about *bad luck*, which only makes matters worse.

The flip side of devious safety play is making sure you don't get snarled in the same traps.

Avoiding these snares is one reason you don't want to get caught with only one or two balls left. Evading ambushes is why you should try to scatter your balls to both ends of the table when you cannot get out. Eluding pitfalls is why you should be careful not to set up easy safety plays on your own balls.

Among good shooters, the first player to get his/her group opened up without selling out is usually the winner, not shooters who gun down every playable ball until they run out of shots.

INTO HARM'S WAY: RE-LOCATING ENEMY BALLS

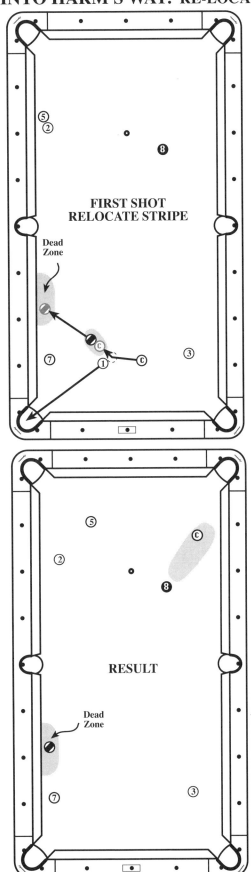

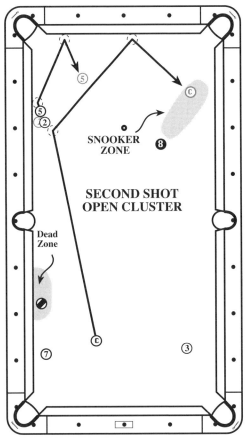

Here's another safety weapon to add to your arsenal. Moves that tie up opposition balls can mean easy victories, if you are alert for the opportunity.

This is a two-step safety where you re-locate an opposing ball to a blocked position to help dispose of an orphan cluster.

Get the best possible position to play a carom to drive the stripe into the ***Dead Zone*** behind the 7-ball.

After putting the stripe in harm's way open up the 2–5–ball cluster and leave your foe snookered or facing a nasty passing bank that even professionals often miss.

The mental focus should be on landing the stripe in the ***Dead Zone*** behind the 7–ball. Playing a snooker is tough but this cost–free move could guarantee a victory. Regard the snooker as a potential bonus, but when attempting a lock–safety is risk–free go for it.

Unless you are playing Godzilla bankers like "Bugs" Rucker, Gary Spaeth or Freddie "The Beard" Bentivegna this move puts the air brakes on the competition and leaves solids in a strong position to finish the game in the next inning.

TWO–STEP BOOGIE

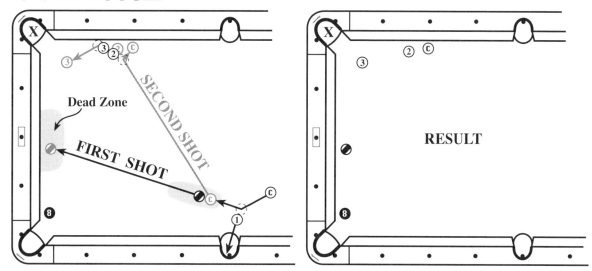

Here's another two–step maneuver. First drive the stripe into never–never land behind the proverbial 8-ball. Then break the 2-3 cluster setting up a winning situation for the next inning. Maximize the shot by parking the 3-ball in front of pocket **X**.

When the cue ball is up close and the angle is right these are effortless shots, but the difficulty rapidly increases when much distance is involved or when the angle is a little off.

MAKING TROUBLE

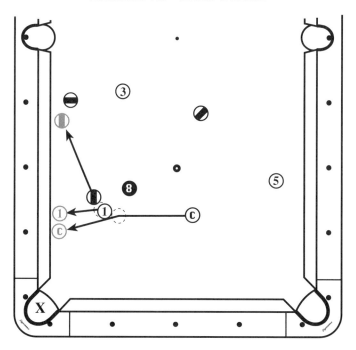

Creating traffic jams among enemy balls destroys opposition chances.

Snookering the newly minted cluster with the 1-ball puts stripes in line for a brain scan, while solids substantially improves their position.

Notice that the 1-ball also blocks pocket **X** for the newborn stripe covey.

Pay attention to chances to tie-up opposing balls when you need a move to handle a problem ball or a cluster.

ORPHAN CLUSTERS

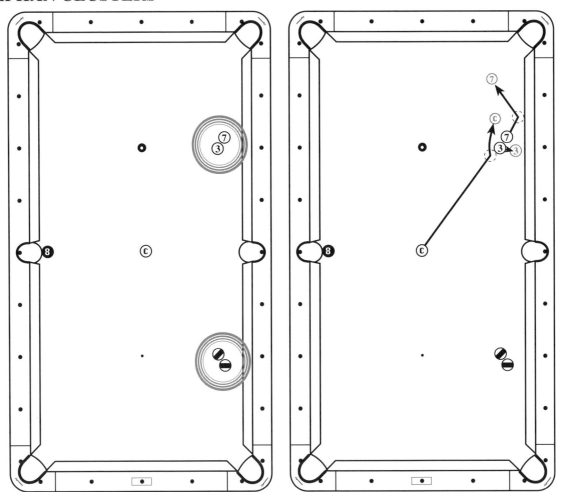

WHO HAS THE ADVANTAGE?

Whoever is shooting is in the catbird perch this time because he/she can open up their balls with impunity while leaving the opposition an ugly *Orphan Cluster* to deal with. Only now the first shooter's balls are open forcing stripes to play a difficult *Safety–Break*.

Needless to say, moves like this should be made much earlier in the game while the natural obstacles provided by your group offer more protection. Leaving a move like this until last is akin to shooting yourself into **One–Ball–Hell** and should be avoided like a plague. This example only illustrates the importance of overcoming roadblocks in your group *before* the other player does, not *when* the shot should be played.

All other things being even whoever gets their balls in the clear first without selling out is most likely to win, so the sooner you take care of problems like this the better.

Great 8–ballers, like Bunny Rogoff, anticipate these moves the instant the balls are broken and their opponents find opportunities denied before they ever get to the table.

DELIBERATE FOULS: The Arguello Solution

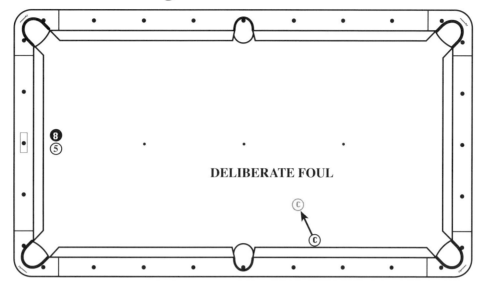

This lesson drives home the stupidity of making a deliberate foul when the balls are tied up. Deliberately fouling the shot at the 8–ball may be tempting, but here's what Carl Arguello does to players who foolishly give up **Ball–In–Hand** hoping to improve their situation.

The Arguello Move

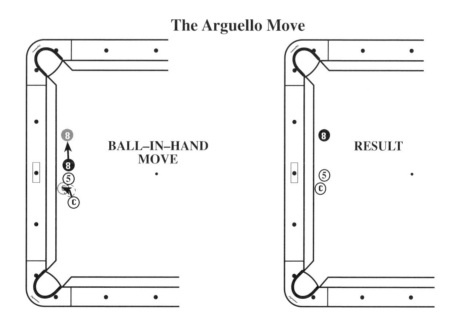

The folly of giving up **Ball–In–Hand** becomes apparent when Arguello instantly turns the tables by separating the cluster a few inches leaving a devastating snooker. Suddenly the foul shooter finds him/herself in a do or die situation where the game can be lost even if the 8–ball is hit.

A deliberate foul hands your opponent the best possible position for an offensive or defensive move. This is not a recipe for victory.

It is almost impossible to imagine a situation where giving up **Ball–In–Hand** improves the shooter's chances. Certainly too few to worry about. Most likely the result will be a crushing defeat. The real solution is to avoid leaving clusters until the end game.

LONE COVEYS SPELL DEFEAT

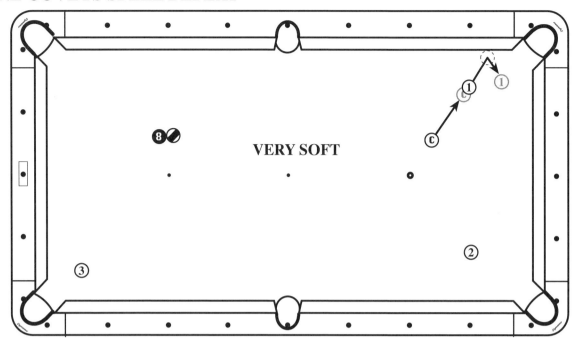

Solids might be able to open up the 8-ball–stripe cluster and win the game, but why bother. Stripes is obligated to hit the stripe and drive a ball to a cushion so the cluster will not be there next inning. The chance of stripes playing a good safety or making the ball and getting out is remote.

Instead of risking a loss, solids **bunts** the 1–ball in front pocket **X** leaving an easy **Starter Shot** that puts the game on ice.

Using an opponent's misfortune to your advantage adds insult to injury and I highly recommend it.

The penalty for marching into **One–Ball–Hell** against anybody who knows the score is almost certain defeat.

SIDESTEP

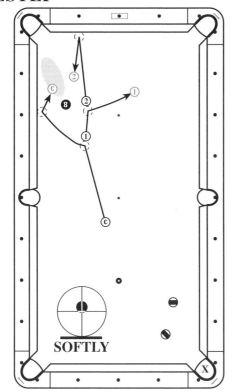

SOFTLY

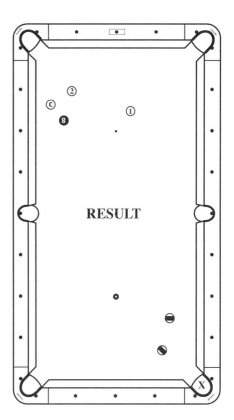

RESULT

Here's a familiar arrangement. Back–cutting the 1–, 2–ball combination is a thankless proposition. There's a very small margin of error and if you do manage to make the 2-ball there's no guarantee of a subsequent shot at the 1–ball. Failing to control both the cue ball ***and*** the 1–ball spells disaster if you go for the shot.

I hate back–cut combinations worse than any shot. Most likely I would miss the 2–ball so in my case a *Safety* or a *Shot–Safety* is a good response to this diabolical leave.

It is relatively easy to land the cue ball in the hidey hole behind the proverbial 8–ball forcing stripes to shoot a difficult ***must–make*** or ***must–get–safe*** shot or lose.

If you have a knack for back–cut combos, by all means run the game out from here, but a *Safety* or a *Shot–Safety* may be the best move. Hiding the cue ball behind the 8–ball leaves stripes a high pressure do or die kick shot that will fail most of the time.

Focus on landing the cue ball squarely behind the 8–ball, ***forcing*** stripes to shoot a tough kick shot. Care is taken not to drive the 8–ball away with the 2–ball. The speed for the shot is figured before taking the stance to avoid unwanted collisions that spoil the snooker.

When you have no choice but to attempt a difficult back–cut combination, try to leave the 1–ball facing a pocket if at all possible. Doing this may be easier said than done.

SWITCHEROO

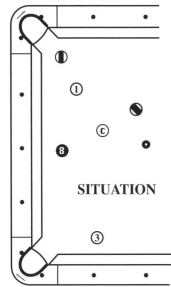

SITUATION

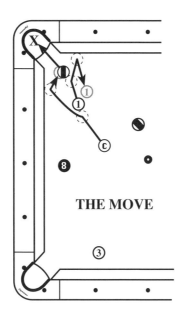

THE MOVE

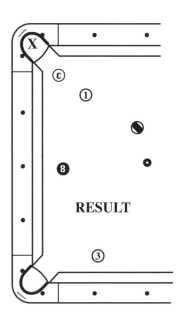

RESULT

Sometimes making an opposing ball completely turns the tables. Here solids has a good chance of clearing pocket X of the obnoxious stripe and unleashing a game winning snooker.

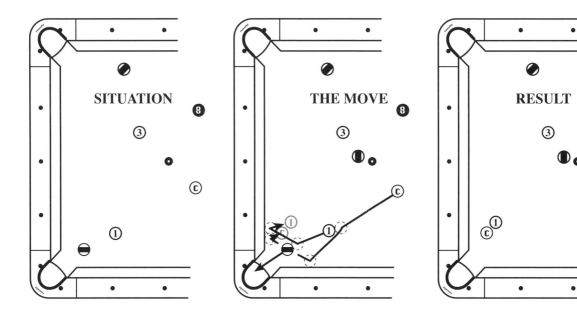

SITUATION

THE MOVE

RESULT

When the balls are sitting right an insidious freeze–up is possible. The reversal of fortune caused by these moves can completely unglue opposition victory plans.

The secret to making these plays is to mentally rehearse the flight of the balls until you get everything right. Use a touch of english to nestle the cue ball up against the 1–ball. When the shot is sitting right the move is relatively simple.

Opportunities for homicidal safeties like these often occur on tables with very slow cloth where most of the balls remain loosely scattered in the foot area of the table after the break.

Capturing a corner pocket with a safety play is good strategy at any time in the game.

⑧

I am a great believer in principles. I believe that you can adapt any principle to a wide variety of situations. It is as simple as that.

For example, if you realize that the cue ball always goes off the object ball at ninety degrees, **providing the balls have the same weight** and the cue ball is struck with medium speed and no english. Then you can make all kinds of adjustments based on that knowledge,

Grady Matthews World Champion One Pocket Player

⑧

SHOT–SAFETY — THE ULTIMATE MOVE

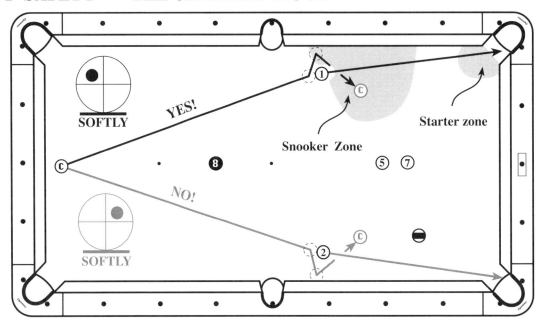

When I discovered the **Shot–Safety**, I thought I had invented the greatest move in the history of the game. Later I found out that the **Shot–Safety** has been around since before 8–ball was even invented. Although I cannot claim ownership of the **Shot–Safety** it is still a mighty game-winning move that offers the chance of playing difficult shots with immunity.

The diagram above illustrates the **Shot–Safety** principle in action. The 1–ball and the 2–ball are exactly equal in difficulty and the pattern play to finish the rack with either shot is identical. However, shooting the 1–ball offers the opportunity to put your opponent in the **Snooker Zone** behind the 5–7–ball if you should happen to miss. Since there's no positional advantage in playing the 2–ball the 1–ball is the obvious choice.

Landing the cue ball in the **Snooker Zone** allows solids to continue the run with shots at the 5– and 7–balls if the 1-ball scores and if you miss stripes has a nasty **Barricade** to contend with. The safety aspect is natural from this angle—just shoot softly.

Leaving the 1-ball in the **Starter Zone** for an easy shot in the next inning if you miss adds muscle to the move.

Once you understand the **Shot–Safety** principle, opportunities to shoot Shot–**Safeties** will occur regularly. Using **Shot–Safeties** in your patterns is a sign of strong 8–ball play because reducing risk while retaining **control** puts you in the winner's bracket.

The secret to good **Shot–Safety** play is identifying areas of the table where the position is good for your group, but safe for your opponent **before the need arises**.

The ideal *Shot–Safety*—

1. Provides a chance of scoring and continuing the run.
2. Leaves the opposition an impossible shot if you miss.

ENCORE

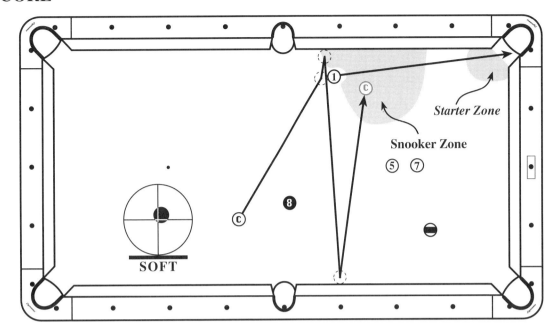

Another version of the preceding shot.

The goal of a *Shot–Safety* is to always leave your opponent in a very bad spot if you miss. If you land the cue ball in the **Snooker Zone** and leave the 1–ball in the *Starter Zone* your opponent isn't going to like it.

Having a hanger waiting if stripes misses gives solids a huge advantage and puts lots of pressure on stripes. Just hitting a stripe won't do. Stripes must get safe or make the ball and get out; both of which are much easier said than done.

Leaving the cue ball in the **Snooker Zone** is essential because if you miss and leave an open shot on the stripe your bacon is cooked.

Stripes is unlikely to recover from this *Shot–Safety* if you miss the 1–ball, but if you make the 1–ball, the 7–5–8–ball (or 5–7–8–ball) sequence will be fairly easy to negotiate.

Protecting yourself with *Shot–Safeties* instead of throwing your fate to the winds adds an important dimension to your game.

When you play a *Shot–Safety* on a difficult shot and run out— take a bow like a tight wire walker crossing Niagara Falls and never mention your safety net.

This is another *1–2–3 System* shot, so get busy and master this logical method of cue ball control because *1–2–3 System* shots come up in almost every game.

(See: *1–2–3 System*)

HIDE AND SEEK

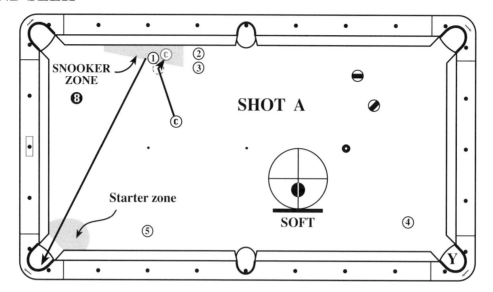

SHOT A: Here are some *Shot–Safety* banks using *barricade* positions. Attempting this bank poses very little risk because stripes will be blinded by the *barricade* in the event of a miss.

On the other hand, if the bank shot falls continue the run as though missing was the last thing on your mind. With the 4-ball sitting pretty, solids will have no trouble getting out with a 2–, 3–, 4–, 5–, 8–ball sequence.

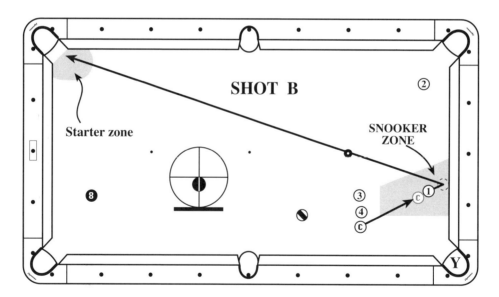

SHOT B: Retaining *control* of the table with bone–crushing safeties makes it impossible for your opponent to get started. The *Shot–Safety* is a great play because you can shut out the opposition while continuing your run if the bank scores. What more can you ask of a shot?

The 2–ball provides an out shot if the bank succeeds.

As usual leaving the 1–ball near the target pocket provides an advantage if you miss.

FREEZE UP

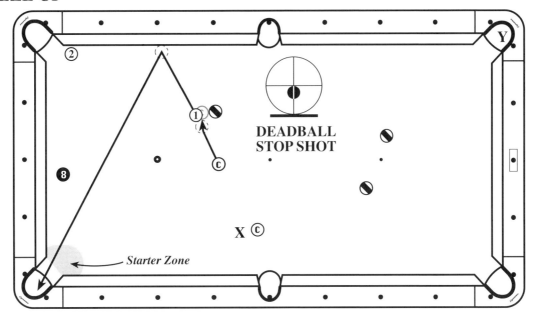

**DEADBALL
STOP SHOT**

X ©

Starter Zone

Here's a *Shot–Safety* where you *freeze* the cue ball on an opponent's ball. Be very careful not to line the stripe up with a pocket and a deadly safety will result if you miss the bank. The cue ball must be fairly close to the 1–ball to maintain good enough control to *freeze* at the angle you want.

Shooting from position **X** would make this a more difficult, but not impossible, shot to *control* so be sure to play good position to stop the cue ball dead. The safety aspect here must come before making the bank, so get the leave whatever it takes. If you can make the 1-ball, fine. If not, try to land it in a good position.

If you land the 1-ball in the grey area it may block the 8-ball and will serve as a *Starter Shot* further increasing your chances of winning in the next inning if you miss.

On the other hand, if you make the bank there will be no problem making the 2-ball and getting a good shot at the 8-ball.

Shooting a strong *Shot–Safety* gives solids a tremendous strategic advantage because in the next inning the 1 and 2-balls will be easy *Starter Shots* for a final sequence.

If stripes fails to make a ball or get a snooker, stick a fork in them because their goose is about to be flash fried.

TAKING ADVANTAGE

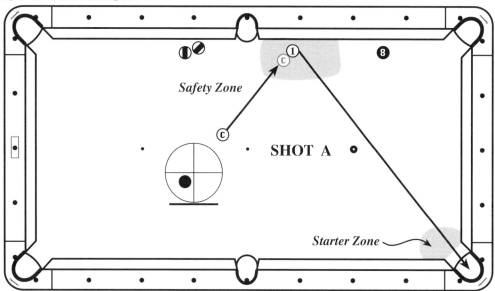

SHOT A: It is not always necessary to snooker an opponent to leave a nasty safety.

Here an orphan cluster allows a low-risk bank that wins the game if it scores. In this case, solids can get safe almost anywhere on the table because a bank is the best shot stripes can get. Besides making a bank stripes must play a very difficult pattern to finish the game. Solids has the catbird seat here.

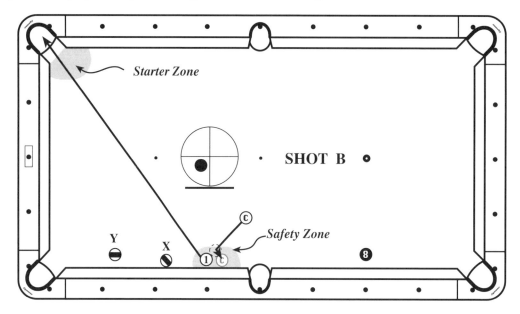

SHOT B: The **X – Y** combination may look easy on paper, but I hate bank–combinations like this and so do most other players. I figure my opponent to miss these shots most of the time because even experts don't have to make these plays.

Whenever possible try to land the 1-ball in the grey area in front of the target pocket. This makes it much tougher for the stripes to get a return safety if you miss. Landing your balls in front of pockets wins a lot of games by providing easy **Starter Shots** for the next inning.

BARRICADES— SHOT-SAFETY STYLE

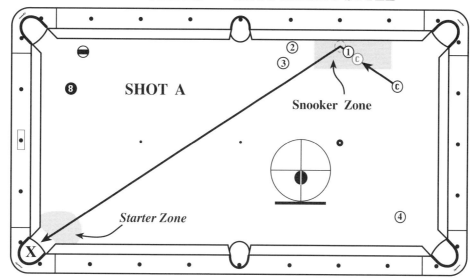

SHOT A: Long cross banks are not my favorite shots, so I love it when I can cover my butt with a strong ***Shot–Safety.*** Lagging the 1–ball up to pocket **X** for a ***Starter Shot*** next inning sends opponents to the loser's bracket. If the 1–ball goes there's a good chance of running out with the 4–ball providing ***insurance***.

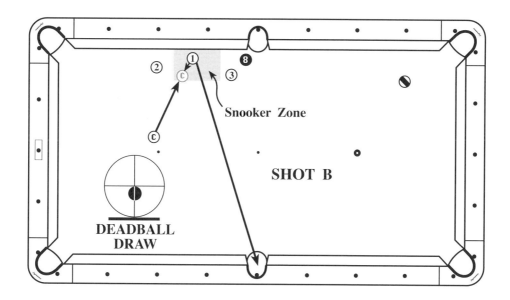

SHOT B: There's an exception to every rule. In this case a side pocket bank is a good move because a ***Barricade*** protects you if you miss.

Side pocket shots on bar tables are treacherous, so a ***Shot–Safety*** is appreciated for this cross side bank. Drawing the cue ball back a couple of inches provides good position to finish the game while leaving your foe a tough kick shot if you miss.

The fewer opportunities an opponent gets the better your chances of winning the game.

(See: ***Sides vs Corners***)

SNUGGLE UP BABY

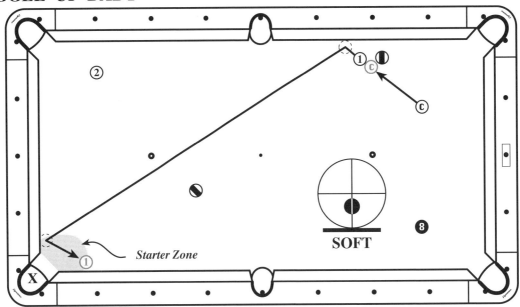

Freezing the cue ball against the stripe will give the opposition a nerve test if the bank misses.

Even champions have a hard time scoring jacked up over a ball at a shot two or three feet from the pocket. Try it a few times and see for yourself.

Most players are guaranteed to screw up such a difficult shot, so this could be a game winner. Not only that, there's the chance of blocking pocket **X** leaving no shot at all**.**

Even if the 1–ball doesn't cover pocket **X,** not many players will finish the rack.

Fast Eddie Felson's smart but evil backer Bert Gordon offers this advice —

> **Look, you wanna hustle pool, don't you? This game isn't like football. Nobody pays you for yardage. When you hustle you keep score real simple. The end of the game you count up your money. That's how you find out who's best.**
>
> **That's the only way.**
>
> **Bert Gordon**
> **The Hustler © 1959 Walter Tevis**

SPEED CONTROL

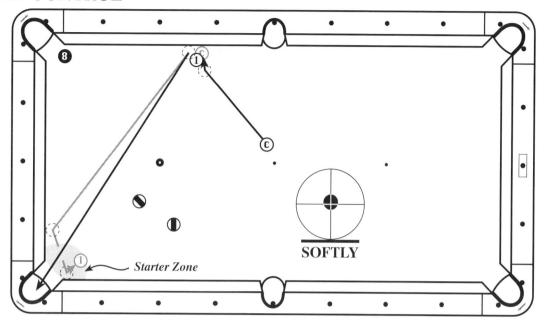

SOFTLY

Starter Zone

Here's a ***Shot–Safety*** I learned watching "Hippy Jimmy" Reid shoot the lights out in Johnston City one year. The idea is to bank the 1-ball softly so that it lands in the grey area blocking the stripes if you miss.

If you sink the bank, you can strut as you run the game out. But if you miss and leave the 1-ball blocking the pocket, your opponent has a headache and most likely you'll get another opportunity to finish the game.

The secret to shots like this is using a ***measured*** stroke to ***control*** the speed. With a little practice intermediate players should be able to either pocket the 1-ball or get safe most of the time. Pay attention to the ***feel*** of the delivery to improve your speed control.

Whether you are playing sharks or run of the mill players combining offense and defense is overpowering.

The ***Shot–Safety*** is my favorite move.

POSITIONAL MOVE

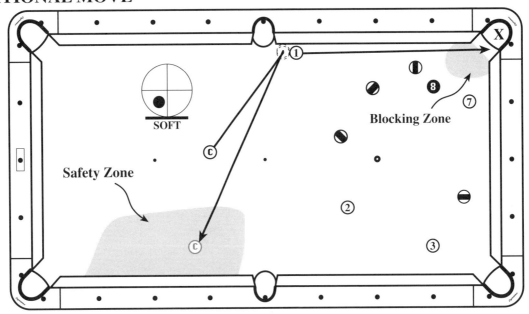

Sometimes the arrangement of opposition balls allows leaving the cue ball in a large area of the table with virtual immunity.

Even though stripes can hit several balls it's going to take some pretty sharp shooting to get a pattern started from this leave because not many players can make off angle combinations like this.

If solids misses and leaves the cue ball in the huge **Safety Zone** and lands the 1–ball in the **Blocking Zone**, stripes will be gasping for air.

On the other hand, if solids *makes* the 1–ball there's a good chance of finishing the rack.

Going after problem balls like the 1–ball as soon as possible is a wise policy. In this case, solids will have the best of it if this shot is played well whether the 1–ball scores or not.

The extra assurance provided by a *Shot–Safety* pays off by pocketing tough shots with more confidence and by finishing more games.

COMING AROUND THE PIKE

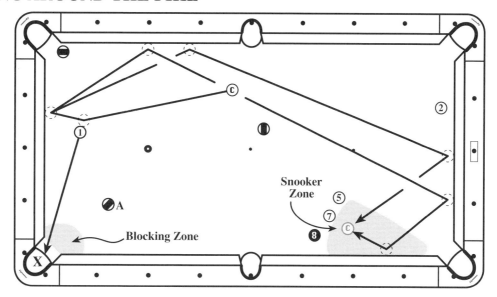

If you practice *3 Cushion Billiards*, shots like these will not be a mystery. Varying the ball action sends the cue ball to the same destination on different position routes.

Besides trying to snooker your foe, play to barely drop the 1–ball into pocket **X** blocking stripe **A** if you miss.

If you make the 1–ball, there's an excellent chance to complete the rack and if you miss and leave the 1–ball in the ***Blocking Zone*** it will add to stripes distress. Nevertheless, getting the snooker should be the priority here.

It should only take a few experiments to get the range on a shot like this. Remembering the ball action and speed that works is essential for consistent results.

Billiard players control these shots by playing to hit a specific point on the second rail that is known to create the exact position route they want. Keeping track of the contact point on the second cushion and remembering where the cue ball lands with different ball actions will teach you these shots.

Protecting yourself with strong ***Shot–Safeties*** prevents needless losses.

INTO THE TWILIGHT ZONE

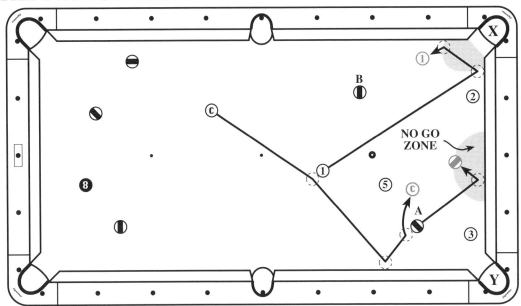

Stripes must be reading this book because they put their balls in the clear and left solids a very tough shot. Since I won't bet on making the cut shot into pocket **X**, a *Shot–Safety* that attempts to drive stripe **A** into the **No Go Zone** between the 2– and 3–balls is in order. At the same time I try to block stripe **B** for pocket **X**.

Care is taken to land stripe **A** in the *middle* of the **No Go Zone** so it does not interfere with a 2–ball or 3–ball shot later on.

If the 1–ball is missed, as will probably happen, and stripes **A** and **B** are blocked solids will most likely get another chance to win the game. Either safety aspect could save the day, but getting both safeties almost guarantees victory because the opposition will have too much work to do.

On the other hand, if the 1–ball goes, solids is home free.

Playing shots like these will earn you nick names with the word *Lucky* in them, but never argue. It's just as well that opponents do not think these moves are on purpose.

BANKS: The Eight–ball Way

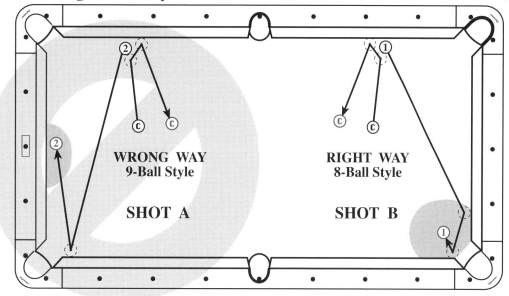

WRONG WAY
9-Ball Style

SHOT A

RIGHT WAY
8-Ball Style

SHOT B

In 8-ball each player can only score with their own group, so the best strategy is to leave bank balls hanging in the pockets if you miss. This means playing bank shots slightly **long** so the object ball lands in **front** of the corner pocket instead of the middle of the end rail. Besides leaving an easy starter shot for your next inning, the object ball may do double duty by blocking opposing balls from scoring.

SHOT B shows the right way to play banks in 8-ball. In 9-ball, banks are played to leave the object ball safe in case of a miss because the incoming player shoots the same ball. Therefore, a 9-baller plays banks slightly short so a missed bank lands near the middle of the end rail forcing the opposition to play a tough cut or another bank. In 8–ball a bank should be played slightly long to leave an easy shot for the next inning if you miss.

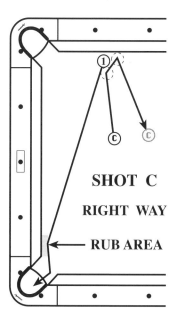

SHOT C

RIGHT WAY

RUB AREA

SHOT C: An added advantage of playing banks slightly long on bar tables is the half ball space leeway for error on the long side of the pocket where a ball can rub the rail in the gray area and still score. From many angles you can miss about one half ball space long and still make the ball.

Softly lagging the ball up to the pocket improves the chance of scoring both now and in the next inning. A ball parked in front of a pocket poses an aggressive threat that cannot be ignored.

The object ball may also block the pocket and leaving your opponent safe.

The sole exception to this general rule is when both players are on the eight-ball. In this singular case, banks should be played for a safety leave in the event of a miss.

Banking like an 8–baller wins games.

KICK SYSTEM: Parallel Method

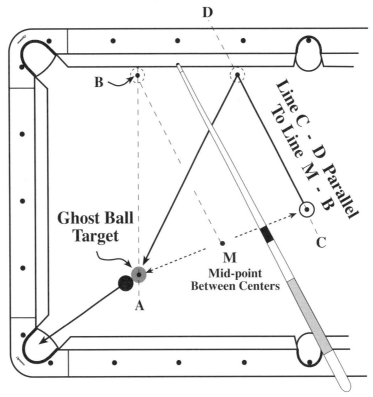

After providing so much information on safety play, it's only fair to give the reader some antidotes to defensive moves. All of the systems in this section work (I carefully checked them.), *providing* you follow the instructions and practice.

Let's begin with a simple method for calculating one–cushion kick shots.

First— draw imaginary **Line A - B** from the center of the *Ghost Ball* Target at a 90 degree angle to the bank cushion.

Second— find the **Midpoint** (**M**) between the center of the cue ball and the center of the *Ghost Ball* and draw **Line M - B** to the center of an imaginary ball at point **B**.

Third— draw **Line C - D** through the center of the cue ball parallel to **Line M - B**.

Holding the cue over **Line M – B** and moving it over the cue ball to **Line C – D** helps in getting the bank line right.

Fourth— shoot into the cushion on **Line C - D** using the appropriate amount of draw and speed to produce **deadball action on impact with the cushion**.

The cue ball must have a **dead slide with no rotation whatsoever at the moment of impact** to attain a perfect equal angle rebound.

THE DEADBALL SECRET

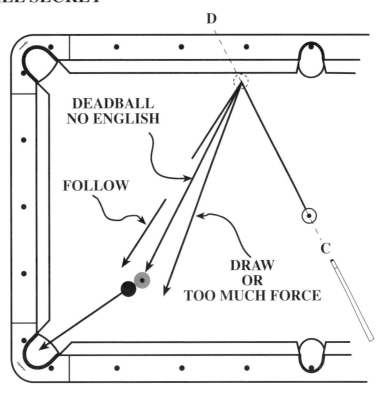

The deadball requirement is the dirty little secret of equal angle banking no one ever bothers to mention. But calculating the correct aiming line is only half the battle in banking because without the right ball action you could miss by a foot!

This diagram shows that the cue ball only takes the equal angle path when it has *zero* draw, *zero* follow and *zero* sidespin at the *moment of contact.*

Follow without english can deflect the cue ball as much as 4-6 degrees *long* of the equal angle bank angle.

Draw at the instant of impact brings the cue ball up *short* of the mark a few degrees.

Using too much force *sinks* the cue ball into the cushion causing the ball to land *short* the same as live draw.

Getting perfect deadball action without excessive force requires using varying amounts of draw which is used up by the friction of the cloth *before* the collision with the cushion. The amount of draw to use depends on the distance to the rail and the friction between the cue ball and the cloth. Players must mentally estimate the right ball action to produce zero follow and zero draw at the moment of impact.

The important thing isn't the action the cue ball starts with, but what it has at the *instant of contact* with the cushion. Everything goes for naught on a bank shot if the ball action isn't right at the moment of impact with the cushion.

PLUS ONE SYSTEM: EXTREME RUNNING ENGLISH

ADD One Diamond Space To Equal Angle Path

The *Plus One System* is very simple. Find the equal angle bank path mid–point, *add* one full diamond and use extreme running english with moderate speed. (In this system all calculations are made opposite the diamonds 1/2 ball space away from the cushion.)

For example, **.5 x 8.0 = 4.0 +1.0 = 5.0**. Therefore, the *Plus One System* target from **8.0** diamonds away is opposite **5.0**. Shooting from **4.0** diamonds away the calculation is **.5 x 4 = 2.0 + 1.0 = 3.0** for the *Plus One System* bank target of **3.0**.

From **1.0** diamonds away the calculation is **.5 x 1 = .5 + 1 = 1.5**.

Once you find the right blend of speed and spin for one angle the same ball action should work for all angles on that table. Just add a whole diamond to the equal angle mid-point and use extreme running english. The cue ball needs a lot of english to make this system work, so don't hold off on the sidespin. *Spin* the cue ball.

The *Plus One System* is very consistent for hitting the target once you get the ball action right.

DEAD ZONE

There's a *Dead Zone* from about 1-1/2 to 2-1/2 diamonds from target where the extreme english system overspins the cue ball. Use the *1–2–3 System* for these shots. At all other distances adding one diamond to the equal angle bank path and using extreme running english works very well.

The cue ball must not be too far off the rail or the angle shift will be too great for extreme english to send the cue ball to target. Within the grey area shown above the *Plus One System* works very well indeed. However, when the cue ball is in the middle of the table, the *Plus One System* does not work.

MINUS 1/2 SYSTEM: REVERSE FOLLOW KICKS

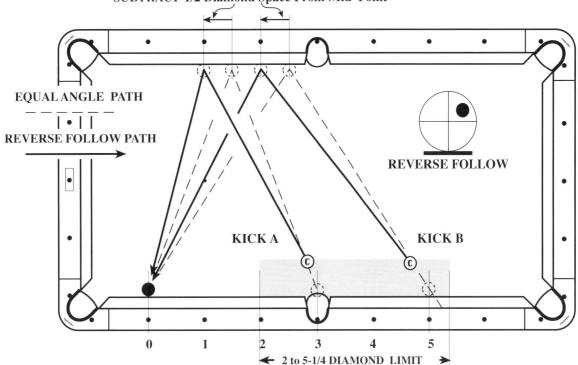

SUBTRACT 1/2 Diamond Space From Mid–Point

EQUAL ANGLE PATH

REVERSE FOLLOW PATH

REVERSE FOLLOW

KICK A   KICK B

0   1   2   3   4   5

← 2 to 5-1/4 DIAMOND LIMIT →

The *Minus 1/2 System* works the same way as the *Plus One System* just discussed. Simply calculate the equal angle bank path *opposite* the Diamonds, only this time subtract 1/2 Diamond from the mid–point and use **reverse follow** english.

Kick A is 3 Diamonds away from target so the calculation to find the Minus 1/2 Diamond aiming point would be **.5 x 3.0 = 1.5 – .5 = 1.0** — making the bank point **1.0** diamonds from the target.

Kick B is from 5 Diamonds away so **.5 x 5.0 = 2.5 – .5 = 2.0** makes the aiming point 2 Diamonds from target.

The *Minus 1/2 System* is useful when you want to **softly roll** the cue ball up to target at a negative angle.

Reverse follow english will adjust the *Minus 1/2 System* bank angle correctly on most tables at almost any speed providing the cue ball is *rolling* when it contacts the cushion. Be sure to hit the cue ball well above center so it *rolls* into the cushion.

WARNING: The *Minus 1/2 System* only works from 2 Diamonds up to about 5–1/4 Diamonds away from target. Farther than that and the angle of incidence becomes too low to allow the reverse english to correct the bank path. Closer than 2 Diamonds and the bank lands short.

Like the *Plus One System* the *Minus 1/2 System* does not work when the cue ball is outside the grey area toward the middle of the table.

It's all very simple, providing you remember the limits.

MINUS ONE SYSTEM — REVERSE DRAW

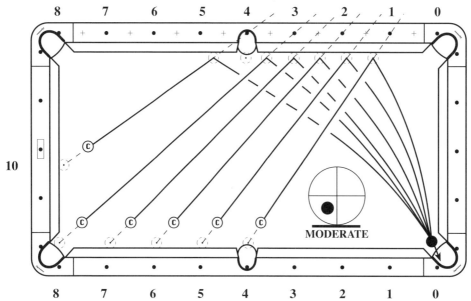

Here's a great inside–draw–english kick system. Aiming is easy — **subtract one whole diamond** from the equal angle midpoint — aim **through** the adjusted diamond aiming point — **use inside draw english** (left above) and moderate speed. Once you get the shot right for one angle, the same english and the same speed works for most angles.

The amount of draw, english and force required varies according to the speed of the cloth, the surface texture of the balls and the "bite" of the cushion, but the english shown above and moderate speed puts you on the right track on most tables. From shorter bank angles use faster draw and less forward speed to allow the curve to take effect.

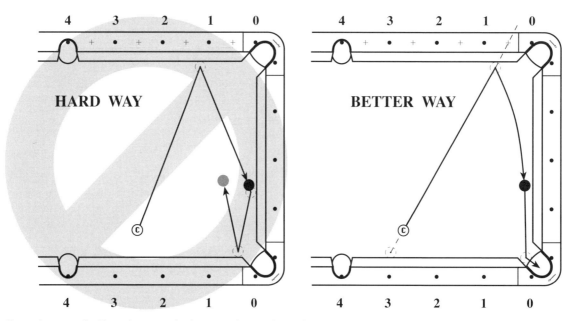

Bending the cue ball trajectory helps on these shots because the more parallel to the end rail the cue ball approaches the object ball the larger the margin of error and the better the chance of making the ball. Making these shots is as much a matter of getting the right **feel** for the stroke as using any system. **Visualize the curve** when you prepare to shoot these shots.

———————⑧———————

The systems I've tried are amazing. It's surprising how accurate they are when you adapt them to the pool table. Naturally, you seldom get a shot where you just figure a point and it comes around and makes a ball, but it puts you in the right neck of the woods.

When you go from table to table or from cloth to cloth that has a big effect on the angles the balls come off the rails. The humidity too — are you playing in a room that's packed with a thousand people or in a room with fifty people.

All of that affects the angles a ball comes off the rails, but it's amazing how well you can adjust.

Using systems is better than guessing from day to day.

NICK VARNER   **Member Billiard Congress of America Hall of Fame**

———————⑧———————

THE SID BANNER SYSTEM

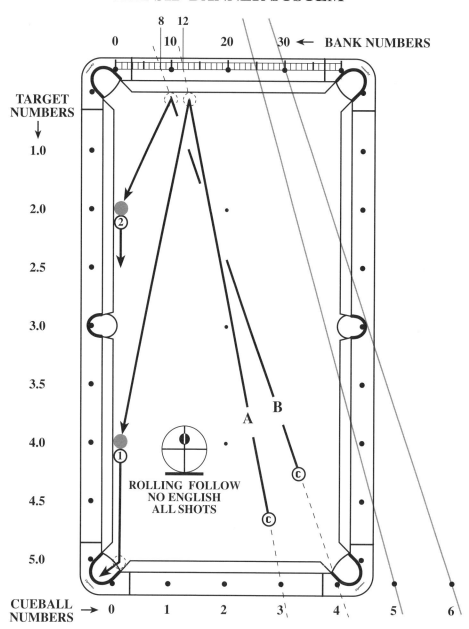

Here's a great system for kicking at object ball targets along the side rails from cue ball positions near or in line with Diamonds on the short rail.

Calculating a kick shot to a target near the long rail is simply a matter of determining the target ball number and the cue ball number and multiplying the numbers to find the appropriate bank cushion aiming point.

Here's how it works. First, memorize the long rail target numbers. The first two Diamond counts on the long rail are whole numbers, 1.0 and 2.0, and after that the target Diamond values increase in increments of one–half Diamond count per actual Diamond i.e. 1.0, 2.0, 2.5, 3.0, 3.5, 4.0, 4.5 and 5.0.

Target numbers represent locations *exactly opposite the relevant Diamonds* as shown. When shots are calculated and executed correctly the cue ball *hits* the cushion *exactly opposite* the target Diamond (*Ghost Ball* positions).

Cue ball numbers on the short rail count in whole numbers — 1, 2, 3 and 4 — and can be mentally extended to 5.0 and 6.0, as shown.

Bank cushion Diamonds are divided into ten parts, making each actual whole Diamond count ten in the *Sid Banner System*. On a 40" x 80" (3.5' x 7') table the Diamonds are 10" apart making each increment on the bank cushion one inch.

In this system shots are aimed *through* the bank cushion numbers to hit points *opposite* the target diamonds, so do not get confused.

CALCULATIONS

SHOT A: To hit opposite Diamond 4.0 from cue ball position number 3.0, multiply 4.0 x 3.0 = 12 providing a bank cushion target of 1.2 actual Diamonds. In other words, the shooter must visualize the 1.2 Diamond position on the bank cushion and shoot the cue ball on a line *through* the bank cushion number.

SHOT B: To hit opposite Diamond 2.0 from cue ball number 4.0, multiply 2.0 x 4.0 = 8 which provides a bank cushion target of .8 Diamond.

Executing a kick once the bank is calculated correctly it is simply a matter of shooting the cue ball on a straight line going *through the bank cushion Diamond* using *follow without english*.

BALL ACTION

It is absolutely essential to use *follow without any english* whatsoever to make the *Sid Banner System* work effectively. Even a small amount of inadvertently applied sidespin is certain to spoil the results.

Points To Remember:

Most mistakes using the *Sid Banner System* can be traced to inadvertently using english, making arithmetic mistakes, poor visualization and failing to aim at a *Ghost Ball* when the player wants to make the target ball.

The biggest cause of mistakes is bad calculations. It's easy enough to multiply whole numbers like **4.0** and **3.0**, but what about calculations such as **2.5 x 3.5** or **2.75 x 4.75**? Do the answers— **8.75** and **13.06** — immediately pop into your mind? Or are you like me having to recalculate the problem several times to be sure the math is right?

Nevertheless, the *Sid Banner System* is one of the most accurate kick systems I've ever seen. It provides good results with very little practice because players with a straight through delivery can quickly raise their kick percentage (hitting the ball) to over 90% for these shots. Think about how many games that will save.

SID SIDEWAYS

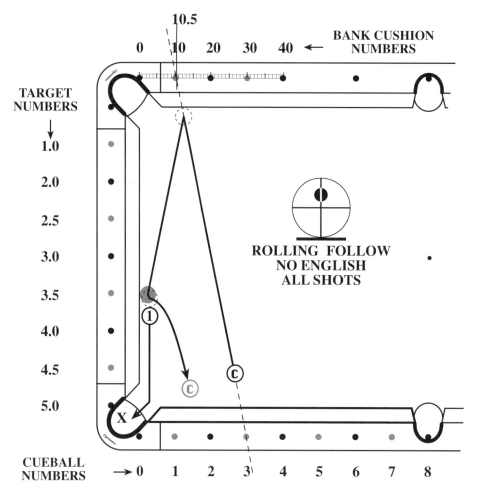

The *Sid Banner System* also works for end rail targets by rotating the calculations and doubling the diamond counts to allow for a *half length table*. When the *Sid Banner System* is rotated 90° each whole bank cushion diamond counts twenty instead of ten. Hence each increment is one-half inch.

If you remember to aim at a *Ghost Ball* positioned to pocket the object ball, you will frequently *make* these shots instead of merely hitting the ball. I see a lot of players who consistently hit balls on kick shots, but seldom make them because they aim to hit the center of the object ball. They often do this with considerable accuracy, but since the contact point is wrong they rarely make the ball unless it's hanging near a pocket.

Using the *Sid Banner System* and aiming to hit a *Ghost Ball* enables you to *make* a lot of these kick shots. You should either *make* the 1–ball or leave it hanging in front of pocket **X** almost every time on shots like these.

Sid Sideways works well up to about 4 whole diamonds away. The main problem is figuring the calculations correctly. This is somewhat harder to do because of the smaller increments on the bank cushion.

While you practice try to get a *feel* for the shots. Good mental imagery is invaluable for refining kick shots to micrometer accuracy. Systems get you into the right neighborhood, but the finishing touch comes from the player's creative mind, not a sterile mathematical calculation.

The intuitive mind that thinks in pictures and sensations is the ultimate shot calculator. Learn to heed this silent inner voice. It is seldom wrong.

SID ANYWHERE

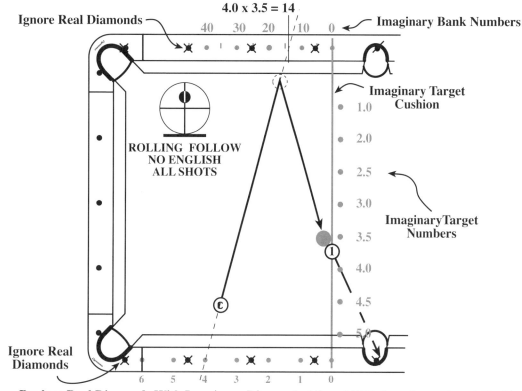

Replace Real Diamonds With Imaginary Diamonds Aligned With Imaginary Target Cushion

Because the *Sid Banner System* is designed to hit points on a plane at a right angle to the bank cushion players with good mental imagery can use the *Sid Banner System* to hit targets anywhere on the table.

The key to using the *Sid Anywhere System* is visualizing the imaginary cushion and imaginary Diamond positions accurately. If you cannot visualize the imaginary positions well, the *Sid Anywhere System* is not for you.

The 1–ball can be made by aiming to hit a *Ghost Ball* at the proper position to score the 1–ball. In this case the calculation is **4 x 3.5 = 14** or **14 *Visualized Bank Numbers*** away from the imaginary cushion.

If you visualize well enough, the *Sid Anywhere System* will shock opponents into submission because you can kick your way out of a lot of safeties.

On tables that bank reasonably well you should hit the object ball almost every time and frequently *make* the ball. Just remember to aim at a *Ghost Ball* instead of the center of the object ball.

SID REVERSED

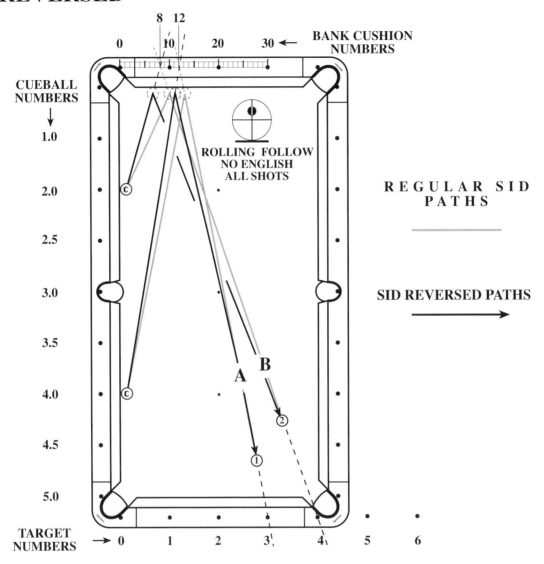

After playing with the **Sid Banner System** for a while the novel thought occurred to try shooting the **Sid Banner System** backwards. In other words, why not place the cue ball on a long rail target position and calculate the kick to short rail locations using the **Sid Banner System** math.

Will the cue ball hit the **Sid Reversed** target? Indeed, it will. However, since the target cushion is **behind** the target ball instead of next to it and in front of it, there is a much smaller margin for error when shooting **Sid Reversed**.

The **Sid Reversed** calculation is done the same as before. The **Cue Ball Number** is multiplied by the **Target Number** and the shot is aimed **through** the **Bank Cushion Number** using **no english** and **rolling** ball action.

Shot A: Shooting from Cue Ball Number 4.0 through 12 on the bank cushion hits 3.0 on the end rail **(4.0 x 3.0 = 12)**.

Shot B: This time the cue ball is at 2.0 and the target is 4.0 on the end rail. **2.0 x 4.0 = 8.0** which sends the cue ball into the 2–ball.

Notice that the cue ball follows an entirely different path when shooting *Sid Reversed*. This is because the *Sid Banner System* aims *through the diamonds* allowing the acquired english to correct the bank angle .

The *Sid Banner System* is **not** an equal angle banking method. The *Sid Banner System* relies on a varying amounts of *english acquired during the collision with the cushion* to adjust the angle of incidence to send the cue ball to the target.

———————⑧———————

A MISSPENT YOUTH

The quaint old saying that "skill at billiards is a sign of a misspent youth" is one of the most arrogantly stupid and slanderous accusations ever made against the cue sports.

Contrary to the dire predictions of Puritan moralists, becoming absorbed in pool undoubtedly kept me (and many many others) from a life of delinquency and crime. Instead of getting involved in thefts, vandalism and juvenile antics, I was busy figuring out how to make draw shots and long cross-banks. Instead of getting into violent confrontations to prove my manhood, I was trying to outsmart and outplay the top dog at the local pool hall.

Pool is a means of confrontation and competition that provides a peaceful outlet for aggressive instincts.

Learning the logic and mental discipline necessary to play pool well provides skills for success in other areas of life. The planning and mental discipline needed to run a rack on a pool table are useful in creating good business plans or in achieving any goal.

Pool and billiards are *skill games* and so is life. The better you play, the better you live.
R Givens

———————⑧———————

1-2-3 SYSTEM: AVOIDING SCRATCHES

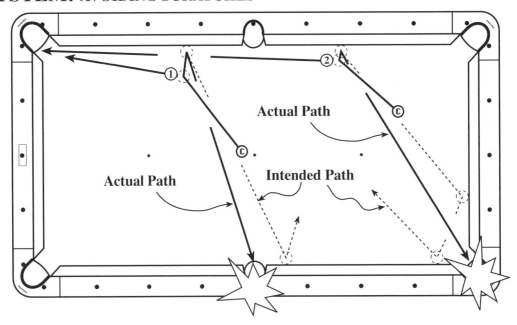

My pal Emmet Clearwater and me were watching a pro tournament a while back when we saw a series of scratches like the ones above. In the space of three games there were no less than 10 cross table scratches. For some inexplicable reason both players mentally shorted out and lost control of the cue ball with such disastrous results that they were apologizing to the audience.   I elbowed Emmet and whispered, "You'll never catch *me* scratching like that." Emmet (my worst critic) rolled his eyes back and snorted, "Yeah, sure," with all the disdain he could muster.

But I'm not kidding. I rarely scratch on shots like these and when I do I know I'm taking a big chance before I shoot, because I have a secret weapon called the *1-2-3 System* that I learned from Bud Harris. This system is so simple, so easy to learn and so accurate that there's no excuse for scratching on simple one cushion billiards.

PROVERBS 4:7 Wisdom is the prime thing. Acquire wisdom; and with all that you acquire, acquire understanding.

─────────⑧─────────

1-2-3 SYSTEM: DRILL I

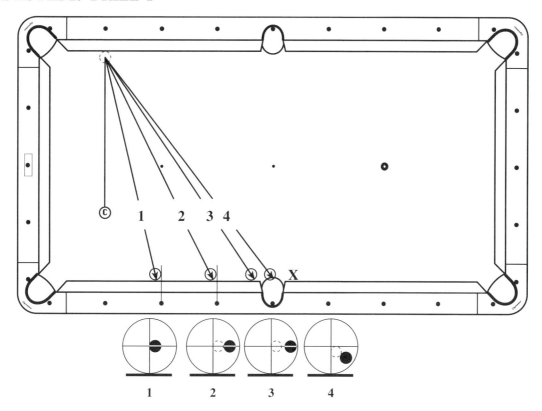

Cross table scratches will be a thing of the past once you learn the *1–2–3 System* because the *1–2–3 System* tells you when there's any danger of scratching and shows you how to avoid it.

Practice the drill above until you can hit target balls dead center with a cross table kick using english to determine the rebound angle. The illustrations above show the ball action *I* use to accomplish these shots. You will need to adjust the exact amount of sidespin according to your stroke and your table. On some tables you can send the cue ball to point **X** with maximum sidespin, but three diamonds is usually about the limit for this type of shot.

The contact points on the cue ball are learned by observant practice. This means paying good attention to where you hit the cue ball. Learn to think like a billiard player. That means **knowing** where you hit the cue ball.

When I showed Emmet the *1–2–3 System* he whooped, "That isn't a system, it's just a method of practice. You don't explain how to adjust for carom angles into the cushion other than 90 degrees or show how hitting an object ball at an angle changes cue ball action. The contact points are all over the cue ball and you don't explain their relationship. These are just practice drills."

Emmet is one of those guys who has an opinion about everything, even when he doesn't know a damn thing about the subject. But this time Emmet has a point. You'll have to practice at a variety of angles to the cushion and different fullness of hits on the object ball to learn the necessary adjustments to control rebound angles using english.

Most players are able to extrapolate these adjustments with very little practice. The main thing is to have regular workouts using the *1–2–3 System*. Set object balls at various points along the opposite cushion and practice hitting them dead center with a kick shot.

1–2–3 SYSTEM: DRILL II

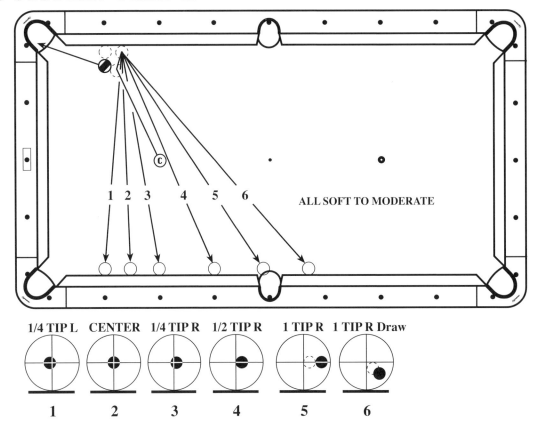

ALL SOFT TO MODERATE

1/4 TIP L	CENTER	1/4 TIP R	1/2 TIP R	1 TIP R	1 TIP R Draw
1	2	3	4	5	6

When shooting off a ball, you must adjust for the carom off the object ball and the effects of the *english acquired* during the collision. These variables drive mathematicians to madness trying to explain the physics involved, but it usually only takes a little experimentation to see what changes are needed to send the cue ball to the desired location.

The secret to using the *1–2–3 System* effectively is sending the cue ball into the cushion as close to a right angle as possible and letting the spin determine the rebound angle. Playing the rebound with a nearly perpendicular impact angle makes the *1–2–3 System* more reliable because you are always trying to play the same shot off the cushion.

The *1–2–3 System* is an extremely valuable tool because many sequences can easily be played using one cushion position routes to place the cue ball where you want it. In fact, it is sometimes possible to run entire racks using nothing but simple one cushion position shots.

Needless to say, you should practice hitting targets in between the examples shown above. And don't be satisfied until you hit the target balls *dead center*.

1-2-3 SYSTEM: DRILL III

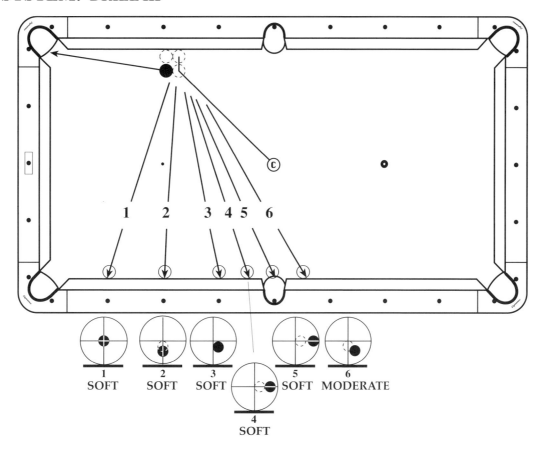

1	2	3	4	5	6
SOFT	SOFT	SOFT	SOFT	SOFT	MODERATE

Here's another exercise to sharpen your cue ball control. Needless to say, the amount of english needed for each rebound angle changes somewhat because the fullness of the hit on the object ball is different. If you practice a few distinctly different angles and different hits, you will soon be able to extrapolate the amount of english required to hit targets according to angle and fullness of hit..

Practice *systematically* so you *remember* how to make these shots in the heat of combat.

The main points to keep in mind are hitting the cushion as close to a right angle as possible, watching where you hit the cue ball and paying attention to the results you get.

More games are lost because of missing simple position plays than because a tough sequence stopped a run. Players who make the simple position shots right *all* the time automatically become tough customers because they seldom beat themselves.

1-2-3 SYSTEM: DRILL IV 3rd Rail Contact Points

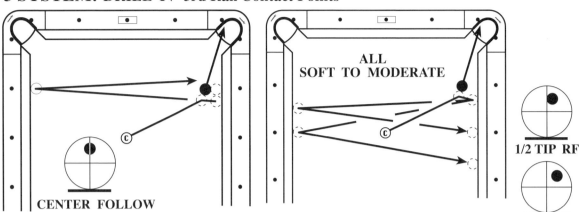

Expand your understanding of position play by learning the third rail contact points for *1–2–3 System* shots. You can easily do this while learning the *1–2–3 System.* Just pay attention.

The biggest weakness most pool players have is not paying enough attention to the effects of english. English is measured in quarter tips and even finer increments because a small error in spin means the difference between delight and disaster. So concentrate when you practice these drills. It'll do your brain good to give it a workout.

English helps on many shots, but you've got to know when sidespin makes things easier and how much to use. You've got to think about exactly where you hit the cue ball and remember the results to master english.

Visualize shots when you are practicing systems because good mental imagery beats any system flat. Combining mental imagery with systematic calculations may enable some of you to get beyond systems altogether and enter the world of master banking— which is the realm of the mentally rehearsed shot.

Pre–see the shot. *Mentally predict* exactly what the results will be. *Feel* the shot. Embed the mental imagery and muscle memory of the shot in your databank.

Pay attention to what you are doing and these exercises are guaranteed to improve your all around play.

1–2–3 SYSTEM: Find it?

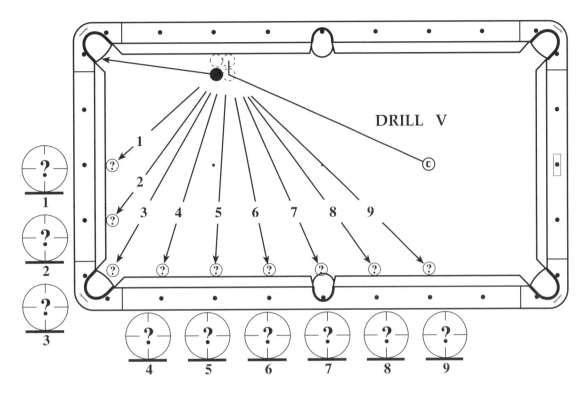

This time readers will have to determine the ball action for themselves because like my smartass friend Emmet Clearwater says you have you practice different shots and different angles to learn to use english effectively. The *1–2–3 System* provides a methodical framework for your practice.

When you encounter position plays you do not understand experiment systematically to see what happens with different speeds and different ball actions. In time, an orderly approach will build up a huge library of plays you know how to make when needed.

Learning to think like a billiard player during *1–2–3 System* workouts will rapidly improve your cue ball control.

1-2-3 SYSTEM: LONGWAY

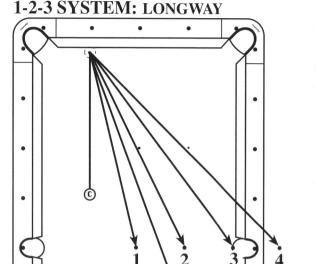

The *1–2–3 System* works equally well for guiding cue ball paths off of the end rails. Just visualize the imaginary diamond positions between the side pockets, determine the amount of english needed to hit the target and you are in business.

I'm sure all of you are familiar with the scratches along the **1.5** and **3.0 Routes**. Using the *1–2–3 System* as a guide makes these mistakes a thing of the past.

The *1–2–3 System* is an extremely valuable tool because so many sequences can be easily played using accurate one and two cushion position plays to place the cue ball where you want it. In fact, it is often possible to run entire racks using nothing but simple one cushion position shots.

---

⑧

UNPLAYABLE TABLES

Some bar tables become so rundown that the game of pool is never seen on them. These tables have worn, pitted, sticky balls that came down from the Trojan Wars. The cloth is slower than molasses in January and cushions rebound like saltine crackers. Washboard slates cause roll offs on almost every shot adding an element of random chance to every play (nothing like seeing a perfect shot roll sideways half a turn stranding you in orbit).

Good bar table players can cope with some pretty bad conditions, indeed, coping with difficult conditions is what makes bar table play challenging. But some tables are simply unplayable. Balls that have lost their resiliency, cushions that are deader than King Tut's cat and cloth that plays like Astroturf can exceed human limits.

When drawing the cue ball two feet from two feet away gets a round of applause and dislocates your shoulder because of the force required, find another table.

There is a limit to the amount of dirt, debris and degraded equipment that I can handle. When that line is crossed I take my action elsewhere.

1–2–3 SYSTEM: ANOTHER USE

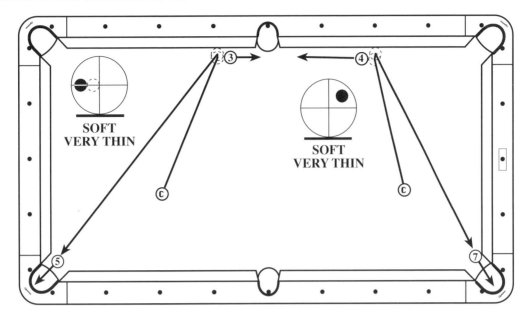

Here's how to use the *1-2-3 System* when you **want** to send the cue ball into a pocket.

Use a very thin hit to keep the deflection off the object ball to a minimum so the rebound angle can be controlled the using the *1-2-3 System*.

Learn the *1–2–3 System* well and you will make most of these shots.

NARROW STREETS

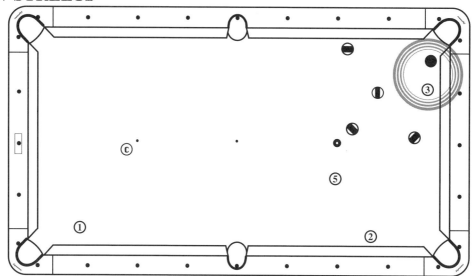

At first glance solids has no way to finish the rack with the 8–ball blocking the 3–ball, but a *1–2–3 System* play untangles the snarl. Getting an angle on the 2–ball permits a controlled landing on the 3–ball shot winning the game. (See *1–2–3 System*)

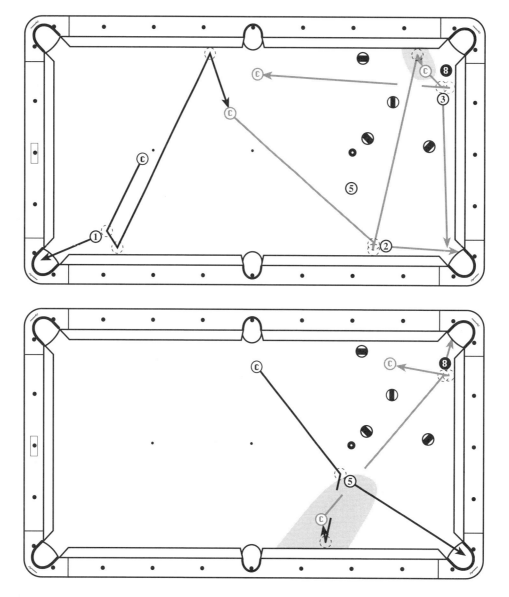

3 CUSHION SYSTEM: *OPPOSITE* THE DIAMONDS

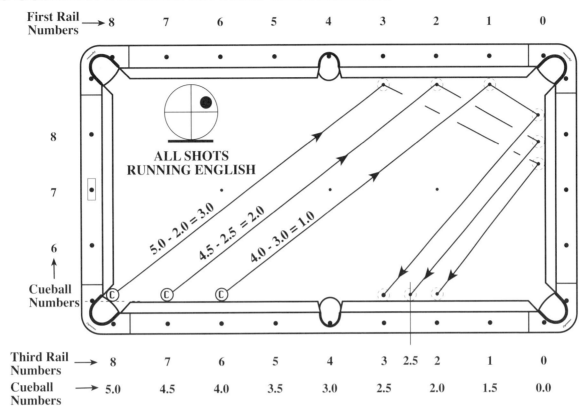

All calculations are done *opposite* the appropriate Diamonds making it possible to predict the third rail contact point very accurately.

Locating the 1st cushion target to hit a point on the 3rd rail requires subtracting the 3rd rail target number from the cue ball number.

For example, a shot from Cue Ball Number **5.0** (the corner) to hit opposite Diamond number **2.0** on the third rail calls for subtracting the target number (**2.0**) from the Cue Ball Number (**5.0**) revealing the first cushion target (**3.0**). Hence, **5 - 2 = 3** making Diamond 3 the first rail target to hit Diamond 2 on the third cushion from Cue Ball Number 5.0. Likewise, **4.5 - 2.5 = 2.0** and **4.0 - 3.0 = 1**.

It takes some practice to do the calculations correctly in the heat of battle, especially when fractions are involved, so don't give up on the *3 Cushion System* if you confuse the cue ball number with the target Diamond or make some other blunder figuring a shot. When you miss a shot by a large margin a mistake in figuring the **System** is the likely cause, so try to correct your arithmetic while you wait for another turn. Once you get the numbers right, the cue ball path will be accurate and consistent on most tables.

ADJUSTING FOR TABLE ERROR

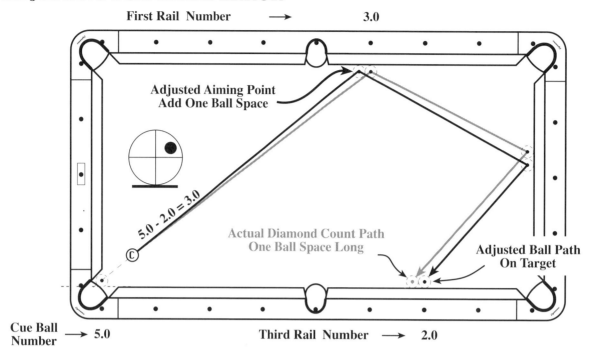

So far as hitting a point on the third rail, the *3 Cushion System* is accurate within a ball space or two on most pool tables I've checked.

The amount of error on a particular table usually remains constant for most angles making an adjustment for *table error* a simple matter of *adding* or *subtracting* the amount of *table error* from the *System* calculation.

In the example above the Diamond calculation sends the cue ball a ball space long. Therefore, the adjustment is to add one ball space to the First Rail Target.

If the cue ball landed one ball space short of the Third Rail Target, the answer would be to subtract one ball space from the First Rail Target.

Providing, of course, that you calculate the shots *opposite* the appropriate Diamond positions as shown. Calculating *opposite* the Diamonds makes it possible to predict the third rail contact point with considerable accuracy.

Now you know what billiard players do when they get on a strange table.

3 CUSHION SYSTEM— ON ITS EAR!

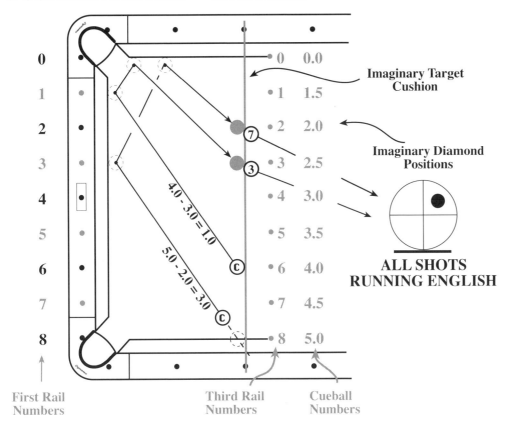

Like the *Sid System* you can turn the *3 Cushion System* on it's ear and use end rail Diamonds to calculate 2–cushion kicks in the end table area.

Just *double* the Diamond count on the end rail and add *Imaginary Whole Diamonds* where the half–diamond spaces are. Likewise picture an *Imaginary Cushion* lined up with the second Diamond.

All of the *3 Cushion System* Diamond counts are *doubled* to compensate for the *half–scale* proportions of the *Imaginary Table*.

The *3 Cushion System* works very well in the quarter–table providing you visualize the *Imaginary Diamonds* accurately. Actually this isn't very hard to do because you can use the real Diamonds on the end rail to help locate the *Imaginary Diamonds*.

SPIN SPIN SPIN

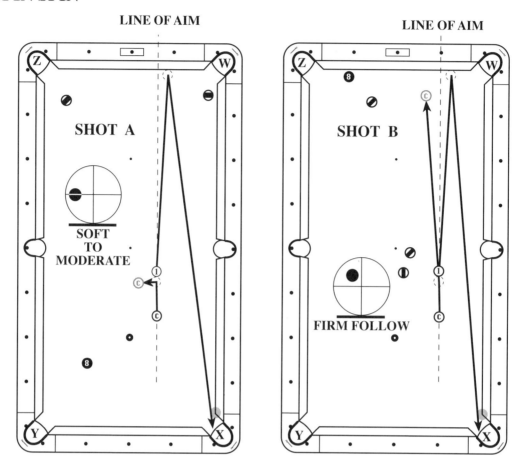

SPIN BANKS are easy to learn. When a bank has a spread of 1.5 Diamonds or less just aim to shoot the object ball straight into the cushion with outside english. The english throws the object ball to the side a bit and applies enough rotation to the object ball to spin it into the correct rebound angle to score.

SHOT A: *Spin Banks* are useful when pocket **W** is blocked or when you need to draw or follow on the line of aim.

The exact blend of english and speed needed varies from table to table, but once you find the right mix of speed and ball action *Spin Banks* are relatively easy to make.

SHOT B: Getting position to play the 8–ball into pocket **Z** after shooting the 1–ball into corner **W** is difficult. A *Spin Bank* enables the shooter to miss the stripes and follow the cue ball near the line of aim for a good shot to finish the game.

Paying attention to exactly how you hit the cue ball is the price you must pay for consistency on *Spin Banks*.

SPINNER DRAW

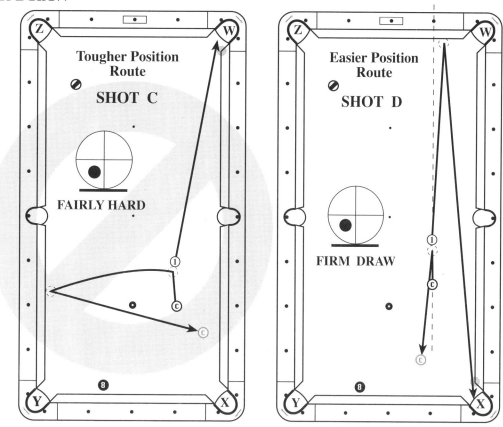

SHOT C: This move should be reserved for times when the *Spin Bank* option is not available. (See *Position Route 3*)

SHOT D: Getting position for an 8–ball shot into corner **Y** is easier using a spin bank that enables the shooter to draw the cue ball back near the line of aim. Remember to shoot the 1–ball straight at the bank cushion. The english will throw the ball to the side and apply enough spin to send the 1–ball into corner. Cutting the object ball toward the bank line needlessly complicates aiming by adding an extra variable to the equation.

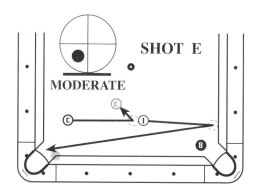

SHOT E: *Spin Banks* also work across the width of the table. A little experimentation will show you the range.

Spin Banks are extremely useful when the carom angle for a cut shot sends the cue ball on a long and dangerous journey that greatly increases the risk of a position error.

When a *Spin Bank* is sitting right the shot converts a tough pattern into a sure thing.

Practicing *Spin Banks* for a few minutes opens up my bank shot database and I begin making all kinds of bank shots with great accuracy. Shooting *Spin Banks* provides instant feedback on the bite of the cushions and their resiliency in a practical way that enables players to extrapolate the effects of speed, english and angle for a wide range of bank shots. If you play Last Pocket or Bank–The–Eight, practicing *Spin Banks* before a match should be *mandatory*.

CLEARING THE POCKETS

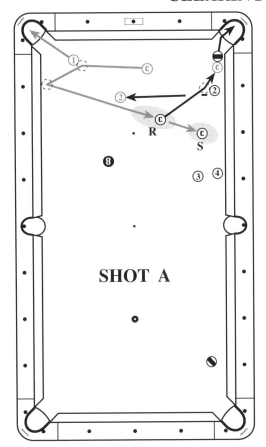

SHOT A

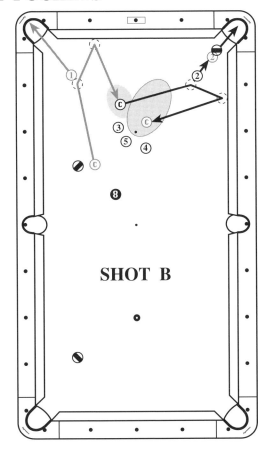

SHOT B

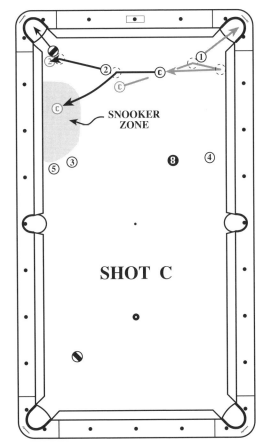

SHOT C

These *planned* safeties show some ways to defeat a pocket blockage. The idea is to get a shot on the 2–ball where you can dispatch the stripe and hide behind a barricade to prevent a loss.

When you block a pocket never think that you have a deed to the real estate. Against strong eight–ballers blocked pockets are usually only good for an overnight rental of one inning. A combination or a carom shot off the blocked ball can eliminate the barrier.

Strategically a blocked pocket is a brief interruption to an opponent's progress. Unless you exploit the obstruction immediately blocking a pocket might work against you.

SHOT A is a two way shot. Playing the billiard [position **R**] is preferable since this avoids blocking the 3 and 4–balls with the 2–ball. A wider scatter also makes it harder for stripes to play a return safety. If the cue ball rolls farther [**S**], a 2–ball–stripe combination is available that also leaves the cue ball behind the barricade.

CLEARING THE POCKETS

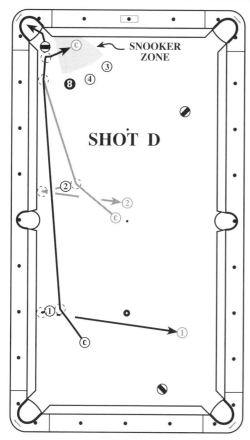

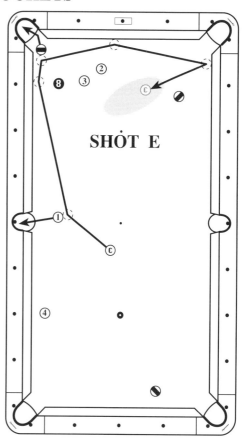

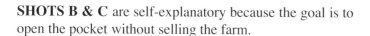

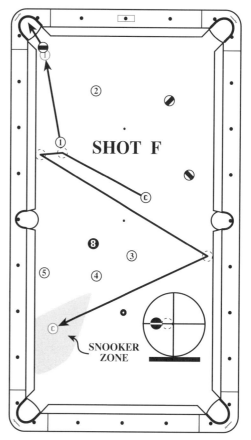

SHOTS B & C are self-explanatory because the goal is to open the pocket without selling the farm.

SHOT D shows a couple of more ways to open a pocket safely. Hitting cushion first reduces the risk of scratching behind the stripe.

SHOT E: Here you can make the 1–ball, clear the pocket and continue your run with an "umbrella" shot that leaves good position to finish the game.

SHOT F: These shots are not difficult after you learn the *1–2–3 System*. Once you get the english right for the angle you want it's only a matter of estimating the speed correctly.

When you make these shots correctly remember the *feel* of the delivery because good mental imagery is essential for repeating plays consistently.

Also See **Bump and Smash Shots**

SHOT-SAFETY PATTERN

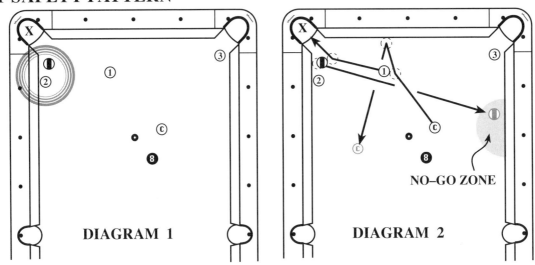

DIAGRAM 1

DIAGRAM 2

NO–GO ZONE

DIAGRAM 1: There's no mystery here. The problem is getting past the 2–ball–stripe tie–up.

DIAGRAM 2: The solution is straightforward. Simply kiss the 1–ball off of the stripe to clear the 2–ball.

Besides clearing the 2–ball a wise shooter plays to leave the stripe the *No–Go Zone* behind the 3–ball. The focus is on landing the stripe in the *No–Go Zone*. *Pre–see* the 1–ball kissing into corner **X**. At the same time, *visualize* the stripe travelling across table into the *No–Go Zone*. Care is taken not to entangle the 8–ball or to block a position route.

Leaving the stripe blocked by the 3–ball adds a layer of security in case anything goes wrong.

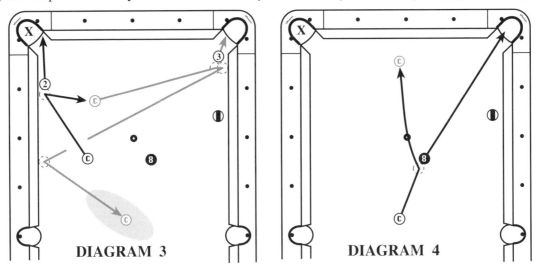

DIAGRAM 3

DIAGRAM 4

DIAGRAMS 3 & 4: Leaving the 3–ball for last keeps stripes in jail to the bitter end.

If solids has two or three balls at the head of the table, the *Shot–Safety* strategy would still be to play the 2–, 3–, 8–ball sequence last if possible.

Putting an opposition ball in a trap is a bonus that should not be passed up when the move improves your chances without undue risk.

KISS ME KATE

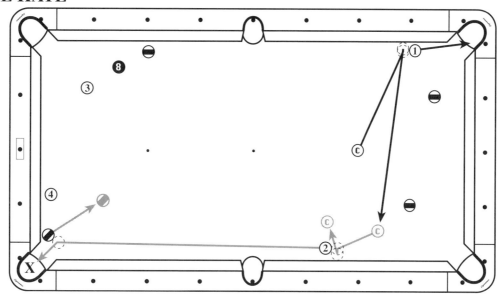

Opening up the 4–ball with a kiss off the stripe will solve solids problems.

The fact that the 2–ball is up table causes many players to overlook possibilities like this, but the shot is not very difficult if you land the cue ball near by.

The shot is played with just enough speed to send the stripe 8–10 inches off the cushion. ***Controlling where*** the stripe lands prevents unexpected tie-ups.

After clearing pocket **X** solids should easily finish the rack.

The main thing is clearing these obstacles with ***control***.

With most of the better players, pressure makes them perform better. It heightens their concentration and gets their adrenaline going. It makes them play better than they normally do.

They may not feel comfortable sometimes, but they get mentally tough and they perform better.

NICK VARNER **Member Billiard Congress of America Hall of Fame**

CHEESY MOVES AND EASY WINS

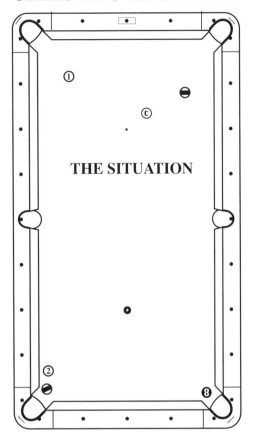

THE SITUATION

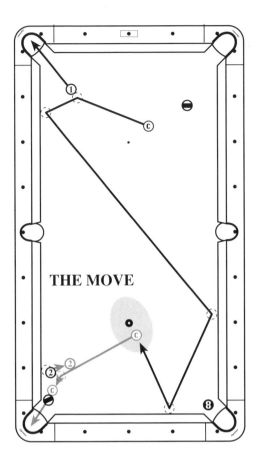

THE MOVE

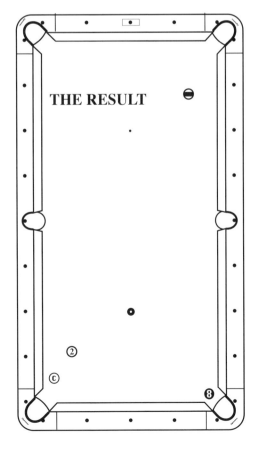

THE RESULT

Look for moves like this when your balls are blocked.

If stripes was shooting the game would be won, but solids has a devastating safety in store that turns the tables.

After this cheesy move stripes will require personal attention from lady luck to win this game.

Practice this pocket clearing play until you *completely* snooker the stripe almost every time.

MIND BUSTERS

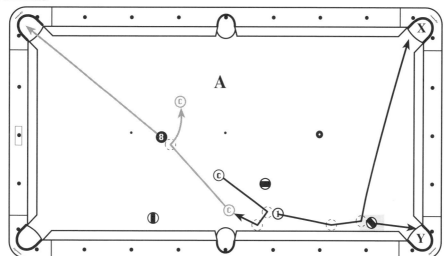

SHOT A: The opposition thinks they played safe, but I make the shot this stunning shot about 80% of the time. When an object ball is sitting close to the cushion about **ONE DIAMOND** from the corner drive the 1–ball cushion first into the face of the kiss–stripe using moderate force. The natural kiss angle takes the 1–ball into corner **X**. When the shot is hit properly the kiss–stripe is usually made in pocket **Y** preventing further mischief in rearranging open balls.

The angle is so natural that only takes a little practice to get the range on this shot. Pay attention to how full the kiss–stripe is hit and visualize the 1–ball flying into pocket **X**.

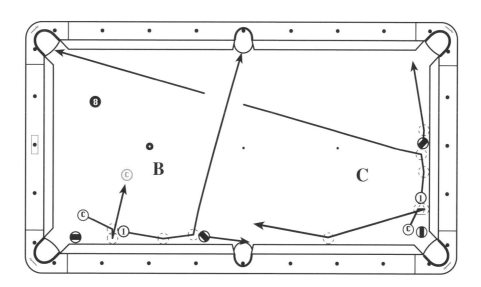

SHOT B: As usual going for a side pocket is tougher because of the smaller size and lack of a adjoining cushion to expand the effective pocket size. Nevertheless, when your back is to the wall the shot is worth a try.

SHOT C: A more difficult version of **SHOT A** because of the distance involved.

> **NOTE:** This shot only works easily when the carom ball is about 1 Diamond from the pocket (for the cross table shot). When the kiss–ball is farther from the pocket or farther off the cushion getting the billiard right is much tougher.

BAD BRAKES and OTHER ROAD HAZARDS

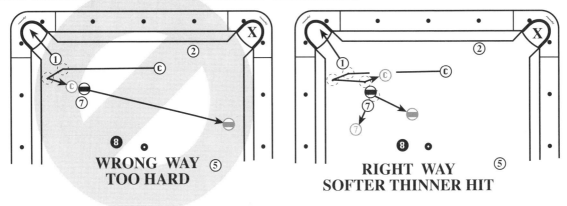

On the next few pages are some bone headed moves that I made dozens of times before I wised up and began playing clusters with a little common sense. On paper these mistakes appear absolutely idiotic, but I've seen some pretty good players make the same errors. The lesson here is to put a little forethought into handling clusters.

WRONG WAY: The biggest mistake in breaking clusters is failing to anticipate where the scattered balls will land. Often players hit the cluster with the wrong speed or at the wrong point causing a secondary tie–up. In this case the errant stripe blocks the 5–ball for pocket **X** creating a needless problem.

RIGHT WAY: It may be very difficult to predict the exact landing place for every ball, but it's usually possible to spot the most obvious troublemakers. In this case driving the stripe too far could block the 5–ball for pocket **X** leaving a nasty pattern to cope with. Shooting softer solves the problem and eliminates the frustration of beating yourself with a half–baked shot.

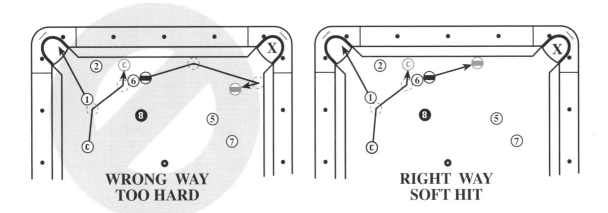

WRONG WAY: How many times have you made a good break only to have a cluster ball create another problem. The cure for this disease is paying attention to where cluster balls might land before blasting away.

RIGHT WAY: The remedy is to merely **bump** the cluster separating the 6–ball–stripe covey by a few inches instead of a few feet. Merely spreading the balls six inches to a foot apart neutralizes most clusters. Shooting softer generally provides more **control** over the scatter so cut down on the speed. Using **controlled** force wins games

Shooting off the 5 and 7 balls **before** dealing with the cluster is another way to avoid a secondary tie–up in this case.

PERILS, PRATTFALLS and PIROUETTES

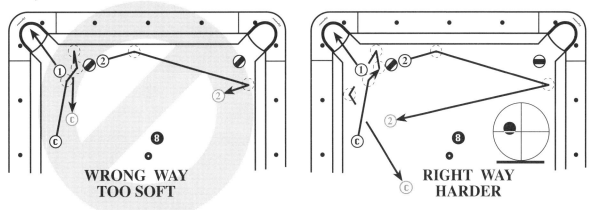

WRONG WAY
TOO SOFT

RIGHT WAY
HARDER

WRONG WAY: Another amateur screw-up. This shot looks so mindless on paper that readers might think only brain-damaged imbeciles make such moves. But rest assured that if you watch carefully you'll see plays like this made regularly by intermediate players.

RIGHT WAY: Avoid leaving the 2–ball blocked by driving the 2–ball back across the table to a good location and landing the cue ball appropriately for the next shot. Use mental imagery to set the speed of the shot according to the force needed to drive the 2–ball into a favorable area.

Use left english, in this case, to spin the cue ball back toward the middle of the table for a more certain shot at the 2–ball. Mentally calculate and recalculate the speed of stroke and ball action until both the cue ball and the 2–ball have the right force and direction to land in good locations. Imagine the shot coming off precisely as you plan it. A good mental rehearsal greatly improves the chance of success.

———————— ⑧ ————————

How you handle clusters wins or loses games, so it is vital to play breakouts with as much *control* as possible.

The day you start breaking clusters with *control* will mark a milestone in your 8–ball progress. Mastering cluster work will take you to the top of your league.

———————— ⑧ ————————

YOU SHOULD KNOW BETTER

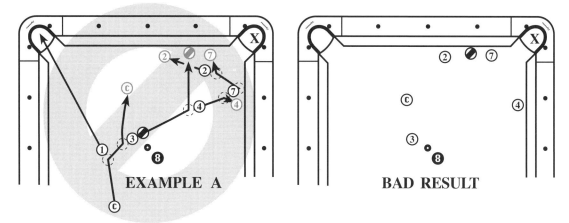

Example A: Sending cluster balls into areas filled with open balls from your group is a stupid mistake that loses games.

Whether you fire an opponent's ball into a covey from your group or vice versa, you are asking for trouble when you send balls into hazardous territory. Only sheer luck will prevent a disaster.

One solution is to shoot off the solids near pocket **X** *before* making the break shot.

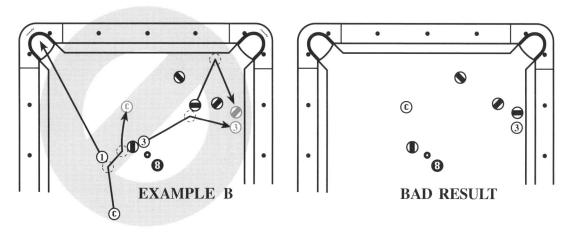

Example B: Sending your ball into the stripes is double dumb. The player should have found a better way to deal with the 3–ball earlier in the rack.

These examples are only *suggestions* of the heartbreak awaiting players who ignore the dictum that open balls should not be disturbed if at all possible and never without *control*.

Years ago when I watched Luther Lassiter, Irving Crane and Eddy Kelly playing I noticed the effort they made to avoid hitting open balls. They had learned from years of high–speed play that accidentally moving a ball can ruin a perfect layout. Whether the cue ball takes a trip into the twilight zone after ricocheting off a loose ball or one of the moved balls gets tied up doesn't matter because you'll be watching your opponent after you sit down.

One other thought. Whenever an opponent shoots into one of these traps and gets away with the felony, never fail to say **"Great Shot!"** and tap your cue on the floor. Remember Maurice Daly's admonition that there is nothing worse for a player's analysis of a position than to shoot it the wrong way and escape punishment. The hope is that your foe will continue playing the shot the same way with less satisfactory results in the future.

HIT THE WEAK SIDE

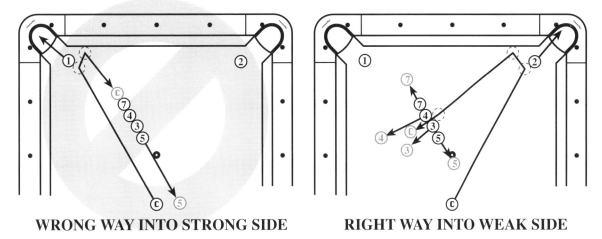

WRONG WAY INTO STRONG SIDE   **RIGHT WAY INTO WEAK SIDE**

Here's a simple concept that is often overlooked. When a group of balls must be scattered always try to hit the cluster on the *weak side*.

WRONG WAY: Hitting the flock at its strongest point where the resistance of all four balls opposes the cue ball is a poor choice.

RIGHT WAY: Attacking the weak side the cue ball only has to overcome the inertia of two balls to spread the clump of balls.

When you have a choice always hit the weak side to open clusters. Less force retains more control and gets a better scatter.

CAN YOU DO IT?

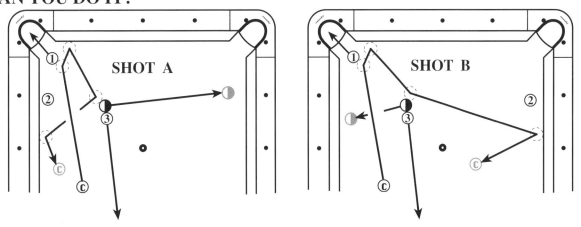

Except for the location of the 2–ball both shots are identical. This difference mandates hitting the carom target on opposite sides to get position. Can you do it?

Controlling where the balls land after breakouts puts you a couple of light-years ahead of cowboy shooters.

Billiard accuracy improves aggressive and defensive play across the board, so work on developing your carom skills.

ACCURACY COUNTS DOUBLE

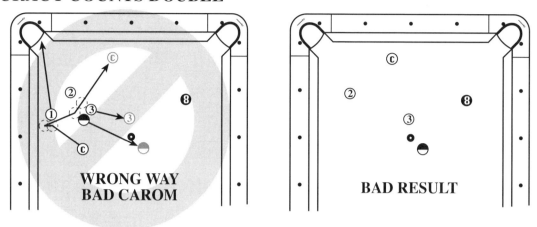

WRONG WAY: A misbehaving billiard can end your hopes in a heartbeat. In this case hitting the wrong side of the target ball leaves the shooter in a difficult situation.

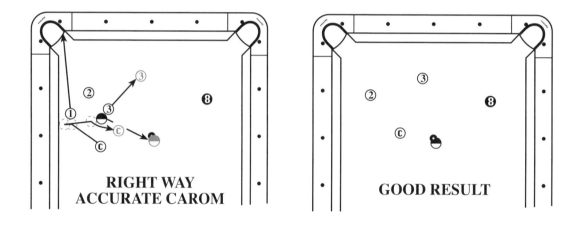

RIGHT WAY: A *controlled* break produces the desired results.

Cluster work is where billiard skills really pay off. Hitting a carom ball at an exact point is a great help in clearing a rack.

BUNT AND RUN

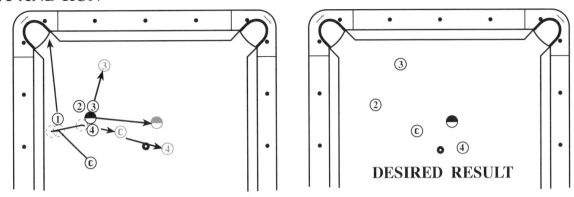

DESIRED RESULT

Concentrate on leaving an easy shot for the 2-ball while spreading the rest of the balls for a playable series. If you slam into these conglomerations, all *control* will be lost. A softer more deliberate stroke scatters the balls enough to get out and keeps them in a playable area.

The desired result leaves an easy pattern to finish the game.

More than half the battle in making good break shots is getting the best possible position to play the shot. Getting the advantageous position necessary to play breaks effectively often requires precise position play for two or three shots before the scatter. It means getting the best angles to make the progression to the critical shot as simple and accurate as possible.

A warrior skilled in attack flashes forth from the uppermost heights of heaven, making it impossible for the enemy to guard against him.

SUN TZU   **THE ART OF WAR**

SMALL DIFFERENCES

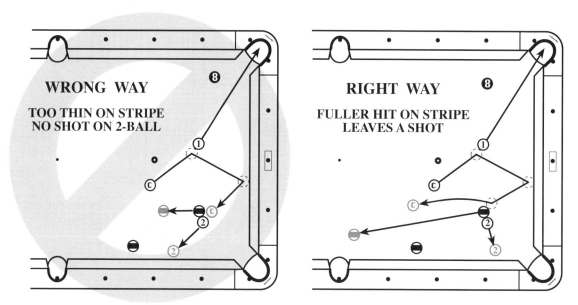

In pool small differences make the biggest difference. Hitting the stripe at the wrong spot leaves solids without a decent shot, while hitting the cluster the right way leaves an easy play on the 2-ball to finish the game.

It takes developed skill to purposely billiard into an object ball on one side or the other, but learning the carom accuracy and speed control necessary to play these shots well adds a mighty dimension to your play. When break shots are executed properly a run continues smoothly without undue problems. Otherwise you are consigned to the loser's bracket.

Practicing on a billiard table (without pockets!) where you can concentrate your full attention on making caroms accurately and driving the first object ball to a predetermined location improves carom skills considerably if you keep at it and practice systematically.

Pay attention to the hit on the cue ball and the force used because simple logic tells us that a player must ***know*** how he/she hit a shot to repeat it consistently. If you pay attention, over a period of time you will build up a huge ***library*** of billiard shots you know how to make. Remembering where you hit the cue ball, the force you used, the angle of the shot and the ***feel*** of the delivery is the price to be paid for developing a good ***billiard sense***.

Situations like these demonstrate the importance of opening up clusters early in the rack when ***insurance balls*** are available after the break shot.

Learning the ***1-2-3 System*** provides an effective reference for one cushion billiards.

TIC TOC

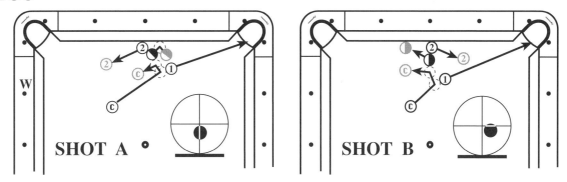

SHOT A   SHOT B

Good straight pool shooters leave insurance balls to continue runs after break shots. Unfortunately, in 8-ball you are constantly faced with breakouts where there's no back up ball. In these situations you must get a shot on one of the balls in the cluster to continue shooting.

With that thought in mind here some typical clusters to practice getting *controlled* position on a ball in the covey after the break shot.

SHOT A: Use deadball draw to carom nearly full into the black and white slightly on the white side of the ball. Apply just enough backspin to pull the cue ball back a couple of inches to clear the black and white ball for a shot on the 2–ball. Try not to drive the 2-ball more than 8-10 inches. If too much force is used the 2–ball lands near cushion **W** leaving you without a good shot.

SHOT B: Hit the carom ball very slightly on the black side of the ball with deadball draw. The 2–ball *springs* off the rail a few inches as shown and the cue ball **forces** the black and white ball out of the way with a double kiss that *squeezes* the 2–ball out for a shot. The cue ball often lands on the spot where the black and white originally rested.

Experimentation will show you the nuances of moves like these if you pay attention to what you are doing.

Straight–Rail knowledge is the greatest aid in making these plays because delicate *controlled* caroms are essential to run more than a hand full of points playing *ball–to–ball* billiards.

When you cannot see how to play a cluster set the balls up later and shoot directly at the clumpet from different angles, with different speeds and using different ball actions until you find a way that works well.

If you are systematic and pay attention to what you are doing, you can add a lot of great moves to your repertoire.

BINGO!

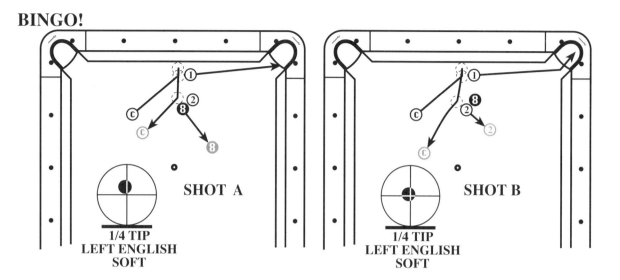

SHOT A: Solids needs to open up the 2-, 8-ball cluster and get a shot at the 2-ball to finish the game. This shot requires carom accuracy and very little speed. Aim for a little more than a half-ball hit on the 8-ball and use a *predetermined* stroke. Accuracy and *measured speed* counts double.

SHOT B: Another version of the same shot. This time you want to hit about 1/4 left on the carom ball (2–ball) to give the cue ball a little more roll after the collision for a good angle on the 2–ball.

This configuration comes up regularly so learning to *control* this shot will win plenty of games. I am so well acquainted with these shots in all of their tenses that my success rate is well over 95%. I cannot begin to count the games I've won with this simple carom shot. Variations of this play come up all of the time, so expend some effort to learn it well.

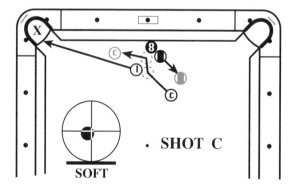

SHOT C: This time solids wants to drive the stripe away and leave an easy shot on the 8-ball. The carom into the 8-ball should be fairly full so the cue ball *kisses off* for a shot while leaving the 8-ball in its original location. When the balls are *frozen* as shown the stripe springs out from the cushion a few inches leaving a simple shot for the 8–ball which remains where it began.

Take care not to overhit this shot or the cue ball is apt to follow the 1-ball into pocket **X**.

ON A DIME

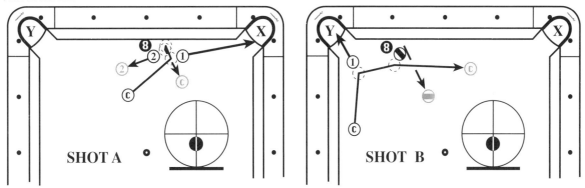

SHOT A   SHOT B

SHOT A: *Bunt* the 2-ball a few inches toward pocket **Y** without moving the 8–ball. Play very softly to maintain a shot on the 2-ball. The cue ball must hit the 2–ball coming out from the cushion without disturbing the eight–ball to insure a good shot for the 2–ball. If you play this shot well, you will be able to make the 2–ball to 8–ball series and finish the run.

My teacher, Bud Harris, often talked about playing "dime position" or "landing the cue ball on a postage stamp." By this he meant that the player was putting the cue ball precisely on target.

If you practice Straight–Rail nursing, precision shots like these present little challenge because Straight–Rail nursing constantly demands driving the second ball in a carom short distances to precise locations to continue a string.

SHOT B: The plan is to clip the stripe leaving the 8-ball in place for an easy shot to finish the game.

Before shooting mentally rehearse the force and carom needed to deadball the cue ball about a foot past the cluster after the collision. Get a firm picture of the intended shot in your mind before stroking. Try to pre–see *exactly* where each ball will land. Focus on using *just enough speed* to get the result you want. *Controlled force*, not muscle, solves cluster problems.

When you screw up a break out, remember how the balls were sitting and practice later until you find a better way to play the shot.

CLASSIC SHOTS

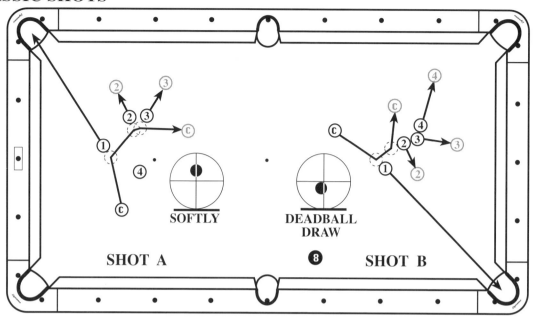

SHOT A: This is a classic pattern with the 4–ball serving as an insurance shot. This type of layout comes up fairly often on bar tables, so keep your eyes open for it. With very little effort solids can guarantee a shot at the 4-ball and probably leave a good shot at the 2-ball as well. A soft scatter leaves the balls in playable positions so why do more?

SHOT B: Here's another example where a little forethought can produce a good scatter leaving easy shots at every ball in the cluster. Providing you break the group **softly** with *control*. The more options you have after a break out the better.

In both examples above putting a little thought into *controlling* the break leaves an easy sequence with multiple ways of running the balls off. Leaving several easy shots to choose from beats cutting a ball backwards because you smashed a cluster to hell and gone.

Controlling the dispersion of clusters makes a huge difference in clearing racks.

The key to effective break shots is using *just enough speed* to get a good scatter. Slambanging break shots surrenders rational thought to the vagaries of chance and taking excursions into the unknown on a bar table almost always ends with a cruel rebuff.

Concentrate on using the *minimum force* needed to accomplish a good break. Generally this means shooting relatively softly.

Replace the lust for raw power with a desire for *control*, accuracy and billiard knowledge. The more insight you develop into breaking up clusters the stronger your game will become.

GETTING THE KEY SHOT

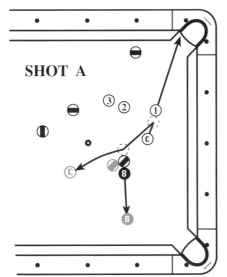

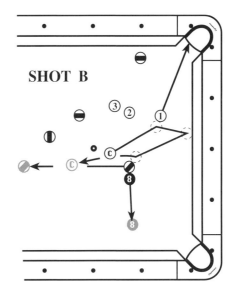

SHOT A: If you open up the 8-ball and get a good shot at the 2–ball or 3–ball, you can get out. The carom to spread the 8–ball–stripe cluster and get position on the 2–ball or 3–ball is delicate, but at close range the shot is definitely playable.

SHOT B: Here's another way of dealing with the 8–ball–stripe cluster. Focus on setting the 8–ball free *and* getting a good sequence on the 2– and 3–balls.

When you are certain that you can negotiate a demanding sequence like this, kick in the afterburners and run out. Just be sure you can go all the way.

A FINE POINT

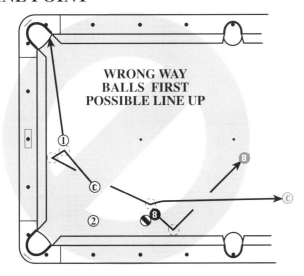

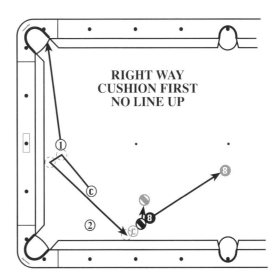

Here's a fine point about handling clusters that wins games. Hitting the cluster directly runs the risk of a line-up and leaving no shot at the 2-ball. Breaking the cluster off the side rail avoids a possible line–up and maintains *control* of the table.

NATURALS

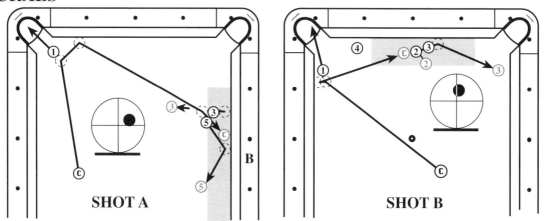

SHOT A   SHOT B

SHOT A is a natural break ball for coveys of balls in the grey area along cushion **B** from the first diamond up to near the side pocket. Practice aiming to hit specific points on cushion **B**.

Pay attention to how changing the fullness of the hit on the 1–ball and differences in speed and ball action alter the cue ball path to cushion **B**. If you *experiment methodically,* before long you'll have enough data in your memory banks to make these shots consistently. English, draw and follow are used to control the cue ball's flight into the misbegotten flock depending on the exact angle and the position of the balls.

SHOT B is a straightforward break shot for stacks of balls along the end rail.

Keep your eyes open for break shots when selecting a group and planning patterns. Easy and effective break shots make runs more certain. Especially if you play the break early in the game when back up shots are available to continue the run.

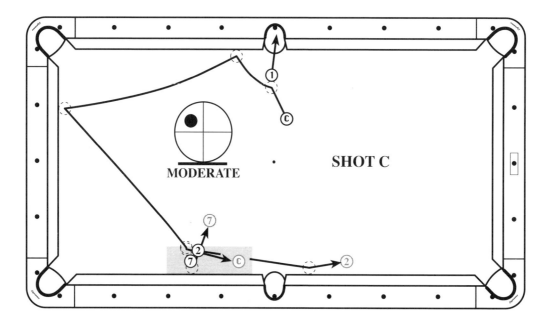

SHOT C: Three cushion players are familiar with shots like this, but there's no reason pool players cannot capitalize on the move when it comes up. If you become acquainted with this shot you will be able to break open clusters in the grey area with confidence.

STRAIGHT–RAIL BILLIARDS— the key to cue ball control

No doubt many readers have been thinking that mentions of billiards in this book refer to the 3 Cushion game, but they are wrong. Straight–Rail is the billiard game for pool players. Three cushion is far less helpful than Straight–Rail because most pool shots should not send the cue ball three rails for position. Most shots in Straight–Rail, on the other hand, are in the same speed range as pool shots or even softer.

If a good (amateur) student of Straight–Rail played carom billiards with most professional pool players they'd win by 1,000 to 100 or *less*. (Unless they are playing Efren Reyes, Jose Parica or one of the other Filipinos who *know* how to play carom billiards.)

The difference is not executional skill or the ability to make billiards, but the fact that a good student of Straight–Rail knows how to shoot each shot without getting him/herself in trouble and would frequently run 100 points or more. (A professional carom player would run a 1,000 and out as soon as he/she got the balls under control![1]) A pool champion, on the other hand, might run 20 or 30 and before long he/she would make an unforgiving wrong choice that Welker Cochran's stroke and an Act of Congress cannot get them out of.

Despite the fact that experts can run points until they keel over from exhaustion, a great deal of billiard knowledge is required to run even 20 points with any degree of control. Players lacking billiard experience will be hard put to run a string of 10 starting with the balls in an ideal Rail–Nurse position. In spite of this, the pool player's goal when tackling carom billiards is to acquire more proficiency in position play and cluster work, not mastering the distinct discipline of Straight–Rail itself.

WHAT STRAIGHT–RAIL DID FOR ME

When I took lessons from Bud Harris I played Gather Shots in sets of 20 while he taught me how to hit the cue ball with good fundamentals. To say that this instruction paid off is putting it mildly. Eight months after beginning my lessons I finished third in the Wisconsin-Northern Illinois Open 8–Ball Tournament (3-1/2' x 7' tables) competing against 384 of the best bar table players in the Midwest. I only missed one called shot in 24 games and ran out in the first inning 20 times.

Since then my high run at Call Shot 8–ball is 13 consecutive racks and my record at Last Pocket 8–ball is 8 games in a row (3-1/2' x 7' tables). At 14.1 straight pool (4–1/2' x 9' table) my high run is 97 and I made a run of 37 left-handed in practice. My 3 cushion average (when in practice) is about .500. I attribute my improvement to Bud Harris's lessons and to my study of Straight–Rail billiards.

Let me be quick to say that I never developed any real competitive skill at Straight–Rail. My high run in open play is about 40 and I've had practice runs of 80-90 starting from Rail–Nurse positions. My best average competing at Straight–Rail is 3.00. This is *not* anything to brag about among billiard players since junior amateurs in Europe are often *required* to make a run of 50 *before* they are even allowed to compete in club tournaments. European players barely out of diapers are running hundreds and rank amateurs average 5 or more.

Nevertheless, my cue ball control in pool improved exponentially because missing a carom by an inch or two in Straight–Rail is a frustrating inning ending error while the same mistake in pool gets a round of applause because the position is still excellent. After studying Straight–Rail for a few months, I rarely landed the cue ball more than 6 inches from target on *any* shot. On simpler plays the rock was on a pinpoint most of the time.

Learning a little Straight–Rail greatly improves cue ball control because the player is always trying to land *dead* on the second ball in the carom without moving it. Instead of playing area position, I began dropping the cue ball on a dime. The accuracy of my position play was sometimes so astounding that I was shocked by the precision.

[1] Straight–Rail was "put to sleep" by master players like Jake "The Wizard" Schaefer who made an unfinished run of 3,005 against Professor J.F.B. McCleery in 1890.

Practicing Gather Shots and Rail Nurses greatly improved my banking because in Straight–Rail a player must figure the bank angle on every shot and try to land the first object ball in a very small area for position. Even though the balls only move a few inches on most nursing shots the shooter must learn the effects of english, draw and follow to control the object ball's bank path. The brain can extrapolate this knowledge to create mind numbing dead center banks on a pool table.

Cluster work also improved dramatically because I could now hit coveys with precision instead of relying on luck and brute force. Being able to hit clusters at ideal angles is a tremendous advantage.

Another benefit of billiard practice is that I did not make a single **Ball–In–Hand** error in the first three years of league competition! Skill at billiards enabled me to overcome dozens of snookers, safety plays and position errors.

Struggling to play Straight–Rail greatly improved my ability to *see* patterns. Constantly trying to anticipate the relative positions of three contrary balls a few shots ahead activates areas of the brain that plan good table runs. Previously I was often at a loss to plan patterns in a logical coherent fashion that had any chance of success. Learning a little Straight–Rail made it much easier to identify where the problems lie and how to solve them.

In part this improved pattern play comes from the huge repertoire of shots a player must acquire to execute Straight–Rail moves with any semblance of orderly play, but the mental exercise of attempting Straight–Rail Nurses definitely activates the brain for pattern play. My 14.1 pattern play (my worst game) got a tremendous boost from Straight–Rail thinking because I began making regular runs of 50–70 balls.

Consistently controlling the cue ball opens up pattern play in a way that weaker players never imagine. Instead of cutting balls backward every few shots, a relatively simple progression can be played. Instead of seeing battle plans demolished by position errors, games are finished. Make no mistake, a good "*cue ball* man/woman" will beat a pure shot maker nine out of ten times.

If you lack the carom accuracy necessary to *control* the break shots and position plays shown in this book, find a billiard table and practice ball–to–ball caroms for a few months. Playing Straight–Rail pays huge dividends in cue ball control.

On the next few pages are some typical Straight–Rail shots from **DALY'S BILLIARD BOOK** and **MODERN BILLIARDS**. Practicing Rail–Nurses and Gather Shots like these is guaranteed to refine your cue ball control to a degree you may not think possible because no Straight–Rail position is worth more than one or two points without controlling the balls. Students must pay close attention to both the cue ball and first object ball on every shot to get anywhere in Straight–Rail.

DALY'S BILLIARD BOOK is probably the best book about a cue game ever written. The old master provides insight into many of the moves needed to play Straight–Rail intelligently. Practicing the Rail–Nurses and Gather Shots used in Straight–Rail will enlarge your cue ball vocabulary dramatically.

I highly recommend that readers get a copy of **DALY'S BILLIARD BOOK** to guide them in a rudimentary study of the carom game.

DALY'S BILLIARD BOOK by Maurice Daly © 1913
Reprinted by Dover Publications, Inc. New York 1971 **ISBN 0-486-22638-7**

New and used copies of **DALY'S BILLIARD BOOK** are currently available from Amazon.com for $6.35–19.95. (http://www.amazon.com/)

Excerpts from DALY'S BILLIARD BOOK

First, in Plate 140, see illustrated the normal rail position, and a series of theoretically perfect shots. Ball No. 2 (on the outside) should travel along a straight line 4 inches from the rail. Ball No. 1 (on the inside) zigzags to and from the rail, and the two stop in a duplicate of the original position each time, but a little bit further along the rail.

In all this discussion of the rail-nurse I refer to Ball No. 1, meaning the ball nearest the rail, and Ball No. 2, meaning the outside ball.

Perfect Execution Not Possible. — So much for the theory of the shot. Sometimes the player will make a series of these perfect shots. But even the most expert players make mistakes in execution. No. 1 (ball nearest rail) is hit too hard or too full or too easily. Sometimes ball No. 2 is forced outside of the five-inch line and it must be flocked back, or the nurse is lost, and so it goes.

The Rail-Nurse a Series of Mistakes. — The rail-nurse, therefore, as it comes into actual play, is for the most part a series of mistakes and shots to correct them.

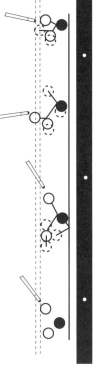

ILLUSTRATING THE PERFECT RAIL SHOT.
BALL No.1 INSIDE . BALL No.2 OUTSIDE

←Line 4–3/4 in. from cushion

Line 5 in. from cushion

PLATE 140

A.- In this ease the cue ball got slightly ahead of Ball No. 1. Cure - Cue ball hit barely above center, with LEFT ENGLISH, kissing back and JUST GRAZING Ball No. 2, scarcely stirring it.

B.- A fine shot. Play very softly not to move No. 2. English left, landing on No. 1 full, but to the LEFT OF CENTER

C.- Cue ball hit top and left, landing on No. 1, like a "half-follow" shot.

D.- Result, the normal rail position recovered.

PLATE 144

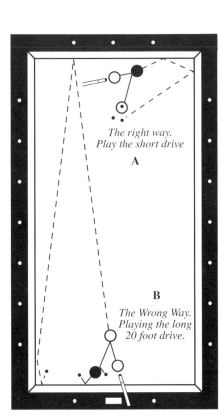

The right way.
Play the short drive

A

B

The Wrong Way.
Playing the long
20 foot drive.

PLATE 51

The Right Way.
Barely reach the
balls leaving several
easy, soft shots.

The Wrong Way.
Hitting too hard, leaving
draw or cushion shot.

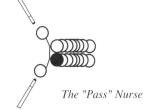

The "Pass" Nurse

The cue ball on each shot just passes the center of the second ball, leaving the same shot coming back. The object balls are hardly moved

PLATE 45

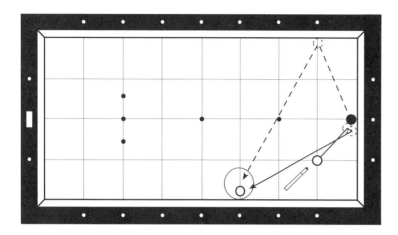

GATHER SHOTS
From MODERN BILLIARDS

One Cushion Shot
Cue level.
Object ball 1/2 right.
Cue ball center.
7 inch bridge.
Moderate stroke.

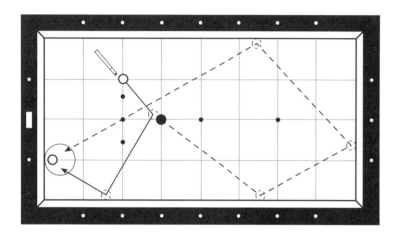

One or Two Cushion Shot
Cue level.
Object ball 4/5 right.
Cue ball slightly below center,
english right.
6 inch bridge.
Moderate stroke.

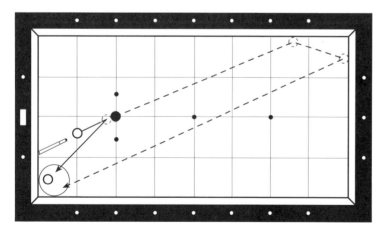

Draw Shot
Slightly elevate butt of cue.
Object ball full, slightly right.
Cue ball 1/2 below center,
english right.
6 inch bridge.
Moderate stroke.

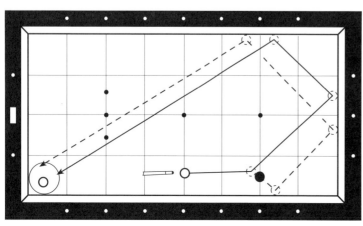

Two or Three Cushion Shot
Cue level.
Object ball 1/2 left.
Cue ball 1/2 above center,
slightly english left.
7 inch bridge.
Moderate stroke.

Practice for Dead Ball
Make these shots repeatedly
until you are not afraid to hit the
object ball FULL enough to take
***all** the life out of the cue ball.*

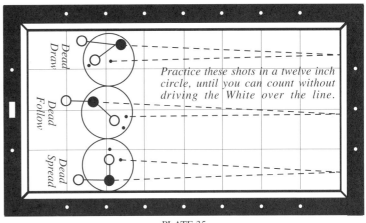

PLATE 35
Daly's Billiard Book

Dead Ball Draw Shot
Cue level.
Object ball 4/5 full right.
Cue ball slightly below center.
5 inch bridge.
Moderate stroke.

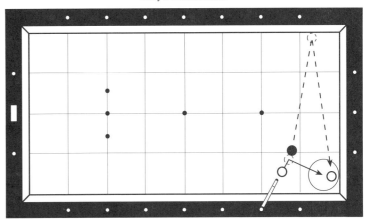

Two or Three Cushion Shot
Cue level.
Object ball 1/4 left.
Cue ball center, english right.
6 inch bridge.
Moderate stroke.

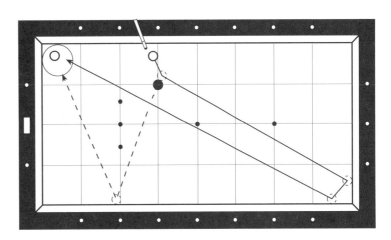

Dead Ball Shot
Slightly elevate butt of cue.
Object ball 4/5 left.
Cue ball slightly below center,
english left.
6 inch bridge.
Moderate stroke.

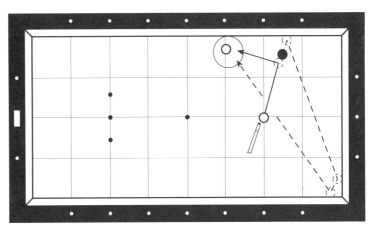

"TOLEDO JOE'S" FABULOUS BREAK SHOT

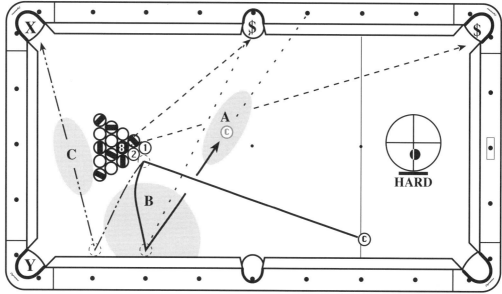

Here's a great eight–ball break shot I learned from "Toledo Joe" Thomas. Aim to hit the 2–ball as *full* as possible *without* touching the 1–ball. If you graze the 1–ball the break usually fizzles. Use a *touch* of inside draw and as much force as you can *control*.

The best results usually come using about 80–90% of maximum speed where you can hit the rack accurately with considerable force. Easing back from maximum velocity a bit prevents a huge energy loss when the 2–ball is hit from 1/4"-1/2" off the mark. A big benefit of *controllable* break speed is that you avoid scratching or jumping the table the way *power–breakers* often do. Controlling the cue ball on the break shot is essential because giving up **Ball-In-Hand** to better players is a good way to lose your bankroll.

On some tables the eight–ball flies out of the rack toward the $ pockets almost every time and once in every 10 or 15 tries the 8–ball finds a pocket winning the game immediately.

This is a powerful break that consistently pockets balls, provides a wide scatter and leaves a good cue ball position. On top of that the 8–ball falls from time to time. What more can you ask for.

Optimum break speed varies according to the friction of the table, the resiliency of the balls and cushions, the temperature, humidity and barometric pressure, the decibel level of the jukebox, global precession, lunar cycles, solar tides, cosmic rays, the greenhouse effect and perhaps the alignment of the planets. I leave it to mathematicians, physicists and stargazers to figure exactly how these factors interact because it is only necessary to *observe* the results to figure the best break speed at the moment. Usually better results come from less speed and more accuracy.

ZONE A: Ideally, the cue ball lands a little past the middle of the table for direct shots into all four corners. Particularly shots into pocket **X** where some open balls are likely to land because of the lateral impact.

On some tables you can overhit the shot and scratch in the $ide pocket, but you can usually add a little to the stroke and draw on a line a whole diamond above the $ide pocket. It is important to focus on the desired cue ball path to maximize the effects of break shots. Pay close attention to the force, ball action and angle used on successful breaks.

Of course, you can't get to **ZONE A** on every table.

ZONE B is perfectly acceptable providing the balls are breaking well. However, shots to pocket **X** are likely be tough combinations or blocked altogether.

ZONE C: When the cue ball lands here you aren't hitting the cue ball low enough, you are missing the correct contact point on the 2–ball or you have some extremely high friction cloth to deal with. You are just a hair away from scratching, so something must be changed. When a break fizzles, next time, try looking at the cue ball last to make double sure you are hitting the cue ball low enough. Many great breakers ***always*** look at the cue ball last. After they line up, they focus on the cue ball and the delivery. On cloth that plays like Astroturf, it may be best to abandon the second ball break because you'll probably get better results hitting the 1–ball first.

HEAD BALL BREAK

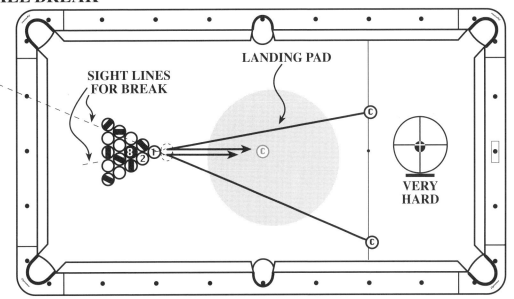

To be a really good player you must develop a reasonably good break. Although the break is not the huge factor in 8–ball that it is in topflight 9–ball (pros say the break is ***everything*** in modern 9–ball), a good break adds to your winning percentage. Among better players the difference between winning and losing on bar tables is often razor thin, so you want to bring your best to every aspect of the game.

The second ball break is my favorite, but on some tables it just doesn't work very well. On these tables you have find the best angle and force to use for a first ball break shot. Here again maximum force can work against you by greatly increasing the risk of scratching without dropping as many balls as a ***controlled*** break using less force does.

The correct force to use is a speed that ***you can control*** that makes balls consistently and leaves the cue ball in the center of the table. If the cue ball is running wild on your breaks, you need to slow down enough to get some control over where it lands because it doesn't matter how many balls you make when the cue ball lands on the floor or ends up in the bottom of a pocket.

Look for "break lines" etched into the cloth because these well-worn paths may indicate optimum break angles for that table. Try to find an angle and speed that makes balls, provides a good scatter and leaves good cue ball position consistently. Refine the aim on the break shot by sighting through balls at the rear of the rack or aiming at diamonds on the foot rail. Sometimes you find a "***sweet spot***" where you make balls 90+% of the time. ***That*** is a tremendous advantage over a series of games.

Hitting the 1–ball dead full from whatever angle you shoot from transmits 100% of the cue ball's forward energy into the rack where it does some good. Hitting less than full leaves energy in the cue ball that sends it flying around the table looking for a pocket to fall into.

English does not help in pocketing balls on the break, but sidespin can cause a scratch or a miscue. Hit the cue ball *slightly* below center to draw it back to the center of the table for maximum second shot opportunities. Because you are hitting the cue ball very hard it is only necessary to strike the ball a couple of millimeters below center to generate enough backspin to bring the cue ball back to the center area of the table. If the cue ball is coming back to the head rail, you are hitting too low. If you have trouble controlling the cue ball on break shots look at the cue ball last to be sure you hit where you aim.

It is an axiom going back well over 80 years that leaving the cue ball near the center of the table is most likely to provide a playable shot after randomly moving balls come to rest. The center area provides the best mathematical possibility for good shots after an open break so work on landing the cue ball between the side pockets on every break shot. Then when you make a ball you'll have the best chance to continue your run.

SCATTER

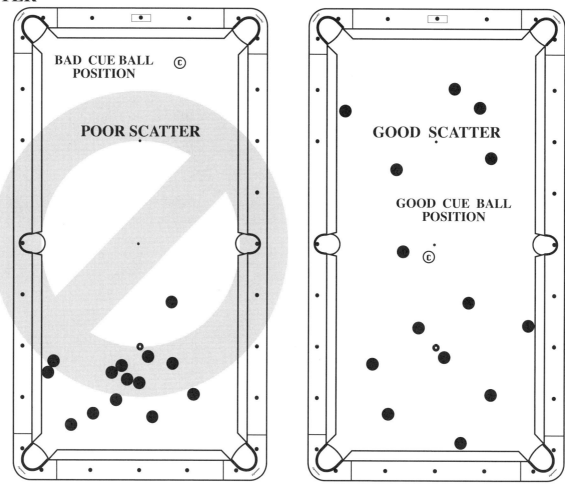

Besides making a ball you want a good scatter and good cue ball position to continue shooting. Getting a wide spread after the break with lots of open shots makes a big difference in how difficult playing a rack will be. A dense clump of balls in the foot area of the table can make it virtually impossible to run the rack in the first inning. More than one safety may be necessary to solve the problems of compactly grouped balls with multiple clusters.

Pay attention to what you are doing and the results you get. When you get a good scatter and make balls, that's the break shot to stick with whether you make any eight-balls on the break or not. A good spread leaves several playable shots and very few clusters. The more options you have immediately after the break the better.

It takes practice to break the balls effectively, so don't give up if you don't get good results immediately. There's a certain *feel* to a good break. When you find it, your break problems will be over.

When you have trouble with break shots watch opponents and see what works for them. If the opposition is pounding balls into the pockets like John Henry driving cold steel and getting a good second shot, imitate them.

A good scatter leaves four or five or even more balls at the head of the table. Up to a point the more balls you drive to the head of the table the better.

Leaving the balls well distributed after the break simplifies things, but it can work against you if you are not making a ball most of the time because your opponent gets first crack at widely scattered balls.

When I start playing cold, it usually takes four or five games to get up to speed, so I make sure I'm stroking well before I make any final decisions concerning the break shot.

BAD RACKS

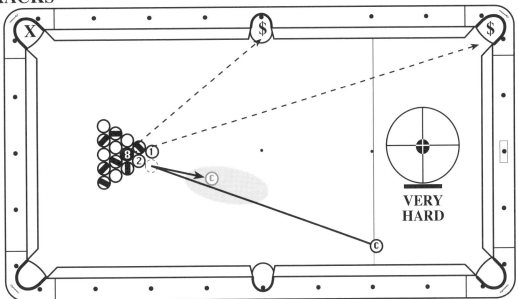

Every so often you match up with players who *refuse* to freeze the balls when they rack.

Whether cheating on the rack works varies because when somebody insists on leaving a big gap between the 1–ball and the rest of the rack, they may be doing me a big favor. If the rest of the balls are fairly tight allowing a full on hit on the 2–ball can backfire when the 8–ball comes flying out of the rack at warp speed toward the $ pockets. The fuller you hit the 2–ball the more effective the second ball beak becomes (up to a point) providing the rest of the rack isn't like Swiss cheese. More object balls tend fall when you hit the 2–ball fuller. If you can hit the 2–ball full enough, draw the cue ball straight back between the side pockets for optimum position.

There are no Sardo Racking Machines in bars, so I am not too fussy about having *every* ball frozen perfectly. Freezing *all* of the balls is difficult when the cloth in the rack area is pitted and torn. So I do not get excited about a couple of 1/32" to 1/16" gaps (the thickness of one to three playing cards) in the rack. Taking a lot of time racking the balls is more debilitating than a less than perfect rack. Of course, when conditions are good, I expect a good rack.

RACK A   RACK B   RACK C

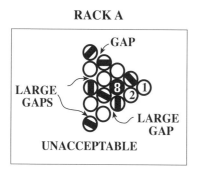 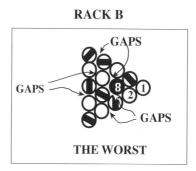 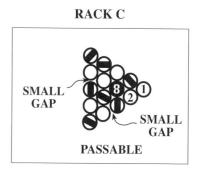

EXAMPLES OF BAD RACKING

Rack A is unacceptable because there are large gaps between some of the balls. Gaps in the rack dissipate the energy the cue ball transmits through the balls weakening the break shot considerably.

Rack B has smaller gaps but this is the worst rack because the gaps are in the middle of the frame right behind the eight ball effectively dividing the balls into two or more groups with a considerable loss of energy to balls in the back of the rack.

Small spaces between the balls interrupt and dissipate the energy flow through the rack. Gaps in the middle of the frame make the worst kind of rack. Leaving small gaps between the 8–ball row and the balls behind it, creates the infamous slug rack or mud rack that breaks like hitting a block of concrete and cream cheese. Creating three or four distinct clusters in the frame makes a good break difficult or even impossible.

Rack C is acceptable because there are only a couple of *small* gaps about the size of a playing card between the balls. On many tables this may be about the best rack you can get without making a huge project of freezing every ball.

WRONG WAY
GROUPS CLUSTERED

The rules only require that a stripe and a solid must be on each foot corner of the rack with the eight–ball in the center, but I take things a step farther by alternating stripes and solids throughout the rack. Here are some ways to evenly distribute the stripes and solids in the rack.

**RIGHT WAY
GROUPS DISTRIBUTED**

I cannot prove it but it seems to me that horrific clusters of one or both groups occur more often when a group is packed into one side of the rack. The same thing can happen even when you spread the balls in the rack, but less often.

A clustered rack can work for you or against you depending on how the balls land, but I prefer to get and give the best chance for a fair spread after the break. There will always be clusters on bar tables, but why magnify the risk.

FAIR PLAY

Unless my opponent is meddling with the racks, I always try to rack the balls as perfectly as possible. That means *freezing* every ball if I can and alternating the stripes and solids so both groups tend to scatter evenly.

On abused bar equipment it is often necessary to *tap* the balls into place with the cue ball to get everything frozen.

Sometimes moving the rack forward an inch or so makes it possible to get a tight rack. As long as the frame isn't moved too far forward this is acceptable.

On some tables it is only possible to approximate a frozen rack.

As long as an opponent is not deliberately bum racking the balls, I give them the best possible rack when their turn to break comes. I expect the same in return.

I do not like petty gamesmanship, but bad racking is a fact of life right up to championship levels. Players who resort to bad racking as a strategy, tell the world they don't think they can beat me with shooting ability alone. Cheating on the rack irritates me, increases my confidence, instills a determination to win and makes it a special challenge to beat the swindlers into the ground like fence posts. Opponents who cheat on the rack openly admit the inferiority of their game. They also guarantee a maximum effort on my part.

A drawn out racking process in every frame breaks your rhythm, so don't let anyone get away with this sort of distraction. The solution to bad racking is to have each player rack his/her own balls! It is preferable to rack for yourself than deal with monkey business on every break shot.

Incidentally, many triangles will only freeze the rack when a particular corner is at the head of the frame. Merely turning the correct point of the triangle to the front often improves the tightness of the rack considerably.

WHAT ARE THE ODDS

For readers who wonder what the chances of making a table run might be here are some statistics from the San Francisco Tavern Pool Association's (SFTPA) Monday and Tuesday leagues for the Fall 1993 season.

Total Games	Table Runs	Odds
3576	132	27-1

The odds against a table run among league players was 27-1.

Expert players do much better. In a Runout Derby among four of the best players in the San Francisco area the group as a whole ran out 30% of the time and one player had 40% table clearance average. Readers can expect top players to run out 30-40% of the time if they are playing an aggression based game, but it's worth mentioning that the leader in runouts did not win the head to head competition.

Leaving such dangerous shooters an open shot is obviously an invitation to disaster.

EIGHT ON THE BREAK

Total Games	8 On Break	Odds
3576	28	128-1

Making the eight on the break is the ultimate one inning game. Out of 3576 games played only 28 single shot victories were scored making the odds against pocketing the eight ball on the break a daunting 128–1.

Among four expert players competing in the Runout Derby there was only one eight on the break in 75 games. This is too small a sample to draw any conclusions, but one would expect expert players to do better than ordinary players. One in fifteen tries is probably the odds for making an eight on the break among better players when they are trying.

However, table runs and eights on the break are not the ultimate 8–ball statistics. What really counts is the won–lost percentage.

I had the highest league average three times in the seven years I played, but never came close to making the most table runs or eights on the break. I believe that I had the most **TWO** inning games though. I also won dozens of 8–ball tournaments using the *Safety–Blitzkrieg* strategy.

Several players in this league make balls better than I do, but I've beaten all of them repeatedly using the strategies outlined in this book. I mention this as a measure of the superiority of the *Safety–Blitzkrieg* style of play.

My experience against some of the best bar table players in the country (Wisconsin–Northern Illinois area) proves that *aggressive planned safety-play* beats pure shooting ability by a couple of light–years. I cannot begin to number the shooters I defeated who had a considerable edge in shooting ability.

In a shot making game like 9–ball, these characters would have pounded me into the side pocket, but playing winning 8-ball on bar tables takes more than the ability to cut a ball backwards. In eight ball, players have to think and if they think wrong they lose every time because the traps in 8-ball are unforgiving and cannot be overcome with sheer scoring ability.

A TALE OF TWO TABLES

There's one table in town where I'd play *anybody* on the planet *if they spotted me the break*. On this particular table I make two or three balls on the break almost every time and scatter the balls like confetti in the wind. I sink a ball on the break over 95% of the time. The eight–ball falls on the break better than 1 out of 10 tries. I run *lots* of racks on this table. I do not know why this table plays so well for me because I seldom get such spectacular results. Indeed, my style of play is designed to anticipate a lot more trouble from the equipment.

This particular table is an arena where cowboy pool rules supreme because of the ease of running out.

I would hesitate to play a top shooter even up on this table because he/she might run a dozen racks at a clip on me.

On the other hand I know of three or four tables in the area where I wouldn't bet a nickel against a quadriplegic in an iron lung. On these tables making a ball on the break and getting the balls scattered seems to be impossible. A run on such difficult equipment requires masterly play on every shot or superlative luck because there are so many clusters and the cloth is slower than #80 grit sandpaper.

The shots in this book relate to tables in what I call the *normal* range. These are the tables *usually* encountered in taverns. This means the equipment is not perfect, but is good enough to execute all of the shots shown in this book without borrowing Mike Massey's stroke.

The lessons are for Valley, Dynamo and most other coin operated tables.

Give It The Brush

When Luther Lassiter played high stakes games years ago he often methodically picked up lint and bits of chalk along the line of the shot. Lassiter made a dramatic performance of creating ideal conditions for his shot and would sometimes repeat this act in several different games.

Lassiter could have had the table brushed and vacuumed between games, but he used a nit–picking routine to put opponents under mind crushing pressure with his showmanship. Especially since he *never* missed any of his nit–pickers.

To get back on track, brushing a bar table can eliminate innumerable problems. The bar tender may have to search for a brush they haven't used since the last time the Cubs won a World Series, but removing accumulated bits of chalk, dirt, dust and debris makes a big difference in how a table plays.

Make it a point to clean the table *before* beginning a session.

SEVEN ROADS TO UTOPIA

STEP 1 — ANALYZING THE BATTLEFIELD

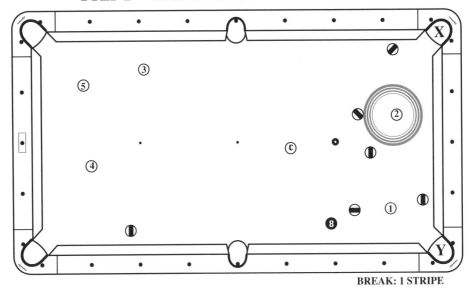

BREAK: 1 STRIPE

Experienced players call set ups like this "Road Map Runouts." However, the notion that there's any need for a chart, a compass or a blueprint is completely erroneous because the balls are scattered so well that all the shooter needs to do is select the order to remove the balls with a little common sense and the game is won. There are multiple simple ways to finish this game.

The pattern is figured by working backward from the 8–ball shot to the first ball you shoot.

STEP 1: Analyzing the battlefield. The only potential problem is the 2–ball with stripes hovering nearby that could make getting position to make the ball difficult. It is critical to get the 2–ball off the table right away because it will be a land mine waiting to defeat solids if left for later.

STEP 2: Find a solution. Taking care of the 2-ball is easy this time because the 1–ball shot provides simple position to shoot the 2-ball into corner **X**.

STEP 3: Clear the table. Once the 2-ball is out of the way, the shooter has several routes to the 8–ball with huge position areas to fit into a pattern. Any halfway decent player should win the game from here.

STEP 4: Finish the game. A simple cushion play brings the shooter into a huge position area for making the 8–ball in pocket **Y**.

There are at least a half dozen good ways to clear the 3–, 4–, 5–, 8–ball sequence. The main thing is to settle on a straightforward plan.

STEP 2: FIND A SOLUTION

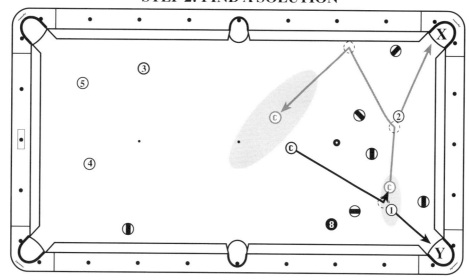

STEP 3: CLEAR THE TABLE

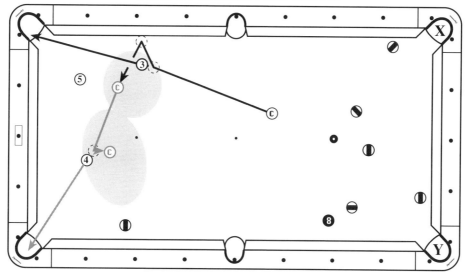

STEP 4: FINISH THE GAME

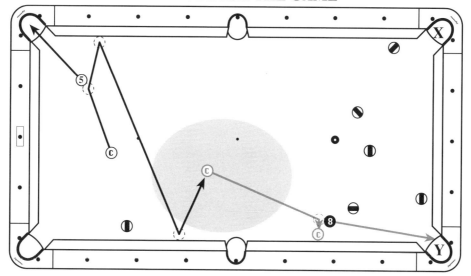

A PIGGYBACK RIDE

STEP 1 — ANALYZING THE BATTLEFIELD

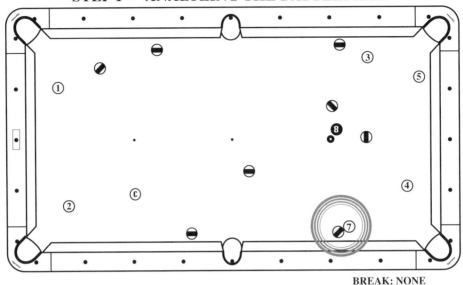

BREAK: NONE

A mental piggyback ride through the process involved in figuring a pattern may help readers formulate more effective game plans.

Ordinary players start by looking at the easiest shots and often shoot off a couple of balls before giving any attention to problems that can stop a run. The aftermath is that solvable situations become impossible because balls are played in the wrong order, position balls for break shots are wasted and break balls are played without opening clusters. These are errors of ignorance or overly aggressive play.

STEP 1: *Identifying the problem.* Winners, on the other hand, begin their planning by accounting for trouble balls first. Champions look for ways to deal with clusters, position problems and badly located balls *before shooting the first shot*.

The 7-ball–stripe–ball cluster stands out like lighthouse beacon because it is the only obstacle to a runout.

STEP 2: *Find a solution.* A good response is to shoot a break shot off of the 4–ball.

STEP 3: *Plan a route to the break shot.* In this case, the 1-2-3-ball series serves very nicely to get position for the 4–ball break shot without any superhuman efforts.

STEP 4: *Plan a pattern to finish the rack.* There are no guarantees where the balls will land on a break shot, so a new pattern may have to be formed depending on how the break shot turns out. With the 5–ball positioned for an "insurance shot" after the break there are several likely ways to finish the rack.

All of this mental imagery is done *before* shooting the first ball. Better players shoot games in their minds *several times* before they hit the cue ball. Experienced players can mentally play several patterns in a few seconds, but *you* should take a couple of minutes if you need to. The important thing is to figure a game plan that *you* can handle with a fair degree of certainty *before shooting the first ball*.

STEP 2: FIND A SOLUTION

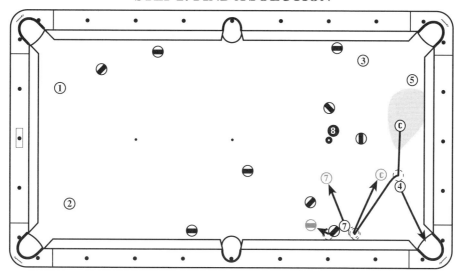

STEP 3 PLAN A ROUTE TO THE BREAK SHOT

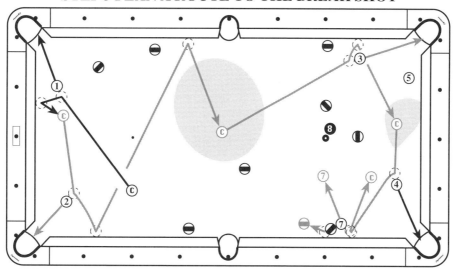

STEP 4: PLAN A PATTERN AFTER THE BREAK

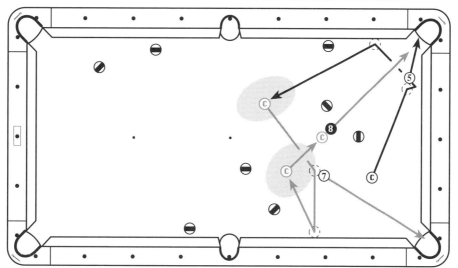

LIKE A CONQUERING GENERAL
STEP 1 — ANALYZING THE BATTLEFIELD

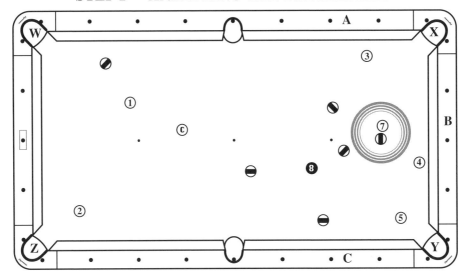

A good eight ball player reconnoiters the battlefield like a conquering general looking for offensive and defensive plays *before* launching an attack. Accounting for difficulties *beforehand* is the mark of a champion.

Step 1: *Identifying the problem.* The 7–ball–stripe cluster sticks out like a sore thumb. It is the only obstruction to a fairly simple runout.

Step 2: *Find a solution.* A break shot off the 4–ball is an obvious response. Using the 3–ball to scatter the cluster might be possible, but driving the stripe toward cushion **C** could easily tie up shots on the 5–ball or the 8–ball or both. Furthermore, the 4–ball break shot offers a much more controllable play.

Step 3: *Plan a route to the break shot.* The 1–2–3–ball sequence delivers the cue ball to the position zone for the 4–ball break shot without any heroic efforts because there are multiple ways to transition from the 3–ball to the 4–ball break shot.

Step 4: *Figure a pattern to finish the rack.* Since the cue ball will land near where the stripe rested it's pretty certain that a 5–7–8–ball series will finish the rack. All of these shots are relatively simple providing assurance that the pattern will succeed.

Step 5: *Play it again Sam.* Before launching your assault, mentally replay your game plan as you stalk the table lining up each shot from where it will be played. Be sure that **you** can make the shots and play the positions required. Good players mentally rehearse games over and over in their mind's eye until they get everything figured correctly *before* bending over to shoot the first shot. Take enough time to get everything mapped out in your head *before* you shoot the first ball.

If your mental battle plan seems too difficult, revise your strategy and consider a safety option to eliminate the obstacles.

Ordinary players lose more games by starting off without a good battle plan than almost any other cause.

STEP 2: FIND A SOLUTION

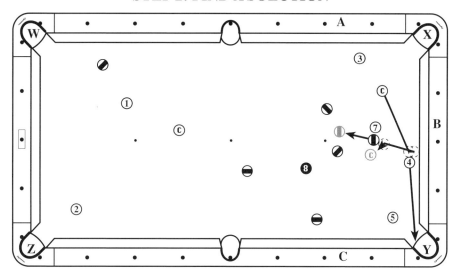

STEP 3 PLAN A ROUTE TO THE BREAK SHOT

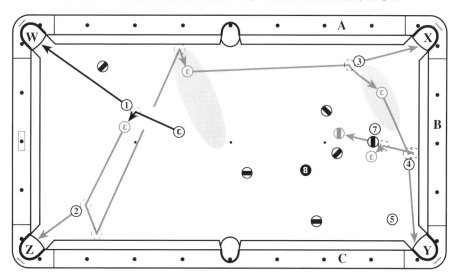

STEP 4: PLAN A PATTERN AFTER THE BREAK

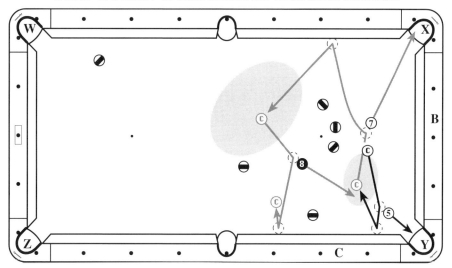

DEMOLITION DERBY

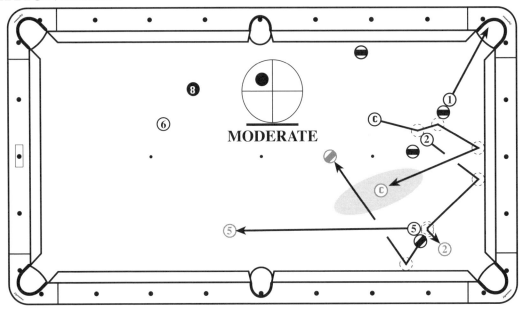

Caroming into the combo while banking the 2–ball into the 5–ball–stripe cluster solves two problems and opens up a potentially game ending sequence.

Try to drive the cue ball back up table a couple of diamonds for possible shots at the 2–ball, the 5–ball or the 6–ball after the break.

Restrain the urge to blast clusters to kingdom come because needless ball travel greatly increases the risk of a secondary tie-up in the confined area of a bar table. So turn down the velocity on break shots.

Finding imaginative ways to use dead combinations wins games.

Combinations greatly expand the possibilities for break shots and position play, so take a good look before popping in a dead combo. You may be able to break the game wide open with a creative combination shot.

GONE POSTAL

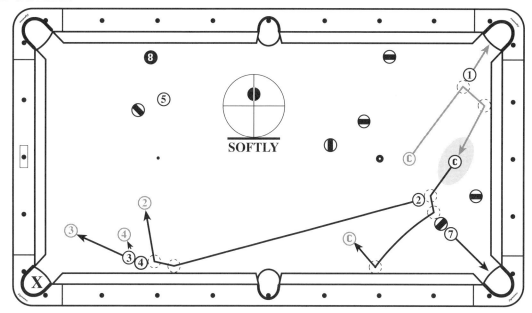

Imagination turns a dead combination into a game-winning cluster busting tool. Breaking the 3–4–ball cluster with the 2-ball while making the 7-ball opens up a game winning sequence.

As long as you hit the 3–4–ball cluster softly the odds are good that you will have playable shots at one or more of balls in the array as well as a likely shot on the 5–ball to continue a run. Blasting the covey throws your fate to the winds while shooting softly confines the scatter to a small area near pocket **X** where a playable shot on one of the balls is almost certain. Overhitting clusters is a sucker move, so stop doing it.

Accuracy and **controlled force** are the keys to handling clusters.

Notice the excellent position played for this shot. Pattern play for power moves must be planned and executed with the same care any other delicate shot requires.

Try to *visualize* where the balls in a cluster will land and play position accordingly. Maximizing shots raises your play a notch or two.

Moves like this send opponents into full-blown mental meltdowns. They know something is going on but they cannot quite figure it out. One minute I'm playing like Whistler's Mother in her rocking chair and the next instant I'm gunning down balls like Annie Oakley "Gone Postal" at the Wild West Show.

Freewheelers do not understand how the sharply contrasting *Safety–Blitzkrieg* style fits in with a consistent approach because they do not comprehend that *control* is the unifying factor in this style of play.

FILIPINO GENE OPENS FIRE

STEP 1 — ANALYZING THE BATTLEFIELD

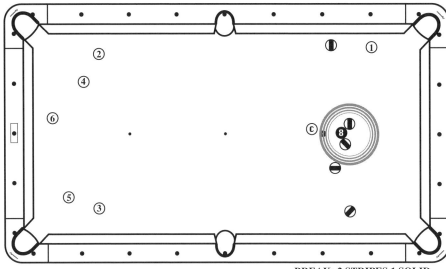

BREAK: 2 STRIPES 1 SOLID

Filipino Gene Ventura shows how to make this a one-inning game.

STEP 1: *Identifying the problem.* Except for the 8–ball solids is in the clear.

STEP 2: Breaking the 8–ball–stripe cluster with the 1–ball shot is the obvious shot.

The danger is hitting the cluster on the wrong side of the **Carom Line** sending the cue ball into pocket **X** (dashed line) or leaving the cue ball buried behind four stripes at the foot of the table. Missing the billiard a little can mean disaster.

STEP 3: *Find a solution.* Filipino Gene only took a few seconds to line this shot up and put the game on ice. If the carom is accurate a moderately hard stroke sends the 8–ball and the cue ball up table leaving an easy pattern to finish the game.

Good players like *Filipino Gene* consider the risks before shooting and seldom make errors on plays like this.

STEP 4: *Plan a pattern after the break.* There are several easy ways to finish the game here. The order of the balls and the pockets *Filipino Gene* chose are shown, but the critical shot is breaking the 8–ball loose. If you get the cue ball into the clear toward the center of the table, there are a dozen easy ways to run out.

Set the balls up and see how you would take them off.

STEP 2: THE DANGER

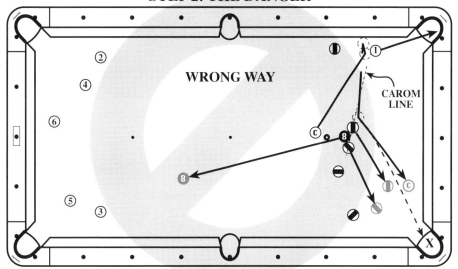

STEP 3: FIND A SOLUTION

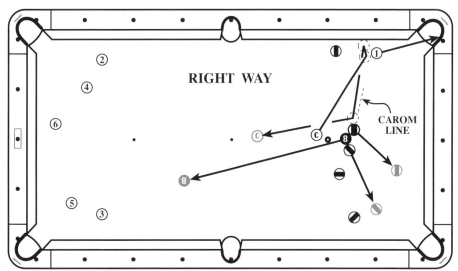

STEP 4: PLAN A PATTERN AFTER THE BREAK

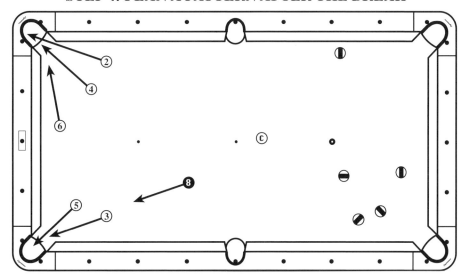

ONE SHOT BOOGIE

STEP 1 — ANALYZING THE BATTLEFIELD

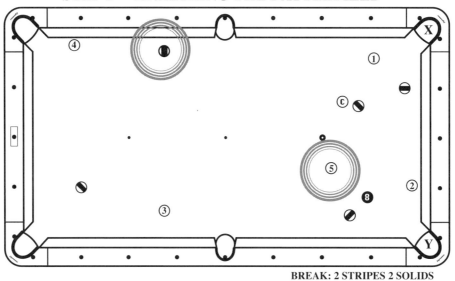

BREAK: 2 STRIPES 2 SOLIDS

STEP 1: *Identifying the problem.* Except for the 5–ball solids is in the clear.

STEP 2: *Find a solution.* The 5–ball is blocked for corners **X** and **Y** but if you can drive the ball toward the center of the table with a billiard off the 2–ball a playable pattern will emerge.

STEP 3: *Plan a pattern to the critical shot.* The route to the key shot is simple and obvious. Just cut the 1–ball softly and land clear of stripe **S** for a cut-shot on the 2–ball. Use a *1–2–3 System Shot* for an accurate billiard into the 5–ball. Drive the 5–ball to the center of the table for a shot into corner **X**.

STEP 4: *Finishing the game.* With no obstacles remaining, finishing the game is simple. Depending on exactly how the balls land after the 2–ball shot a 3–, 4–, 5–, 8–ball sequence or the 3–, 5–, 4–, 8–ball run (shown) can finish the game. The large position area for making the 5–ball assures success.

STEP 2: FIND A SOLUTION

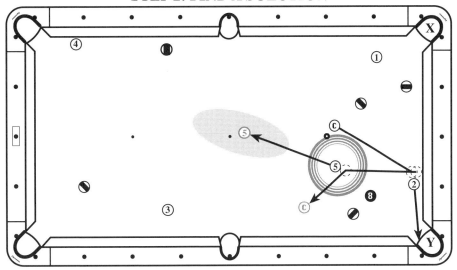

STEP 3: PLAN A PATTERN TO THE BREAK SHOT

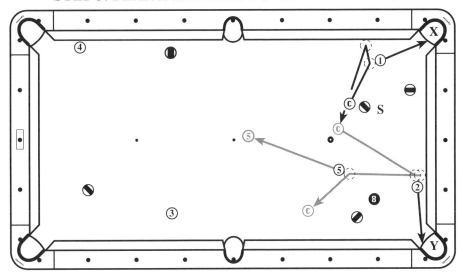

STEP 4: FINISHING THE GAME

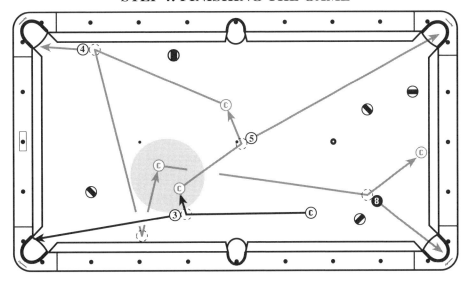

COMING AROUND THE BEND

STEP 1 — ANALYZING THE BATTLEFIELD

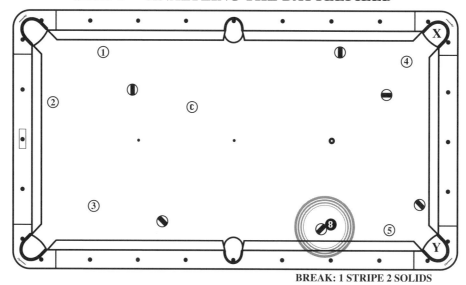

BREAK: 1 STRIPE 2 SOLIDS

STEP 1: *Analyzing the battlefield.* Except for the 8–ball solids has clear sailing.

STEP 2: *Find a solution.* The 4–ball makes an excellent break shot for the 8–ball–stripe cluster. There's a good-sized position area to play the break from. If you practice the nuances of english, follow, draw and fullness of hit for this shot you will have little trouble breaking out the 8–ball–stripe cluster.

STEP 3: *Plan a pattern to the break.* The break shot could be played right away, but prudence dictates clearing the balls at the head of the table before making the break out. There's a large position area to shoot the break shot from, so there will be no problem getting a good angle for the critical shot.

STEP 4: *Finishing the rack.* Completing the rack is simplicity itself for those who know the *1–2–3 System*. Just shoot the 5–ball in the corner and rebound off cushion **X** for an easy shot on the 8–ball. The huge position area for making the 8–ball provides assurance of victory.

Notice that four *1–2–3 System* shots are used in this rack. Get busy learning the *1-2-3 System*. This invaluable method of cue ball control will make you a winner.

STEP 2: FIND A SOLUTION

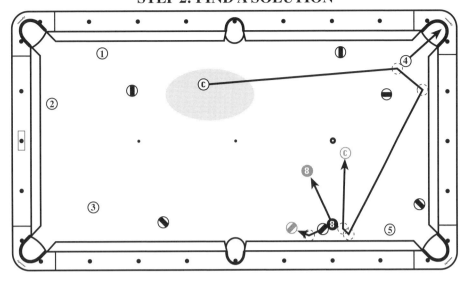

STEP 3: PLAN A PATTERN TO THE BREAK

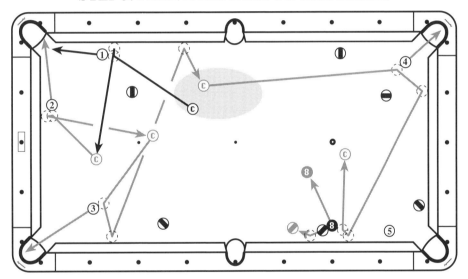

STEP 4: FINISHING THE RACK

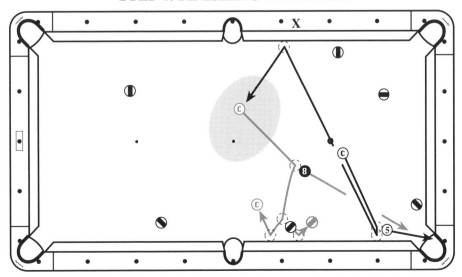

MICROMETER POSITION

STEP 1 — SCOUTING THE BATTLEFIELD

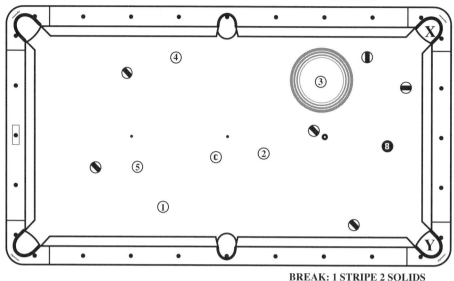

BREAK: 1 STRIPE 2 SOLIDS

STEP 1: *Scouting the battlefield.* Solids must to find a way of dealing with the 3–ball which is blocked for pocket **X**.

STEP 2: *Find a solution.* If solids is up to playing the pinpoint position required on the 2–ball and 3–ball, shooting the 3–ball into corner **Y** solves the problem.

STEP 3: *Find a route to the key shot.* Getting position on the 2–ball for a deadball shot to send the cue ball into the tiny position area for the 3–ball shot is the primary problem to solve. Strong cue ball control is needed to get a good angle on the 2–ball shot to play deadball position on the 3–ball. But if I'm warmed up, I'll get a good angle on the 2–ball and land the cue ball on a dime for the 3–ball shot into pocket **Y** most of the time.

Take care to get perfect position for the 2–ball to 3–ball transition. The game rides on making this shot well.

STEP 4: *Finish the rack.* A 4–5–8–ball pattern completes the game without undue difficulty.

Critique: Players who lack the cue ball control to get position for the 3–ball shot must find a safety that rearranges furniture.

STEP 2: FIND A SOLUTION

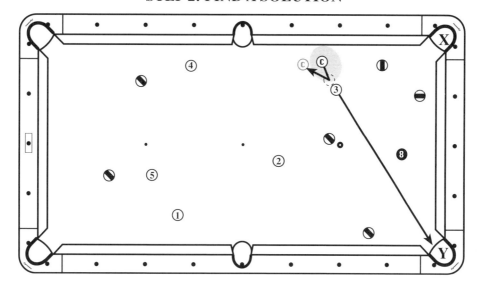

STEP 3: FIND A ROUTE TO THE KEY SHOT

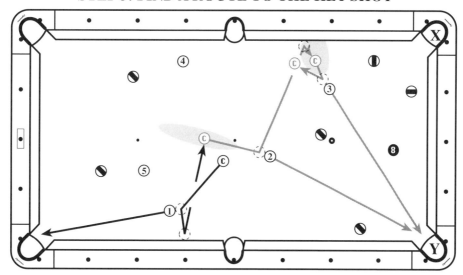

STEP 4: FINISH THE RACK

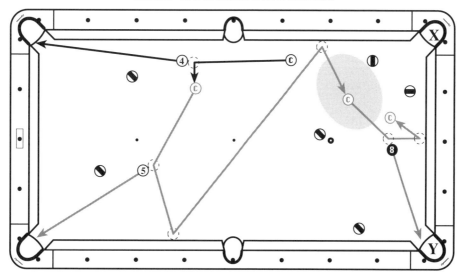

DOUBLE TROUBLE

STEP 1 — ANALYZING THE BATTLEFIELD

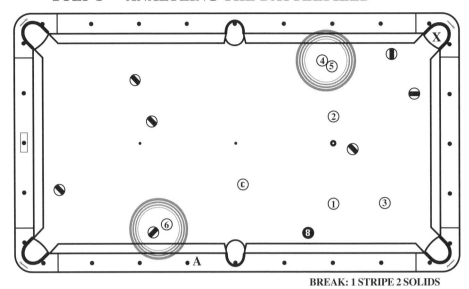

BREAK: 1 STRIPE 2 SOLIDS

STEP 1: *Identifying the problem.* This time solids has double trouble. There's a 4–5–ball cluster and a 6–ball–stripe covey to deal with.

STEP 2: *Find solution one.* A *1–2-3 System* shot will serve to open up the 6–ball–strike cluster. The goal here is to hit cushion **A** before colliding with the 6–ball. Figure the speed to drive the 6–ball about one diamond out from cushion **A**.

STEP 3: *Find solution two.* An old friend will solve the 4–5–ball enigma. This two–rail break shot is a regular workhorse, so familiarize yourself with all of its tenses.

STEP 4: *Plan route to first problem.* The first item to dispose of is the 6–ball–stripe cluster. A short draw shot leaves a *1–2–3 System* shot on the 2–ball to scatter this little convention.

STEP 2: SOLUTION ONE

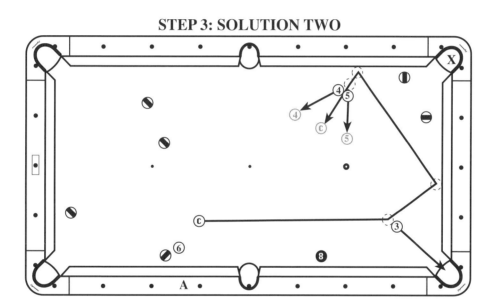

STEP 3: SOLUTION TWO

STEP 4: PLAN ROUTE TO FIRST PROBLEM

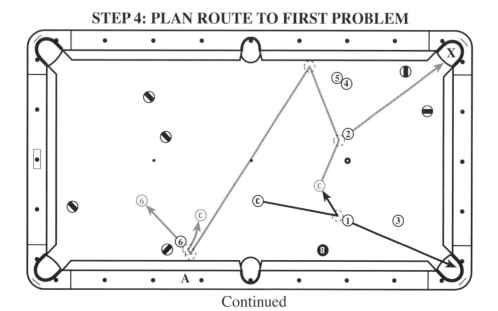

Continued

STEP 5: FIND ROUTE TO SECOND PROBLEM

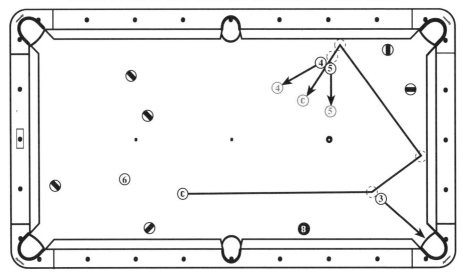

STEP 5: *Finding a route to the second problem.* Opening the 6–ball–stripe covey should leave adequate position on the 3–ball to break up the 4–5–ball duet. Try to drive the 4– and 5–ball out toward the middle of the table where the chance for subsequent shots at these balls is better.

STEP 6: FINISHING THE RACK

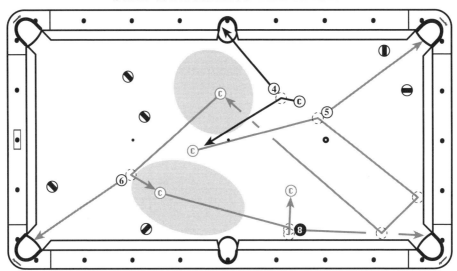

STEP 6: *Finishing the rack.* A 4–5–6–8–ball pattern will complete the rack. The position areas for the 6–ball and the 8–ball are large enough to provide assurance of finishing the game.

Critique: In real life break shots and position plays do not always land as perfectly as shown in this book. This is to say that no one makes break shots perfectly every time. Good results are shown here to give the student a goal to strive for, but there's always the risk that the balls will land badly. The important thing is to keep track of your hits and misses on different types of break shots until you have a good idea of what your chances are on any particular shot.

Transitioning from one problem to the next can be extremely difficult when the balls are not sitting well, so think twice before committing to a run when there are multiple clusters to cope with. Unless the balls are positioned well a two-cluster game often requires a *Safety–Break* to handle the situation.

———————⑧———————

A REASONED DOCTRINE

Many players can make all of the shots in this book, but lack a workable strategic concept for playing competitive 8–ball. They understand aggressive play to some extent, but get lost at sea when it comes to solving difficult situations where sheer shotmaking cannot succeed.

The *Safety–Blitzkrieg* concept provides a powerful logical structure for dealing with problematic situations because this philosophy provides immediate guidance for responding to almost any contingency.

Once a shooter gets over notions of being an invincible runout machine, the door opens to a strategic game that dominates purely aggressive play.

Understanding the tortoise and hare nature of 8–ball is vital for those with championship ambitions because defeating better players who use the *Safety–Blitzkrieg* strategy without a well–reasoned tactical foundation is unlikely.

Balancing safety and aggressive play is essential for becoming a top 8–baller.

———————⑧———————

DEAD PUNCH

BREAK: NONE

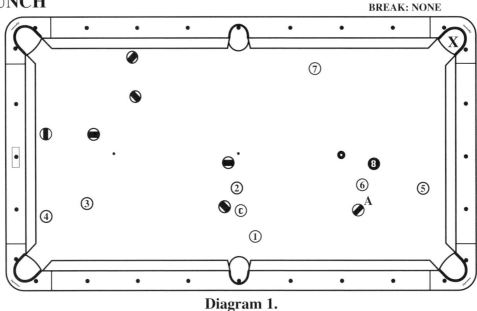

Diagram 1.

Diagram 1: The less than desirable 1–ball shot is the best move available because shooting stripe **A** courts disaster by giving the 8–ball a ride toward pocket **X.**

Diagram 2: The slow rolling cue ball squeezed between the 6–ball and adjoining stripe leaving an awkward shot for the 2–ball.

Diagram 3: An ungainly stretch for the 4–ball cannot stop excellent position for the 5–ball. However, unless you are as tall as this shooter (6'), you might want to get an angle for the 4–ball shot that is easier to reach.

Diagram 4: A soft two–cushion play off the 6–ball leaves a classic key shot off the 7–ball for perfect position to make the 8–ball.

Playing two–cushion position for the 7–ball is more reliable than trying to land on the money going one rail.

Critique: A well played game. This is a dangerous shooter.

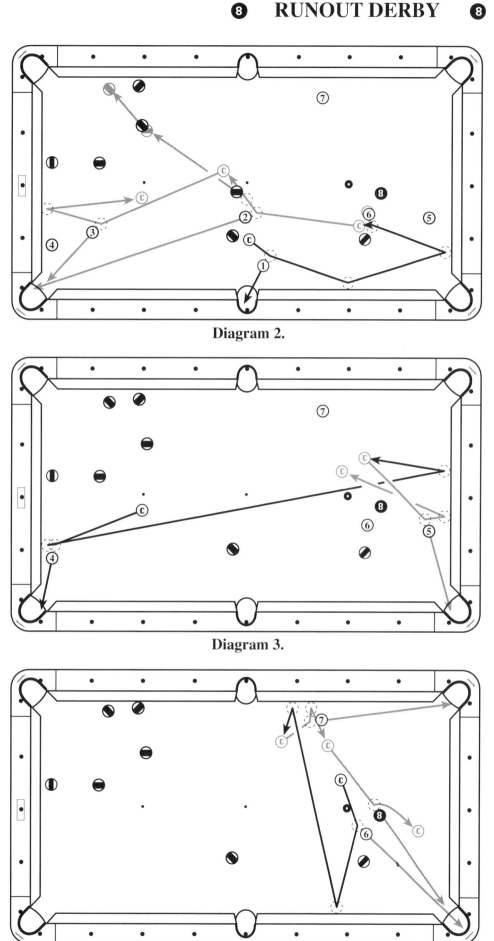

Diagram 2.

Diagram 3.

Diagram 4.

THE NINTH RING

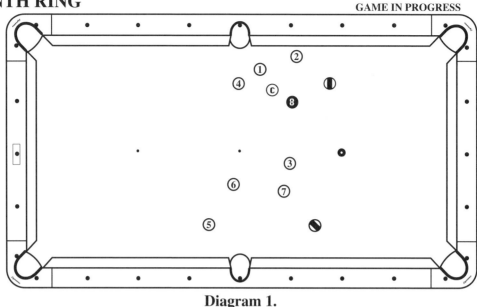

Diagram 1.

Diagram 1: Stripes had fun making five balls, but the shooter may as well hang up his/her cue after this failed runout attempt because there are no prizes for yardage in 8–ball.

Without any stripes to obstruct the pattern solids has a dozen easy ways to clear the board.

Diagrams 2-3-4: As you can see the opposition easily won after stripes *gave* them the game. Don't count games like this as victories. Your opponent beat him/herself.

Critique: When you see that a run is impossible, there's no choice but to try to a *Shot–Safety* or a *Safety–Break*.

Continuing to make balls until you have no more playable shots only digs you deeper in the hole.

Playing safe is simpler when you have more balls on the table, so wise up and stop shooting yourself into **One–Ball–Hell**.

Your opponent may be stymied by the same conglomeration that dampens your progress to the 8–ball. A judicious safety early in the game is often the winning shot.

Readers must learn to stop surrendering games with uncompleted runs. I repeat the earlier admonition that ordinary players beat themselves four out of five games. Keeping your *give–up percentage* down to an acceptable level will make you a winner.

Everyone makes game losing mistakes, but better players keep fatal errors to a minimum. Tempering combativeness with a realistic estimate of the chances of finishing a rack makes you a tougher competitor.

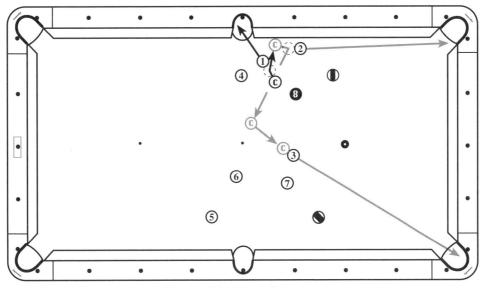

Diagram 2.

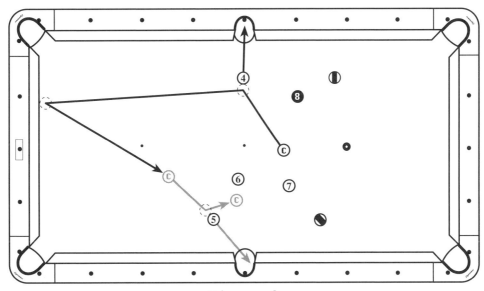

Diagram 3.

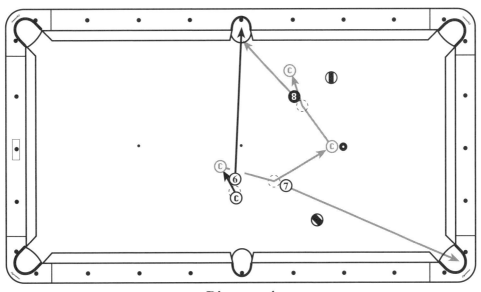

Diagram 4.

JUST SO

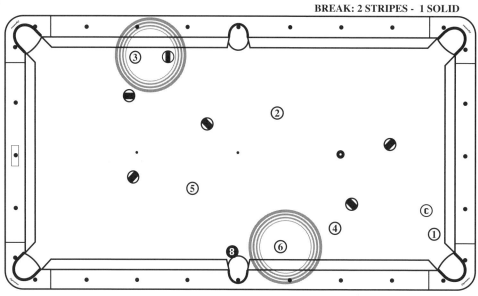

Diagram 1.

Diagram 1: The 3–ball and the 6–ball are the biggest obstacles to clearing the table because the approach to the balls is small and hard to get to.

Diagram 2: The first priority is getting a shot at the 3–ball where the run can be continued. Perfect position on the 2–ball solves the difficulty and puts solids on the road to victory.

Diagram 3-4: The 4–ball shot is played with a good angle on the 5–ball to connect with the 6–ball to 8–ball conclusion.

The 8–ball shot is a *tap* shot hit just hard enough to send the cue ball a foot or so past where the 8–ball rested.

Critique: The shooter made no mistakes. A well played run.

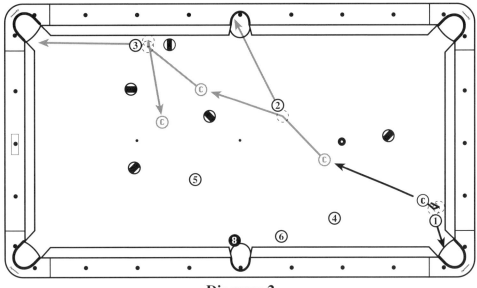

Diagram 2.

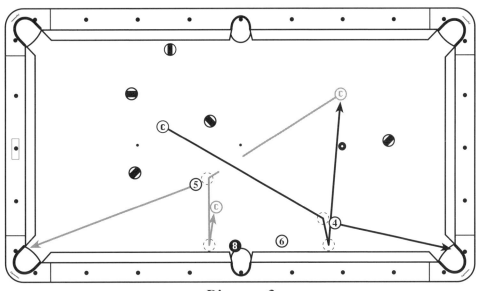

Diagram 3.

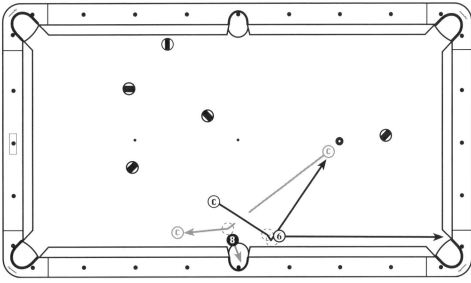

Diagram 4.

TEFLON

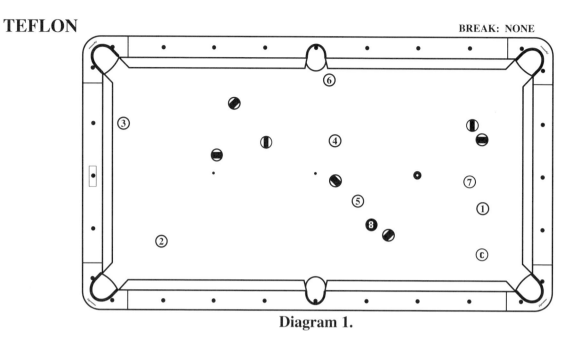

Diagram 1.

Good planning takes care of this fairly easy pattern. Getting the sequence right makes the transitions from ball to ball simple and surefire. Exercising reasonable care should finish this rack 90+% of the time.

Notice that the shooter has viable back–up shots for almost every play. Also the shots get easier as this player advances toward the 8–ball.

None of the witnesses doubted that this player had a definite plan in mind from the beginning of this relentless march to victory.

It will help readers to "play" these games by hand. Removing the balls and moving the cue ball to the next position manually helps imprint the pattern play into your right–brain memory for future reference.

After making a dry run, set the balls up again and try shooting the pattern.

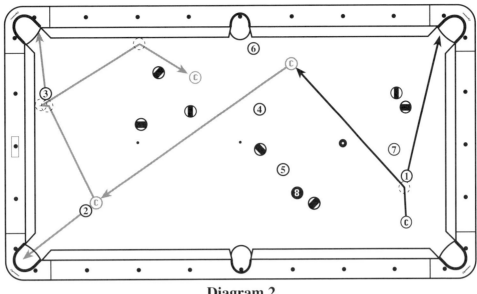

Diagram 2.

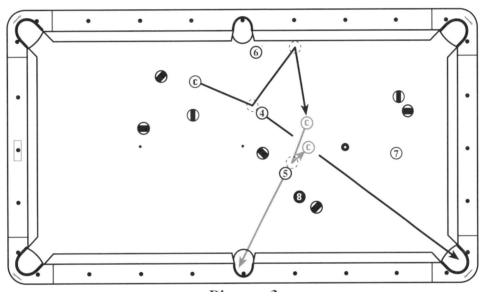

Diagram 3.

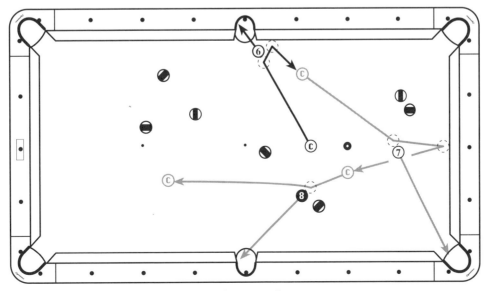

Diagram 4.

PING PONG

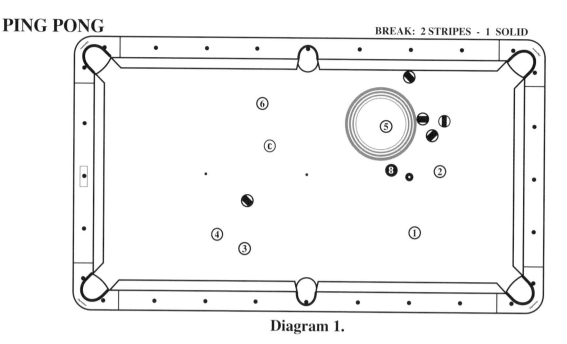

Diagram 1.

Diagram 1: Stripes has a nasty cluster to cope with while solids only has the 5–ball to negotiate, so the solids are the obvious choice.

Diagram 2: The player immediately identifies the key shot on the 1–ball that sets up a 2–ball shot that opens up the 5-ball setting the stage for a table run. A simple shot on the 1–ball floats the cue ball into position to set the 5–ball free.

Diagram 3: Putting the 5–ball in the clear is definitely the critical play. With the 5–ball in playable position, solids is firmly planted in the catbird seat for a relatively easy victory,

Notice that solids has three potential shots after moving the 5–ball. As long as the cue ball lands in mid–table there is an excellent chance to complete this rack.

A minor positional error on the 5–ball shot prevents getting an angle on the 6–ball to draw back into the **Intended Position Zone** for an easy shot on the 8–ball in corner **X**. Therefore, the shooter accepts a less than perfect line up for the 6–ball to avoid the risk of shooting over one of the stripes in the cluster and getting an even worse position for the 8–ball.

Diagram 4: This player demonstrates confident shooting by drilling the black ball dead center in the corner and drawing the cue ball between the stripes for a ***controlled*** landing.

Avoiding collisions with the clustered stripes increases the difficulty of the 8–ball shot somewhat but eliminates any chance of a pinball shot that sends the cue ball ricocheting into a pocket.

Fine points like this add up to superior play.

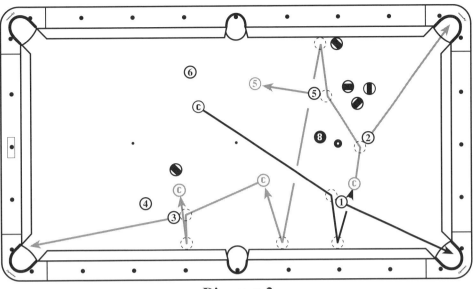

Diagram 2.

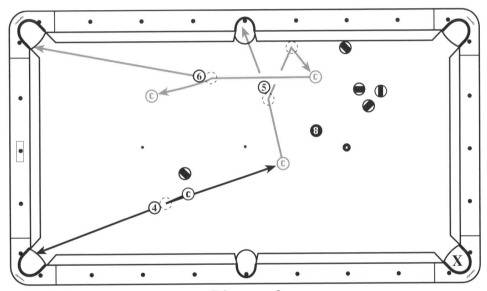

Diagram 3.

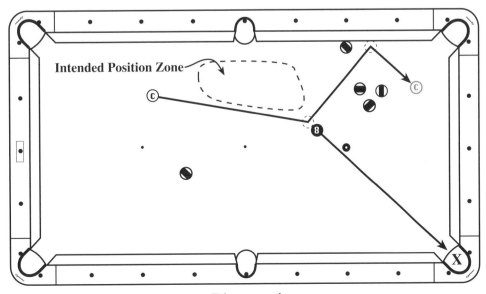

Intended Position Zone

Diagram 4.

WINDOW JAM

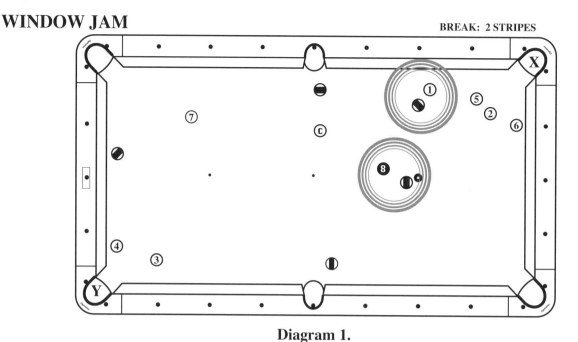

Diagram 1.

Diagram 1: Solids has two problems. The 1–ball's proximity to a stripe makes it essential to clear this ball as soon as possible. The 8–ball's location mandates playing it in either pocket **X** or pocket **Y**.

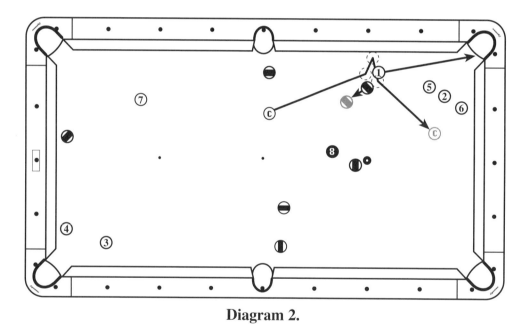

Diagram 2.

Diagram 2: Fortunately, position after the break allows for making the 1-ball right away.

Diagram 3: The 2–ball shot is played with a potentially dangerous carom into the 5–ball, but the shooter escapes unscathed.

Diagram 4: The two-cushion drive off the 4–ball requires excellent speed control to land in the window for a 5–ball shot that enables the 6–, 7– and 8–ball series.

Diagram 5: The shooter takes off the 7–ball and 8–ball as planned. Notice that the shooter draws the cue ball to the side rail on the 8–ball shot avoiding any nasty surprises from colliding with the adjoining stripe ball.

Critique: *Insurance shots* covered the risky plays in this tour de force.

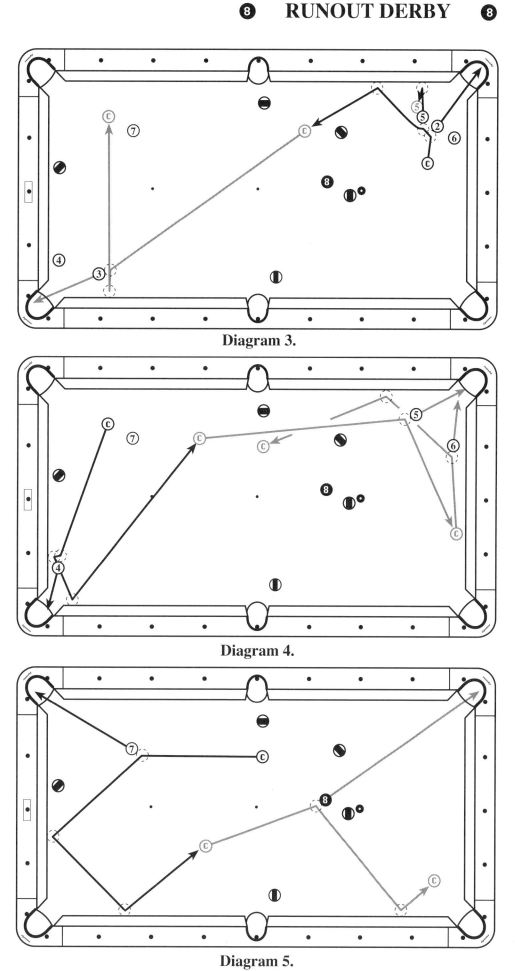

Diagram 3.

Diagram 4.

Diagram 5.

BUMPERBOOM

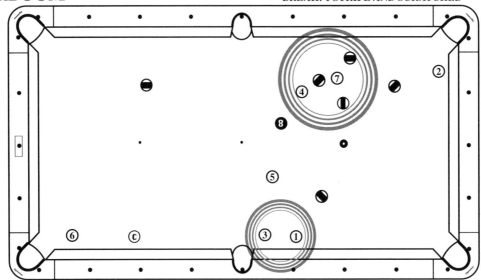

Diagram 1.

Diagram 1: Solids is the best selection because there is a potentially playable 4–ball and a possible break shot using the 2–ball.

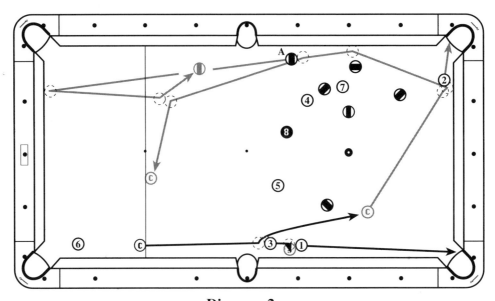

Diagram 2.

Diagram 2: Having **Ball–in–hand**[1] gives the shooter confidence to eliminate the 3–ball–1–ball covey on the first shot with a simple combination play. The 1–ball shot yields position to break the 4–ball–7–ball–stripe–ball cluster with the 2–ball shot. But the shooter misses the cluster and the cue ball crashes into stripe **A** hitting the ball twice before landing near the headstring.

Diagram 3: The shooter plays the 3–ball and uses the 4–ball shot to clear a path to the 7–ball.

Diagram 4: Easy 5–ball and 6–ball shots deliver position for the 7–ball to 8–ball finale.

Diagram 5: A deadball shot off the 7–ball sets up an unmissable straight in shot for the 8–ball.

Critique: Opening up the 7–ball with the 4–ball shot was the key to victory.

[1] The rules in this contest required shooting behind the head string after a scratch on the break.

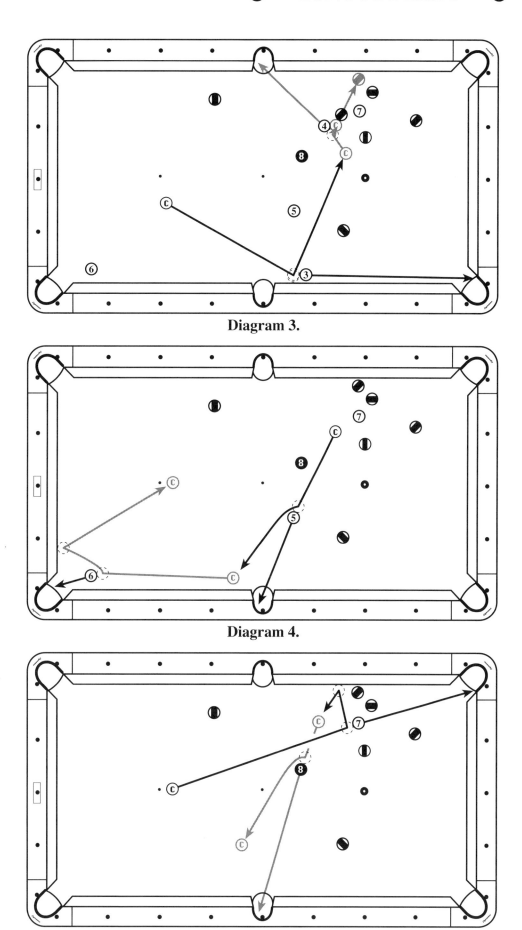

Diagram 3.

Diagram 4.

Diagram 5.

GEORGIE PORGIE

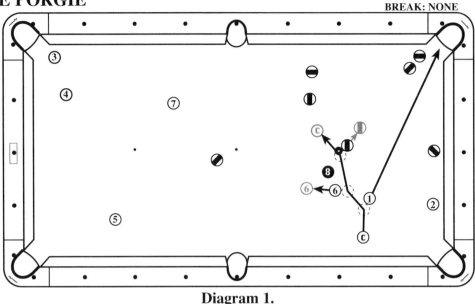

Diagram 1.

Diagram 1: The 1–ball shot brightens up the 6–ball and 8–ball and leaves several shots to continue the run.

Diagram 2: The shooter wavers on the 3–ball shot and very nearly ends up in deep trouble when the cue ball almost lands behind the 5–ball for a run stopping snooker. The angle left for the 4–ball shot is not good, but a draw shot gets things back on track.

Diagram 3: Overhitting the 5–ball shot and smacking into a stripe courts disaster. Suddenly the player is faced with an awkward back cut on the 6–ball and a tough position play to get on the 8–ball.

Diagram 4: For most players the mishap on the 6–ball position would mean defeat, but this feckless shooter regains composure and fires the 6–ball into corner **X** like Daniel Boone at a turkey shoot. Left–hand draw brings the cue ball straight off the cushion for perfect position to shoot the 8–ball in the side.

Critique: The remarkable recovery from less than perfect position on the 6–ball warns an observant player that serious competition is at hand.

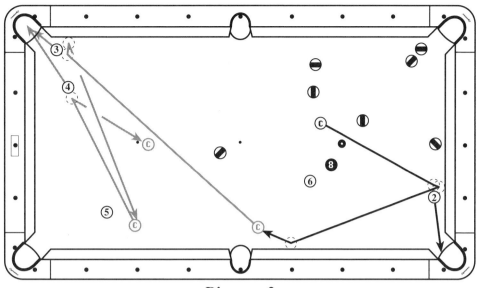

Diagram 2.

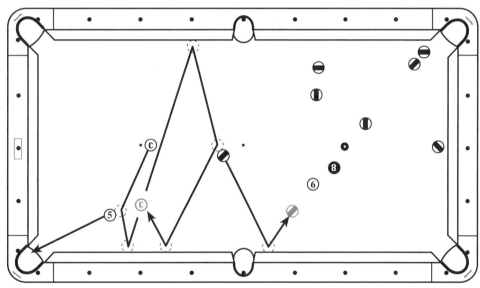

Diagram 3.

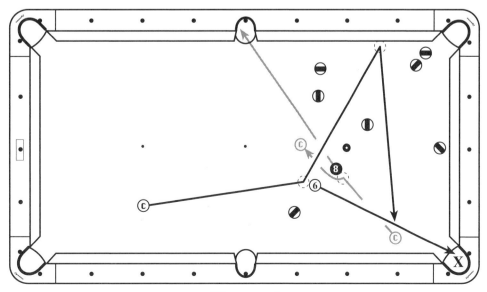

Diagram 4.

SUPERSONIC

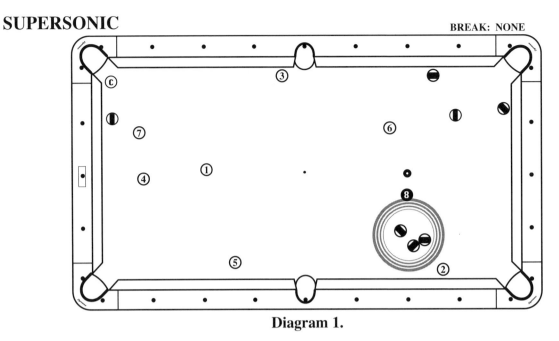

Diagram 1.

Diagram 1: The triad of stripes near the 8–ball precludes taking stripes. The 1–ball shot is not an easy play shooting from the mouth of the pocket, but this guy can shoot.

Diagram 2: The 1–ball shot requires a dead straight stroke.

The 2–ball shot is a subtle cushion first play enabling the shooter to escape the consequences of landing dead straight in on the ball. The shot was played with enough speed that the cushion first hit was only apparent when the tape ran in slow motion. This astute move shows billiard skill.

Getting good position on the 3–ball eliminates a problem ball with a natural angle on the 4–ball to continue the run.

Diagram 3: The 4–, 5– and 6–balls are removed with simple one–cushion position plays.

Diagram 4: The 7–ball shot is less than ideal, but definitely playable as this straight stroker demonstrates by using inside english to recover position for the 8–ball.

Critique: This was a *controlled* run. Other than a minor slip playing position on the 7–ball there were no errors in this logical pattern. Position for the 8–ball shot was excellent, so this player gets a gold star.

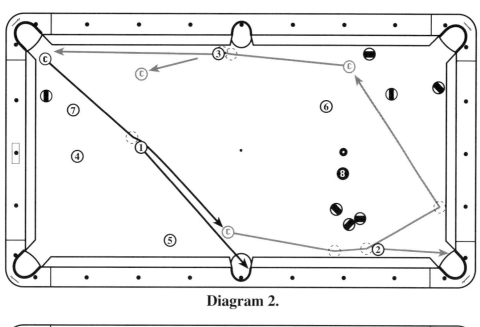

Diagram 2.

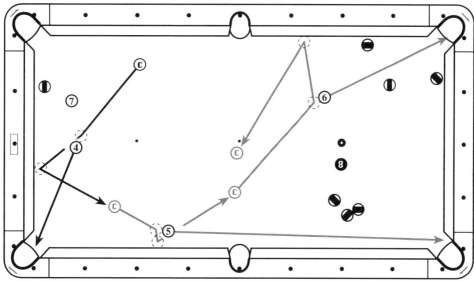

Diagram 3.

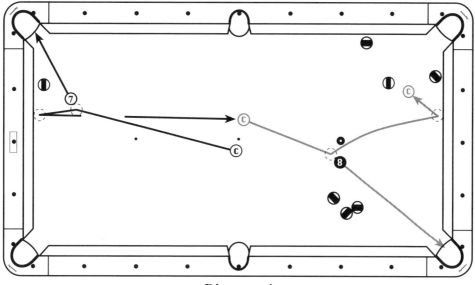

Diagram 4.

KICKBALL

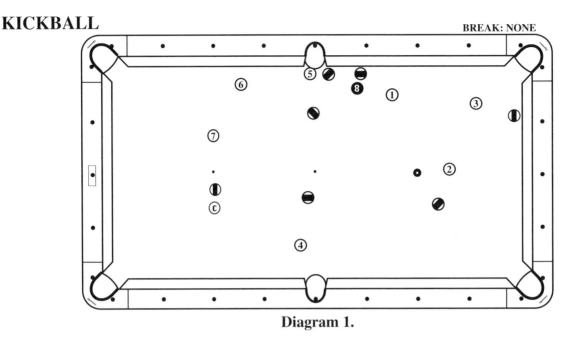

Diagram 1.

Diagram 1: Solids has no real problems. All the shooter needs to do is find a logical sequence to clear the table

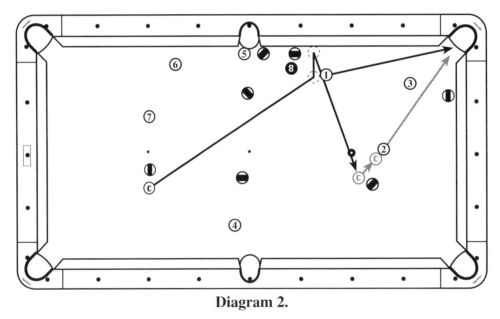

Diagram 2.

Diagram 2: The 1– and 2–balls are played leaving good position on the 3–ball shot to go up table for the 4–, 5– and 7–balls.

Diagram 3: The 3–ball is played leaving a simple shot to start the 4–, 5–, 6–, 7–, 8–ball pattern. Hitting a stripe could have caused a disaster, but the shooter gets away with the impropriety this time.

Diagram 4: The shooter takes off the 4–, 5– and 6–balls as planned leaving a good shot at the 7–ball to get on the 8–ball.

Diagram 5: The 7–ball and 8–ball are easily played.

Critique: This virtually risk–free battle plan covered every nexus for error with back–up shots and alternate patterns.

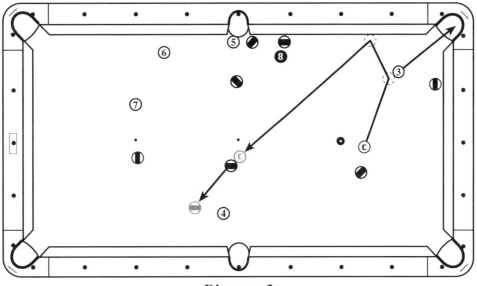

Diagram 3.

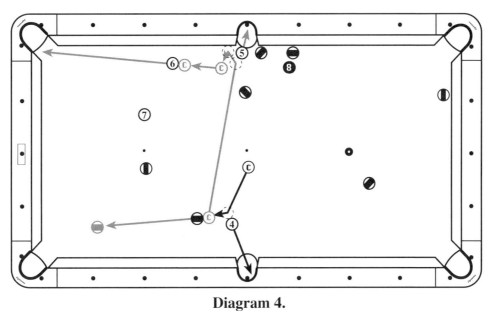

Diagram 4.

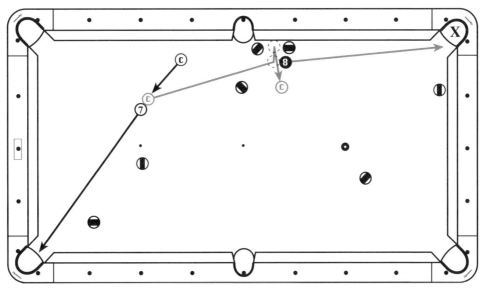

Diagram 5.

SQUEEZE PLAY

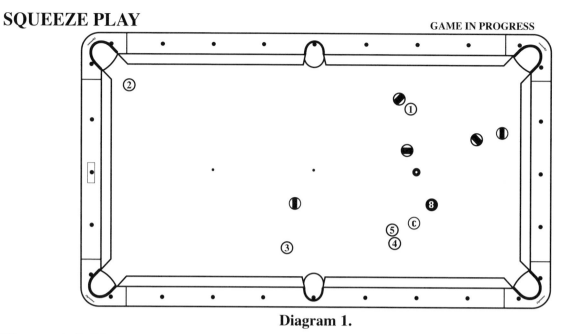

Diagram 1.

Diagram 1: Solids faces a very difficult pattern.

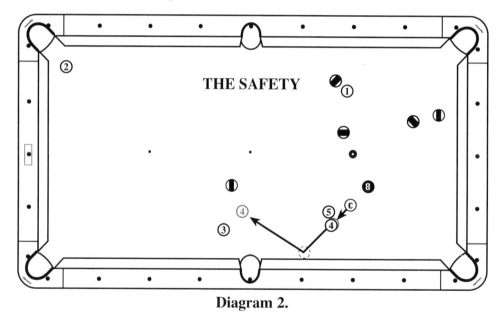

Diagram 2.

Diagram 2: There is a clear shot at the 2–ball, but instead of making a valiant and most likely failed attempt to clear the table, solids locks up stripes by *freezing* the cue ball against the 5–ball. Since the 4–ball is only a couple of inches away this is very easy to do. (The cue ball stops where the 4–ball rested, so **Diagram 2** only shows a sliver of the cue ball leave. See **Diagram 3**.)

Diagram 3: The 5–ball and the 8–ball snooker every stripe. Stripes hits a ball with authority almost making it, but close only counts for hand grenades and nuclear weapons. Solids is left in perfect position for the 1–ball shot and there is also a shot at the 2–ball.

Diagram 4-5: Solids puts a string together clearing the table with relatively simple shots. The 5–ball shot is a natural carom dead into stripe **A** leaving perfect position on the 8–ball.

Critique: The *Safety–Break* on the 4–ball shot put stripes at a tremendous disadvantage because it is tough to do anything positive *from* a safety. The player who makes the first move in safety situations usually has a big advantage.

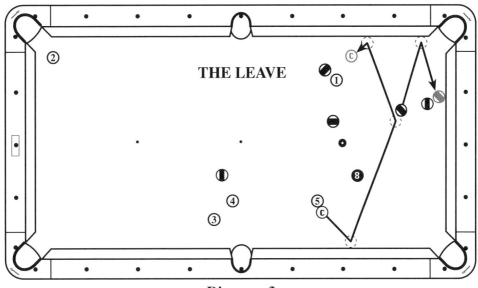

THE LEAVE

Diagram 3.

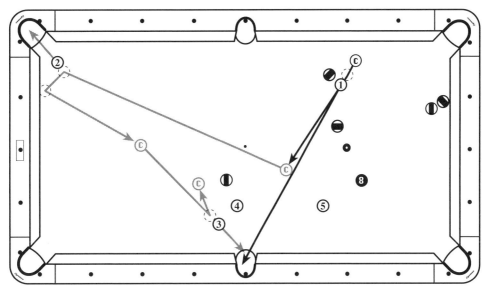

Diagram 4.

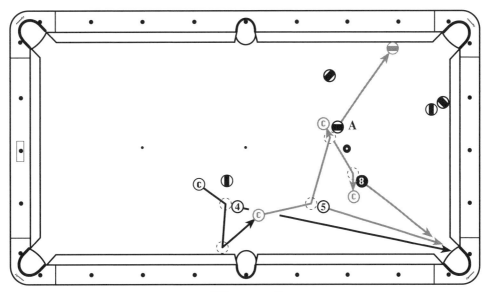

Diagram 5.

AIRBRAKES

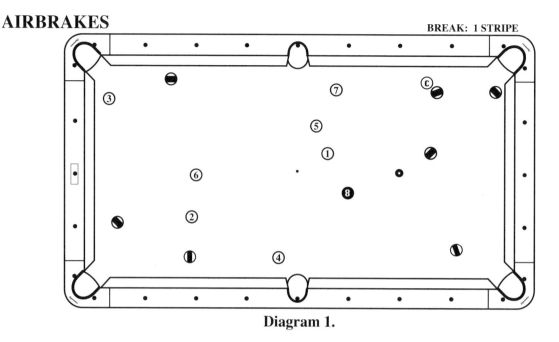

Diagram 1.

Diagram 1: The shooter is snookered on every reasonable shot except the 1–ball. The 1–ball shot is played without hitting another ball avoiding a potentially game ending collision. In fact, this player never hits anything except the object ball being played during this run.

Diagram 2-4: This game is an exception to avoiding side pockets because stripes has the corners blocked. If it had been possible to make a stripe after the break they would have been the preferred choice because they control the corners. This time solids must muddle through making three side pocket shots which present the risk of a misplayed position.

Critique: All things being equal shooting three or four balls into the sides is a bad idea. This time things are not equal so the shooter exerts some effort and finishes the rack anyway.

Don't let a successful run like this lull you into false notions about side pocket shooting. The sides are dangerous targets that can cost games. (See: **Sides vs Corners**)

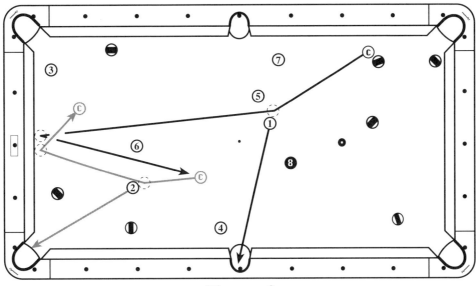

Diagram 2.

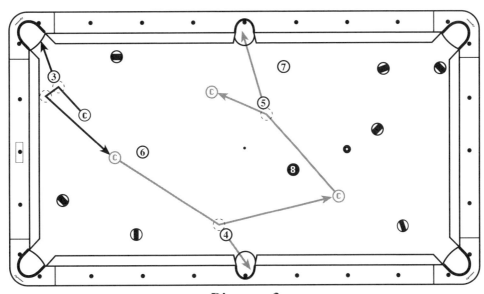

Diagram 3.

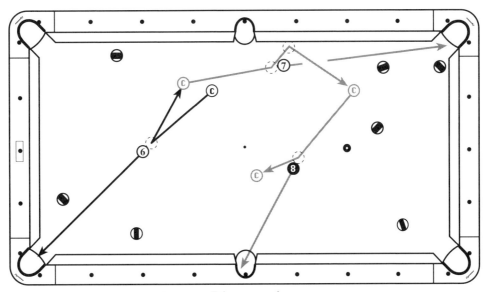

Diagram 4.

BYE BYE

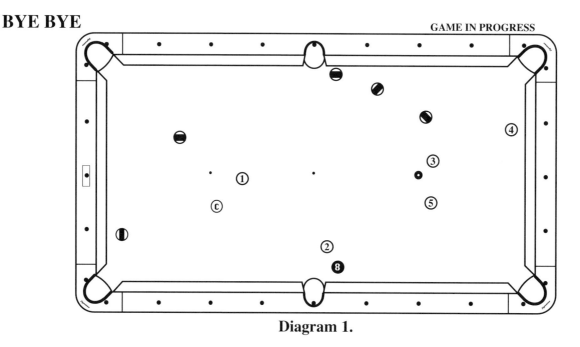

Diagram 1.

Diagram 1: Here's another real–life example of what happens when you leave a good shooter open balls on a bar table.

Diagram 2-3: This runout is so simple and so foreseeable that no commentary is necessary. Solids has so many options that it would take an anti–tank mine to stop this run.

Critique: Stripes lost because of committing the sin of leaving solids a good ***Starter Shot*** and a wide-open group. A playable shot at ***any*** solid can lead to a simple runout pattern, so failing to get safe is suicidal.

No one should expect to win against better players when they leave golden opportunities like these. Winners on bar tables have to clear scattered balls or play a good safety almost every time to compete with superior players.

The importance of ***not*** beating yourself cannot be overstressed in bar play because self–defeat is the average player's biggest failing. Players who do not learn to protect themselves with planned safety play are consigned to the ranks of pushovers.

Overreaching your skills actually lowers your competitive level because failed runs leave opponents easy wins. Prudent safety play enables players to overcome difficulties using strategy instead of relying on pure shooting ability.

Needlessly surrendering games is a difficult handicap to overcome, but reducing the number of games you give away makes you a tougher competitor, so stop doing it.

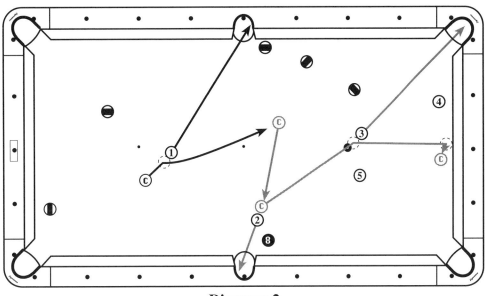

Diagram 2.

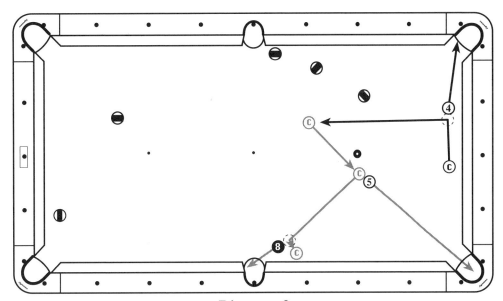

Diagram 3.

CORNERPLAY

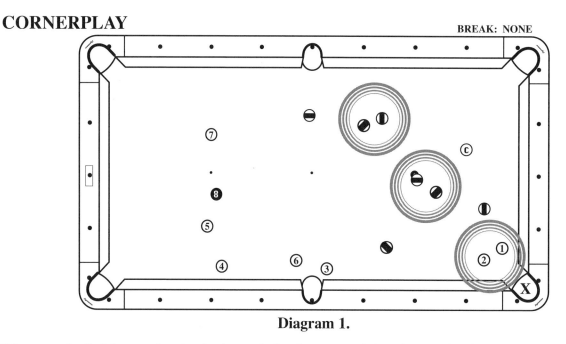

Diagram 1.

Diagram 1: Solids are clearly the best choice because of the clustered stripes and the fact that the 1–ball and 2–ball have pocket **X** covered.

Diagram 2: Many players forget the Open Table Rule after the break and pass up combinations and caroms off the 8–ball or the other group, but this shooter knows the rules and plays a combination on the 1–ball using a stripe. Solids then takes off the 2–ball and 3–ball with well played shots. (See **Rules**)

Diagram 3: The 4–ball and 5–ball are easily removed. Notice that the 6–ball serves as a back up shot

to recover position if anything goes wrong with the 3–, 4–, 5–ball series.

Diagram 4: Shooting the 6–ball into corner **X** avoids the brick wall of stripes blocking position routes off the foot rail using a side pocket shot to get on the 7–ball. Shooting a corner shot insures a simple

7–ball shot with an easy rebound for perfect position on the 8–ball.

Critique: Cue ball *control* made this elegant pattern look as easy as ABC.

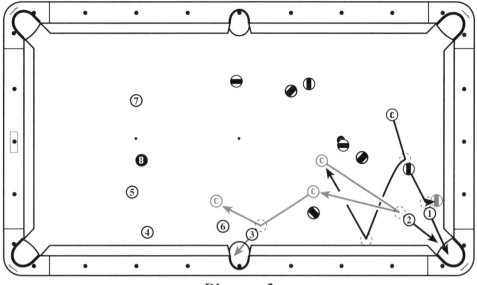

Diagram 2.

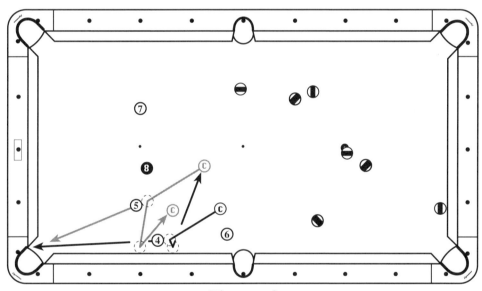

Diagram 3.

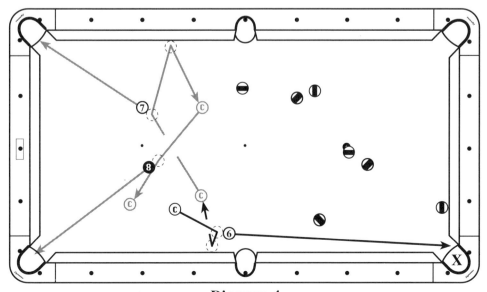

Diagram 4.

SPADEWORK

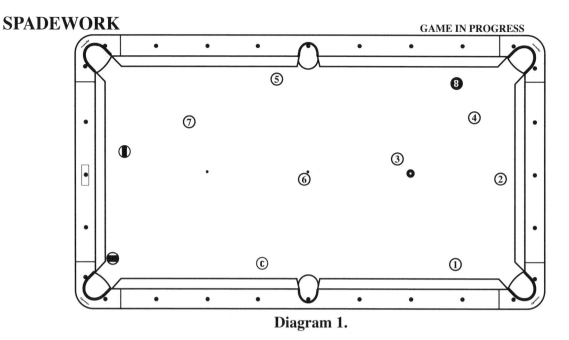

Diagram 1.

Diagram 1: Another example of the peril of shooting oneself into **One–Ball–Hell**. Stripes dug themselves into a hole and now it's time for the funeral march.

Diagram 2-4: Once solids figures a logical pattern the party is over. Without obstructions and with no challenging moves required stripes can hand over the deed to the ranch because this real estate has been sold.

Critique: Solids demonstrates good shot selection because every play is simple and easy to execute.

Readers will benefit by setting up the patterns in this book and taking the balls off by hand. Doing this imprints the visual pattern into your right–brain memory banks where it can be called up for future reference.

Try to understand the logic behind each shot. Consider the english that must be used to play position for the next ball in the sequence. Imagine how hard the shot must be hit to follow the path shown for each shot.

Mentally rehearse the pattern before actually shooting the balls off. Imagine yourself playing each ball with precise results. Then try shooting the set up.

Fitting shots into a simple framework, eliminating as many difficult shots as possible and keeping cue ball travel to a minimum is the signature of topflight 8–ball play. Good patterns flow smoothly from one shot to the next using simple follow shots, stop shots, short draws and easy position routes.

Embedding good patterns into your memory bank spills over into improved game plans.

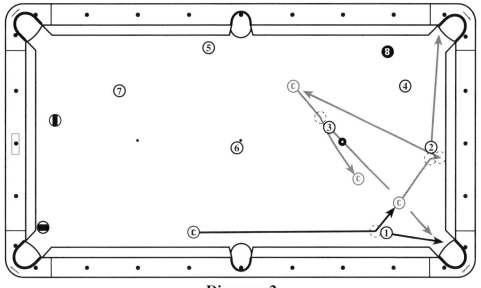

Diagram 2.

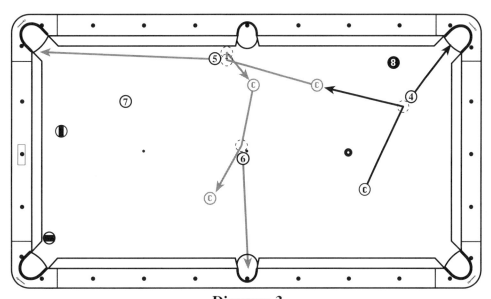

Diagram 3.

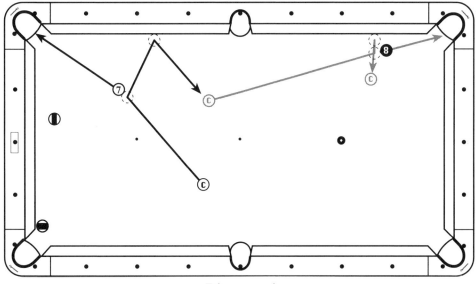

Diagram 4.

DRUMBEAT

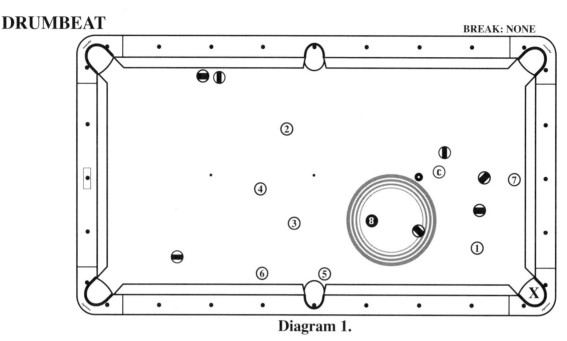

Diagram 1.

Diagram 1: Solids are well scattered offering an excellent opportunity to clear the board. The single problem is the stripe blocking the 8–ball for pocket **X**.

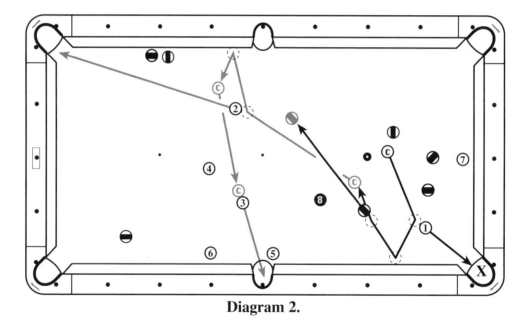

Diagram 2.

Diagram 2: The 1–ball shot opens corner **X** for the 8–ball. The shooter figured on having an easy shot at the 5–ball, but the cue ball landed behind the 8–ball forcing a change of plans by inserting the 2–ball into the pattern at this point. Shots like the 2–ball play shown are simple moves that a better player should make over 90% of the time. The lessons on avoiding side pocket scratches show that there is no danger of scratching unless you draw the cue ball on this shot. (See: **Great Escapes p 54**)

A stop shot on the 3–ball provides perfect position on the 4–ball for a draw shot back to the 5–ball.

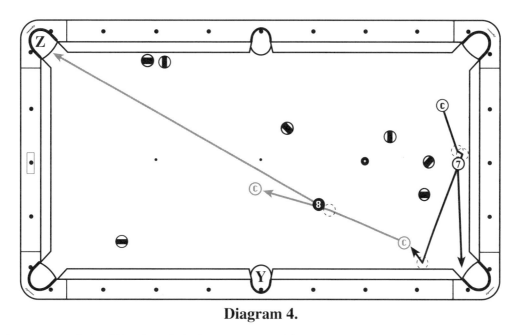

Diagram 3.

Diagram 3: A short draw off he 4–ball for position to play the 5–ball in the side sets up a simple pattern to clear the table.

A *1–2–3 System* shot with a touch of draw brings the cue ball to the foot of the table for the 7–ball.

Diagram 4.

Diagram 4: Because of the difficulty of playing precise position to shoot the 8–ball into side **Y** with a spin shot, this shooter opts to drop the cue ball a few inches off the second cushion for an 8–ball shot into corner **Z**.

Critique: A well played run that avoids needless problems. Going for the 8–ball in corner **Z** after the 7–ball avoids a tough side pocket position play that could go wrong with cataclysmic results.

GRAVY TRAIN

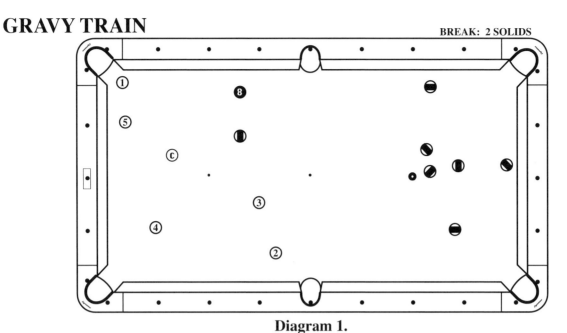

Diagram 1.

Diagram 1-3: A simple series of logical shots clears the 1–, 2–, 3– and 4–balls

Diagram 4: The only shot worth notice is the classic two or three rail 5-ball to 8-ball position. This position route is a workhorse shot for balls in this configuration.

Critique: This break is so good that a runout is mandatory. The shooter made two solids on the break and all of the solids are at the head of the table, well scattered and obstacle free. The cue ball is nearby so finishing the rack is merely a matter of selecting a logical sequence out of a dozen rational possibilities and exercising reasonable care.

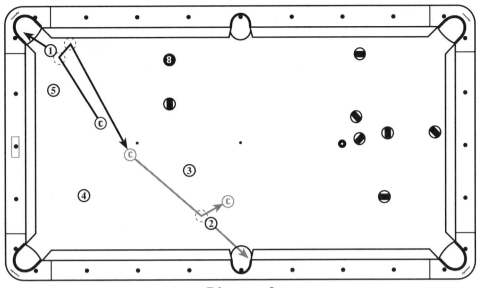

Diagram 2.

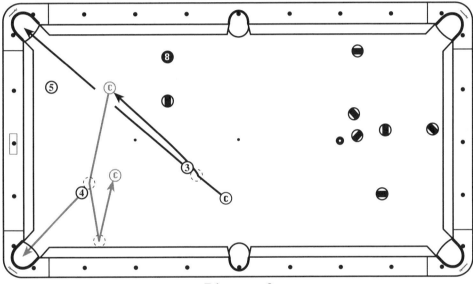

Diagram 3.

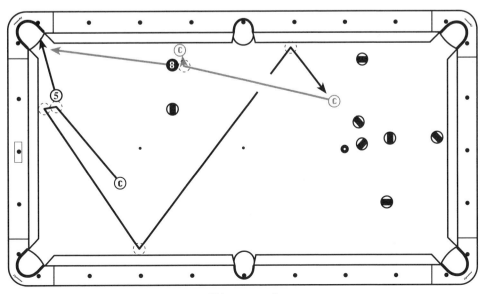

Diagram 4.

COUNTERPOINT

Diagram 1.

Diagram 1: Despite making three stripes, solids is still the best choice because there is no playable stripe. The only problem solids has is the 3–, 8–ball–stripe cluster. As we will see this shooter has a plan.

Diagram 2: The 1–ball and 2–ball shots get position for the problematic 3–ball.

Diagram 3: The 3–ball is played with a nice draw shot off the rail for a go at the 4–, 5–, 6–ball series. The 5–ball shot positions the cue ball perfectly for the 6–, 7–, 8–ball sequence.

Diagram 4: The 6–, 7– and 8–ball are easily played.

Critique: Solids played a good game with no major slips. The only change I would have made is to play the 8–ball in corner **X** instead of the side. (See: **Sides vs Corners**)

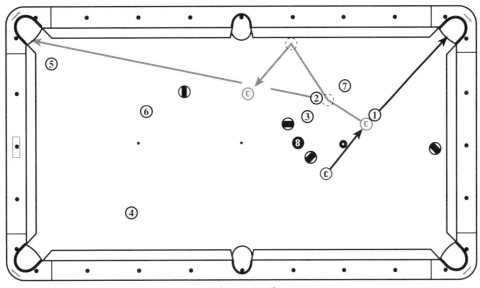

Diagram 2.

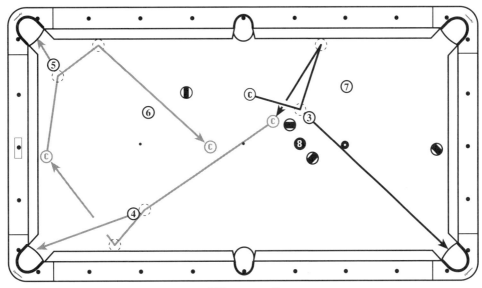

Diagram 3.

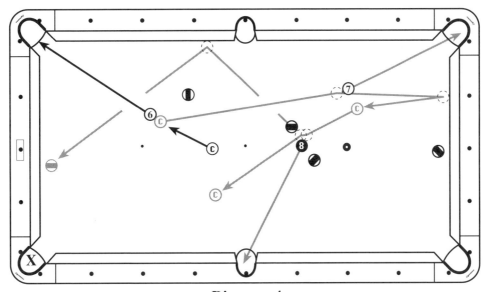

Diagram 4.

NUDGE 'EM

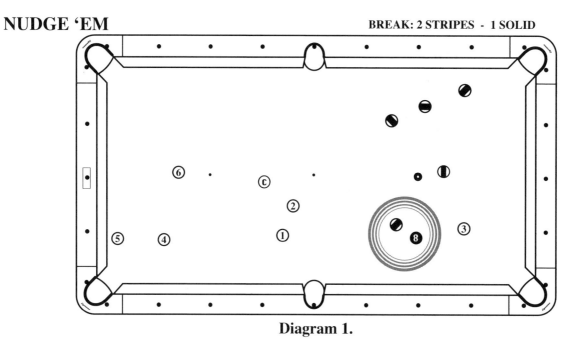

Diagram 1.

Diagram 1: The only problem solids has is the 8–ball–stripe cluster. With several simple *Starter Shots* to choose from and lots of wide open space to maneuver in there should not be much trouble opening up the 8–ball.

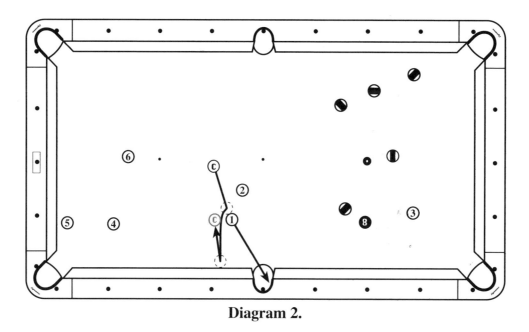

Diagram 2.

Diagram 2: The 1–ball shot gets position for a break attempt using the 2–ball.

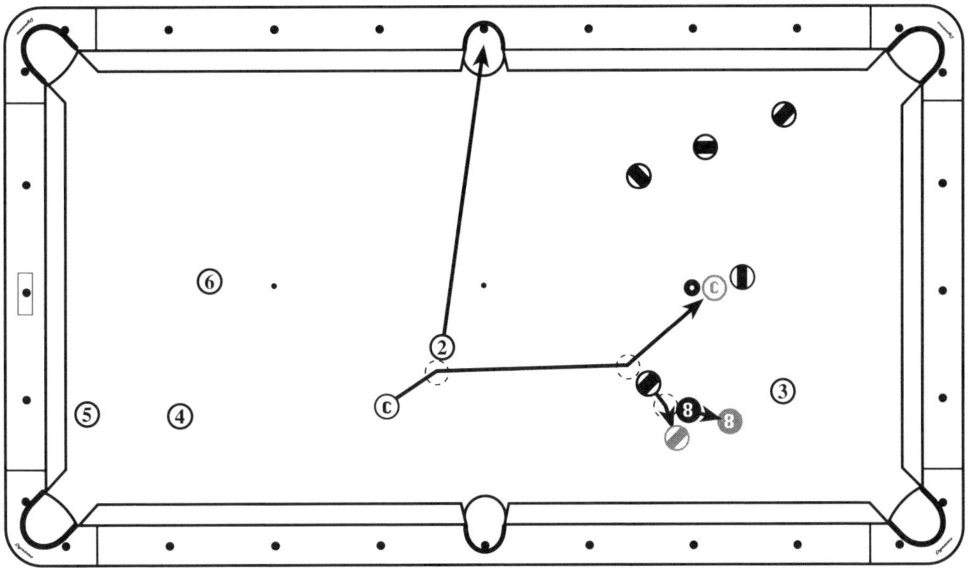

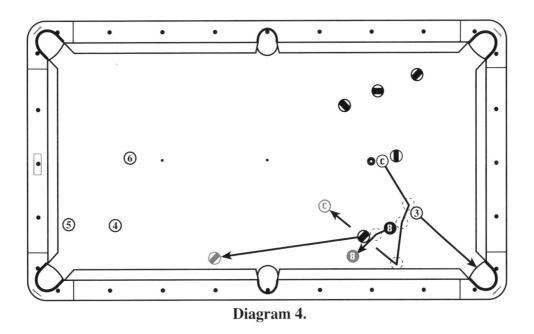

Diagram 3.

Diagram 3: The 2–ball shot separates the 8–ball–stripe cluster

Diagram 4.

Diagram 4: The cue ball lands next to a stripe forcing a shot at the 3–ball that breaks the stripe and 8–ball farther apart leaving the 8–ball completely in the clear and while setting up an easy shot for the 4–ball.

continued

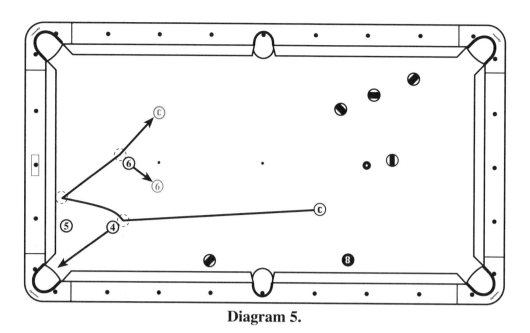

Diagram 5.

Diagram 5: The cue ball accidentally bumps the 6–ball on the 4–ball shot and leaves a good pattern. But make no mistake; these little *accidents* cost a lot of games.

Diagram 6: The 5–ball, 6–ball and 8–ball series is played without a hitch.

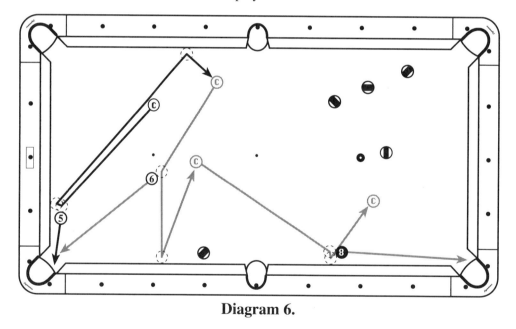

Diagram 6.

Critique: This was a well played run. Breaking open the 8–ball on the second shot is clever pool because playing break shots while you have back up balls in play offers more assurance of success. Break shots can beat you later in the game if there's a mistake because there are no open balls left to cover a positional accident.

The only slip was hitting the 6–ball on the 4–ball shot when there was no need for it. Collisions with balls not involved in the shot are a major source of error, so take care to avoid ramming the cue ball into innocent bystanders who can waylay game plans in a nanosecond.

Every great player I've ever seen takes pains to avoid unnecessary contact with open balls. When a collision is unavoidable they do their best to control the outcome by planning the result.

He will win who knows when to fight and when not to fight.
SUN TZU   THE ART OF WAR

KISSEROO

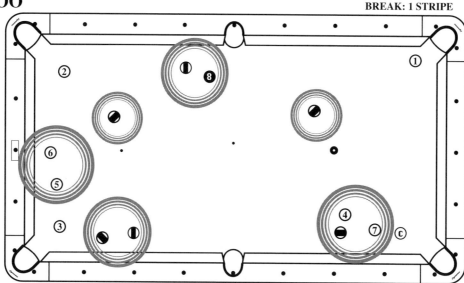

Diagram 1.

DIAGRAM 1: The shooter made a stripe, but all of the stripes have problems and there's no decent shot except playing the 1-ball first and taking solids.

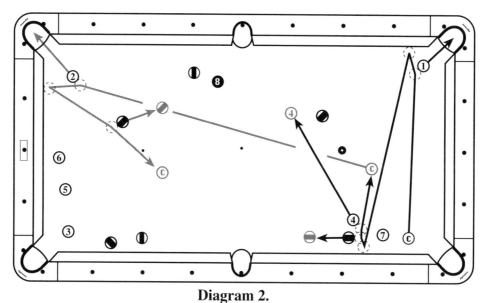

Diagram 2.

DIAGRAM 2: Identifying the 4-, 7-ball-stripe cluster and the 5-, 6-ball layout as problems leads to an immediate play to open up the 4-, 7-ball-stripe cluster with the 1-ball shot.

The 1-ball shot appears to have solved all of solids major problems, but chance and circumstance turn this into demanding runout sequence.

DIAGRAM 3: The trouble begins when the cue ball glances off a stripe leaving a dead straight-in shot on the 3-ball. A long awkward shot on the 4-ball is followed by a hard to control play on the 5-ball.

DIAGRAM 4: Unfortunately the cue ball ends up dead straight-in on the 6-ball persuading the player to accept a long difficult drive around the table after making the 7-ball.

DIAGRAM 5: Good position on the 8-ball closes out this difficult string.

Critique: This straight shooter isn't bothered by long shots, but most of us would be more comfortable playing the 3-, 4-, 5- and 7-balls from better positions.

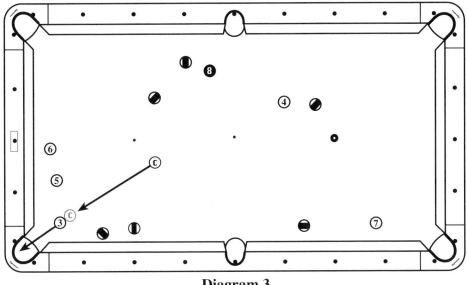

Diagram 3.

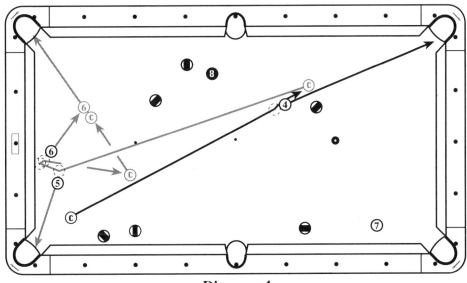

Diagram 4.

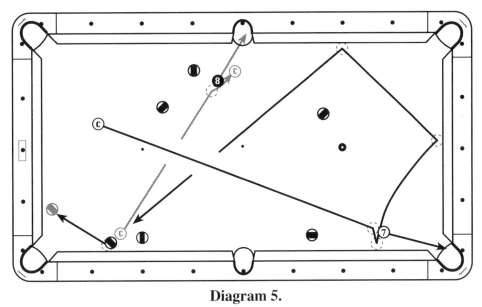

Diagram 5.

PINBALL WIZARD

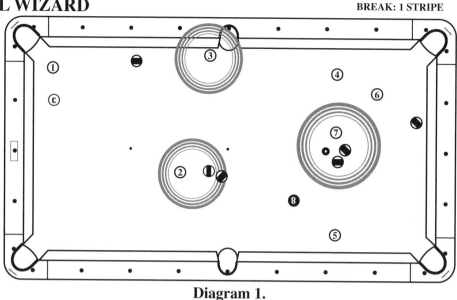

Diagram 1.

Diagram 1: The clustered stripes leave no choice but to take solids.

Diagram 2: The shooter opens up the 3–ball for a corner shot right away. However, the cue ball lands at an angle on the 2–ball that permits position to shoot the 3–ball into corner **X**.

Diagram 3: The 4–ball shot clips the 5–ball and leaves solids snookered on the 6– and 7–balls. Showing skill in the face of adversity the shooter slices the 5–ball into the corner.

Diagram 4: Unfortunately the position only allows a slightly off angle combination on the 7–, 6–ball layout. The shooter makes a serious mistake playing the combination and leaves a tough bank on the 7–ball.

A Tortoise and Hare Game

Understanding the tortoise and hare nature of good 8–ball play is the hardest lesson for average players. Gunslinger types think the game should be based on pure aggression, while safety players want to run and hide until they have a perfect set up. Neither approach wins in high-speed competition.

To compete against top shooters an eight–baller must be able to recognize the appropriate tactics for the situation at hand. Attempting a run that cannot be made almost guarantees defeat and too much safety play loses out of excess caution.

Learning when to turn on the afterburners and when to apply the air brakes is essential to advance to the highest levels of 8–ball play. Every game must be judged according to the possibilities and according to each player's particular skills.

Good 8–ballers regulate safety and aggression according to the lay of the table, not unrestrained ego.

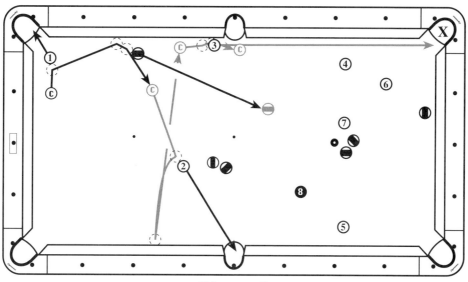

Diagram 2.

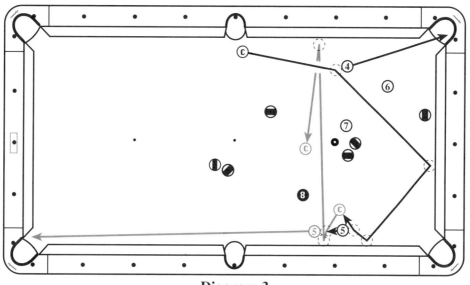

Diagram 3.

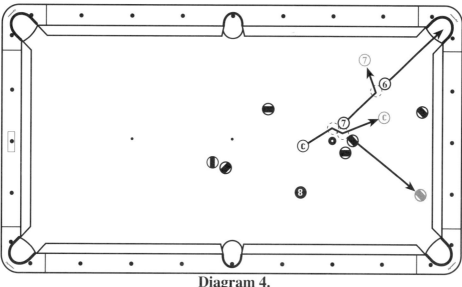

Diagram 4.
Continued

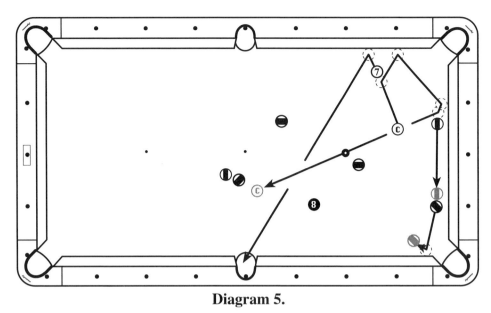

Diagram 5.

Diagram 5: This would be a *Friday The 13th* ending for most players because there is no obvious position play to get on the 8–ball. With nothing to lose this unflappable shooter plays an incredible two–rail kiss shot for position on the 8–ball while banking the 7–ball into the side.

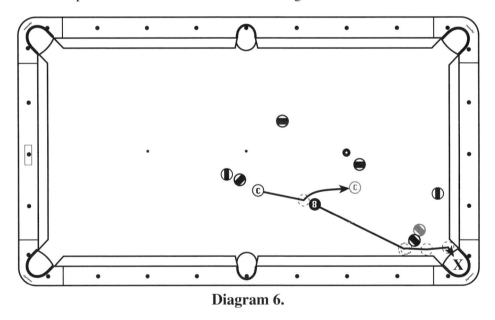

Diagram 6.

Diagram 6: The bank is made and the shooter has a shot at the 8–ball, but more trouble is at hand because a stripe is bumped into a blocking position for corner **X**. Nevertheless, solids is able to make the 8–ball with a cushion first tickie shot.

Critique: The shooter never gets the game under control so the best that can be said is that the player muddled through a series of difficult shots to win.

When I was taking lessons from Bud Harris and I made a shot like the 7–ball bank, instead of congratulating an outstanding shot, Bud would set the shot up again and ask me to make it three or four times to prove that I *knew* how to make it. If I could not repeat the shot a few times, Harris put my feet back on the ground with the terse verdict, "You got lucky."

---8---

A skillful combatant puts himself in a position that makes defeat impossible and does not miss the moment for defeating the enemy.

The victorious strategist only seeks battle after the victory has been won, whereas he who is destined to defeat fights first and then looks for victory.

So much for tactics
SUN TZU   THE ART OF WAR

---8---

BANK JOB

BREAK: 2 STRIPES - 1 SOLID

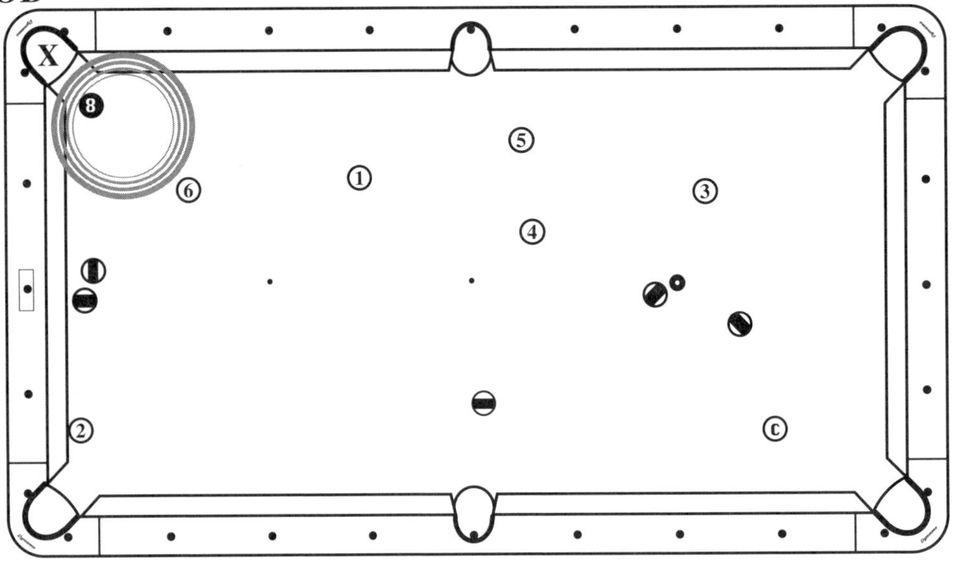

Diagram 1.

Diagram 1: Solids is the best choice because of stripe's ***Orphan Cluster*** near the head rail.

Diagrams 2: Solids doesn't have a clear shot because the 8–ball, which nearly scored, blocks corner **X** for the 1–ball and 6–ball.

A cushion first kiss off the 8–ball with the 2–ball shot solves all of solids problems.

Diagrams 3: The 2–ball shot delivers perfect position for a 3-, 4–, 5-, 6–, 8–ball progression.

Diagrams 4: Solids finishes with three simple shots.

Critique: A well played game, but again I would choose corner **Y** instead of a side for the 8–ball shot. (See: **Sides vs Corners**)

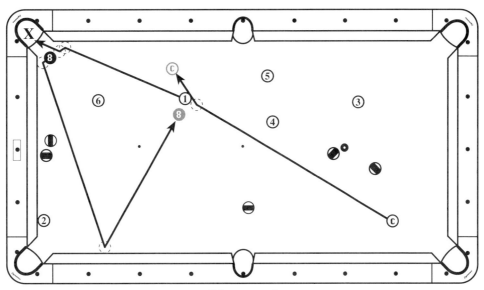

Diagram 2.

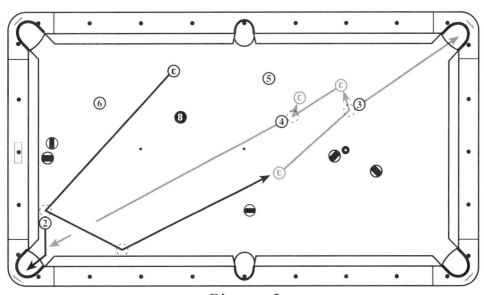

Diagram 3.

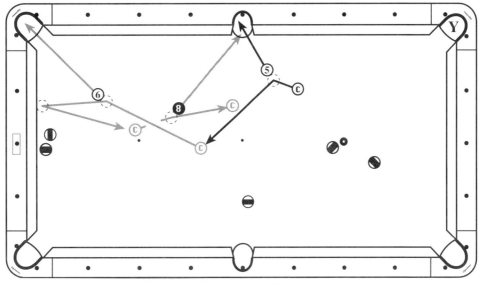

Diagram 4.

SLIP, STUMBLE AND BANK

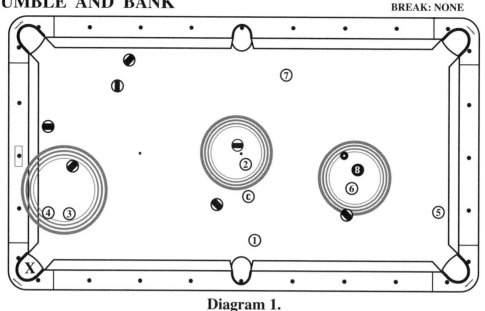

Diagram 1.

Diagram 1: Solids is the choice because of the 3-, 4–ball blockade on corner X.

Solids faces a potentially difficult rack because several balls have limited access.

Diagram 2: The 1–ball shot leaves less than perfect position for the 2–ball, but the shooter fires it in. Then the 3–ball shot goes astray by hitting the wrong side of the stripe leaving a thin cut on the 4–ball.

Diagram 3: The player misses the angle to get an easy shot on the 5–ball and nearly spoils the run by moving the 8–ball.

Nevertheless, the shooter soldiers on making the 5- and 6–balls.

Diagram 4: The angle on the 7–ball does not permit easy position for the 8–ball, so the cue man attempts a two–cushion play to shoot the 8–ball into corner **Y**. Unfortunately a miscalculation sends the cue ball crashing into a stripe leaving a long bank on the 8–ball.

Critique: The shooter never got the game under control. The player was unable to break a sequence of deteriorating positions, but managed to bank out anyway.

When you cannot get things moving in a positive way you must either find a safety or do your best to muddle through.

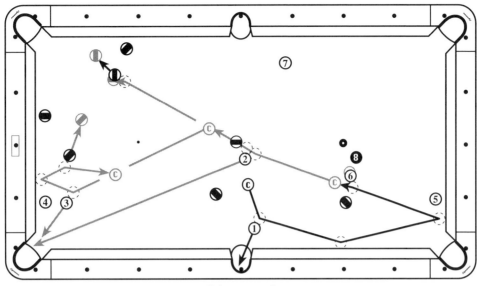

Diagram 2.

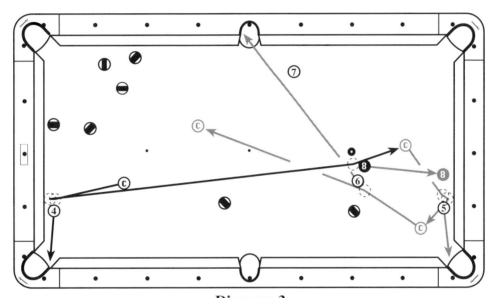

Diagram 3.

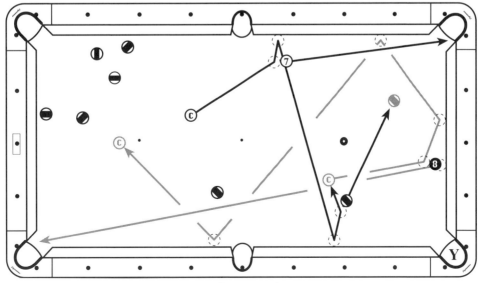

Diagram 4.

CONSEQUENCES

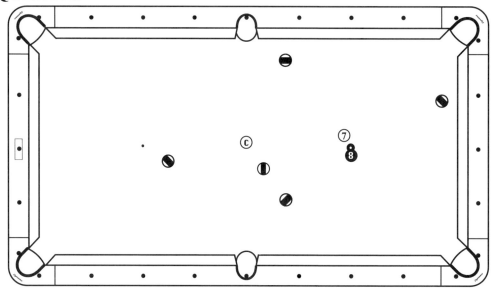

Readers who are getting notions that unrestrained aggression is a winning strategy should take note of the disaster awaiting them when uncompleted runs leave the opposition an open road to victory.

Here's a fairly typical result of a failed runout attempt. Solids made some spectacular shots on a one–way trip to **One–Ball–Hell**, but the party is over. Does anyone doubt that solids has sold out and will lose this game way over 95% of the time to any fairly good player. Solids is not going to get another shot.

The only way solids can win from here is for stripes to have a heart attack.

A good *Safety–Blitzkrieg* player, on the other hand, pays attention to leaving the opposition in bad situations when an inning ends.

Hell for leather play often costs a cowboy shooter three or four games in a row because intelligent players don't give these freebies back.

Instead of coming back to a wide open table in the next inning gunslingers will most likely face a strong safety or an unrunnable conglomeration. Overly aggressive players might not get another playable shot until a break shot fails and then they face the full rack with all of its perils.

Unless a player can string several table runs together, all-out aggression is apt to be a losing strategy.

Being sure you can get *all the way out more than half the time* before committing to a runout attempt eliminates a lot of give up games.

Knowing that many professional class players cannot runout as much as 40% of the time on bar tables should temper combativeness because 60% of the time the opposition gets a shot. If that shot comes after shooting down to the last few balls, the shooter is in trouble.

---------- **8** ----------

A clever fighter not only wins; he excels in winning with ease. He wins by making no mistakes. Making no errors establishes the certainty of victory, for it means conquering an enemy that is already defeated.
SUN TZU   THE ART OF WAR

---------- **8** ----------

LAST POCKET 8-BALL

Last Pocket 8–Ball is a challenging version of 8–ball where everything revolves around the requirement to make the 8–ball in the same pocket where the last ball from a player's group is made.

Playing Last Pocket 8–Ball well requires skill, imagination and the ability to create effective patterns.

The admonition not to shoot down to your last couple of balls and then miss counts tenfold in Last Pocket 8–Ball. Unskilled players with an iota of comprehension of the nature of Last Pocket can easily frustrate champions who ignore this advice because it is often very easy to leave a player with only one or two balls open shots that do not lead to a Last Pocket. Running down to your last two or three balls without finishing the game usually means a loss against a knowledgeable opponent.

RULES
All the rules of regular 8–Ball apply with these revisions:

TO WIN: The shooter must sink the 8–Ball with a legal shot in the same pocket where the last ball from the player's group was made. It is not necessary to call or mark the 8–Ball pocket since making the last ball designates the 8–Ball pocket..

UNPLAYABLE 8–BALL

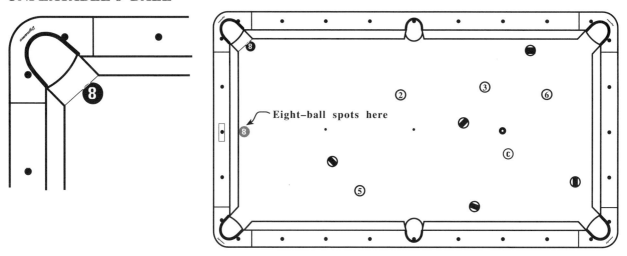

When the 8–ball lands in the jaws of a ***neutral*** pocket where the edge of the 8–ball touches a line between the points of the pocket the ball is deemed unplayable and spotted frozen to the center of the head rail.

If the head rail position is occupied by a ball the 8–ball is spotted in the center of the foot rail. The players can also agree to replay the game.

The 8-ball is spotted immediately ***after*** the player who moved it to the unplayable location finishes his/her turn.

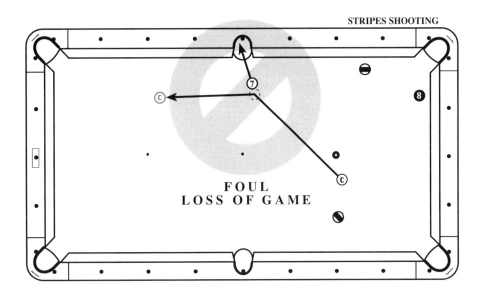

LOSS OF GAME: Making an opponent's last ball with an illegal shot forfeits the game.

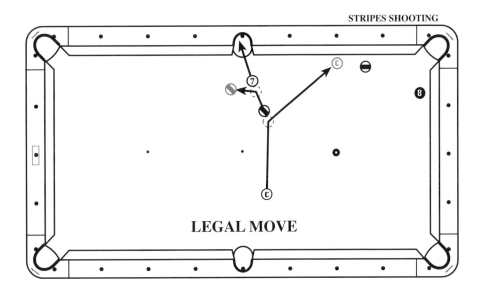

However, if a shooter makes an opponent's last ball with a legal shot (i.e. a combination or a carom off their own ball) the incoming player is stuck with that Last Pocket.

This rule prevents players from illegally assigning opponents a bad Last Pocket with a foul shot.

It goes without saying that missing your last ball can have dire consequences.

Last Pocket #1

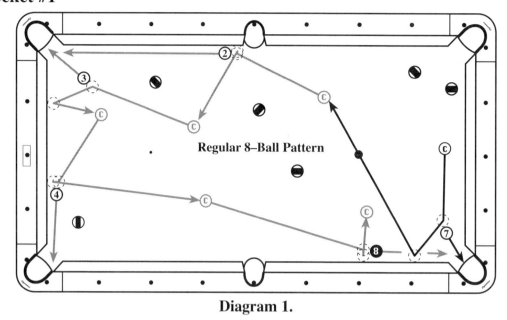

Diagram 1.

The need to leave a good last ball–Last Pocket–8–ball sequence dictates shot selection in Last Pocket 8–Ball.

Diagram 1: If the game was regular 8–ball, shooting the 7–ball would be the right shot to set up a simple table run.

Diagrams 2-3: However, in Last Pocket shooting the 7–ball first eliminates the only decent shot to set up a Last Pocket shot on the 8–ball.

In Last Pocket, the 2–ball is the right shot. Shooting the 2–ball from near the cushion is somewhat tougher than the 7–ball shot, but most of the difficulty is in the player's mind. In any case, there's no choice.

If the 2–ball scores the rest of the Last Pocket sequence will be relatively simple, but if the 7–ball is played first solids is plunging headfirst into shallow water.

The importance of leaving a last ball that provides easy position for an 8–ball shot into the same pocket overshadows other considerations to such an extent that all planning and strategy must bend to exploiting or creating a playable Last Pocket twosome.

Last Pocket #2

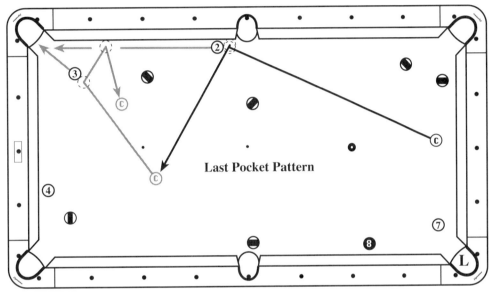

Last Pocket Pattern

Diagram 2.

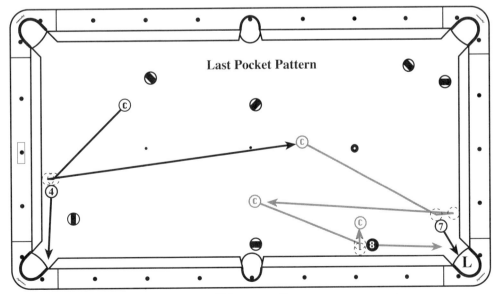

Last Pocket Pattern

Diagram 3.

Last Pocket #3

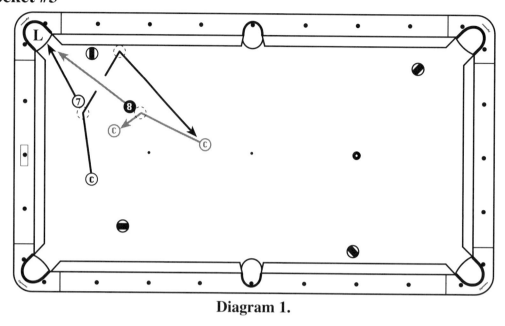

Diagram 1.

Diagram 1: Here are some simple Last Pocket out shots to watch for. When the 8–ball and one of your balls are near the same corner pocket use the setup to finish the game.

In Last Pocket 8–Ball formations like these are worth their weight in latinum. All the shooter needs to finish the game is a decent angle on the 7–ball.

When you are fortunate enough to get lay outs like these do everything in your power to preserve the Last Pocket sequence until the right time.

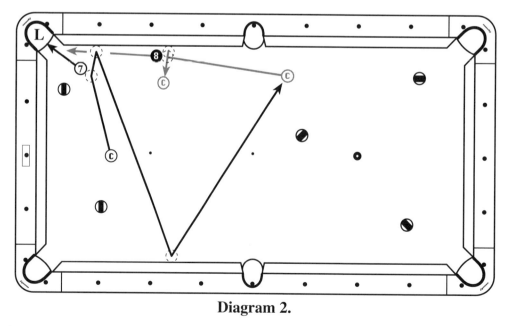

Diagram 2.

Diagram 2: Here's a classic Last Pocket end game shot. When fortune smiles like this seize the opportunity.

Last Pocket #4

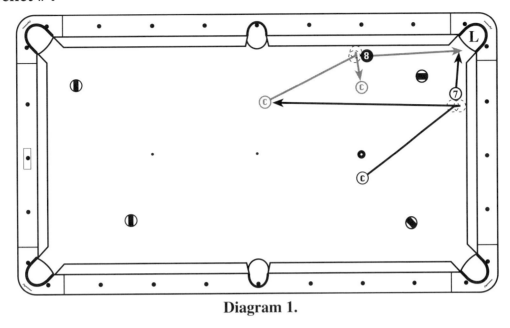

Diagram 1.

Diagram 1: Save set ups like these until the end game.

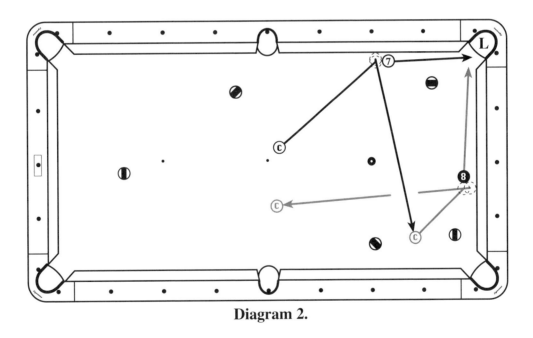

Diagram 2.

Diagram 2: This is the same shot rotated 90 degrees. If you learn to use english in a businesslike fashion by practicing the *1–2–3 System* these moves will present no special problems.

Last Pocket #5

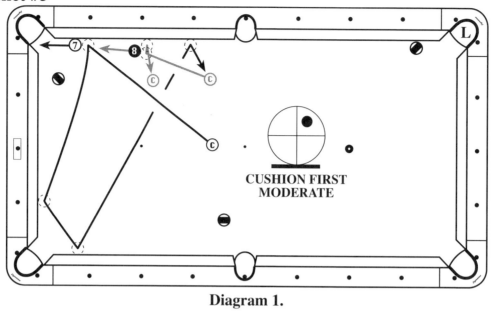

Diagram 1.

Diagram 1: The 7–ball is frozen. Hitting cushion first with some reverse english creates this useful position route.

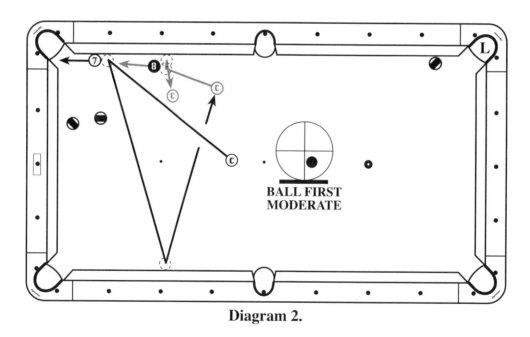

Diagram 2.

Diagram 2: Knowing alternate position routes comes in handy when enemy balls block one way.

Last Pocket #6

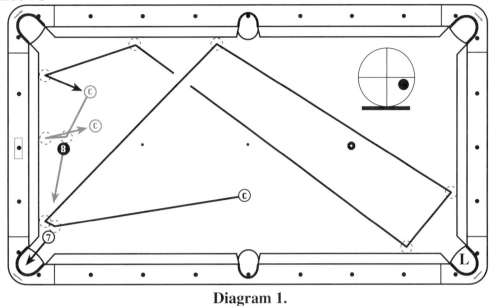

Diagram 1.

Diagram 1: Three Cushion players are familiar with round the table shots like these.

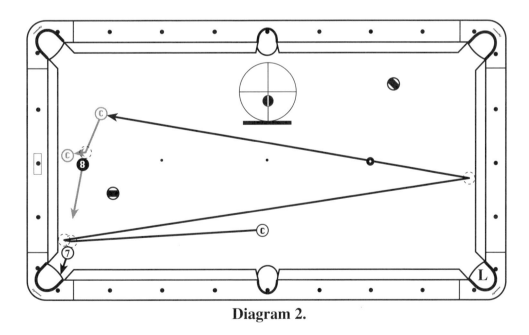

Diagram 2.

Diagram 2: Here's an alternate Last Pocket route when a stripe blocks the six cushion path. Use a little draw without any sidespin for this shot.

File good Last Pocket arrangements in your memory banks for future reference.

Last Pocket #7

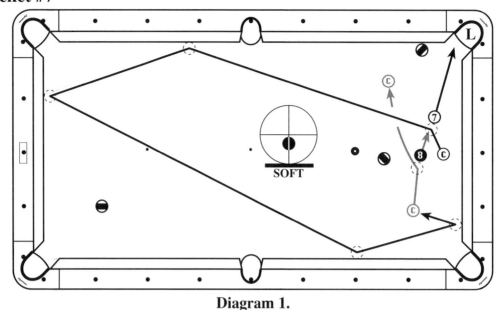

Diagram 1.

Diagram 1: This position route is unknown to most players. Deadball without english creates this useful play. Very little force is needed.

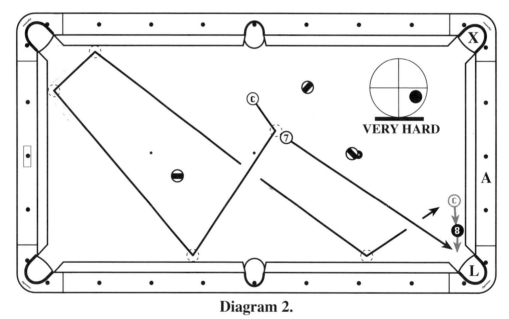

Diagram 2.

Diagram 2: Landing on the wrong side of the 7–ball forces a difficult shot requiring about 3/4 break shot speed—this is just about the maximum speed for a ***controlled*** pool shot. The cue ball must be moving and spinning at a good clip when it hits the first rail, so don't spare the horsepower. Getting a fix on the speed before lining up the shot improves high speed accuracy.

On new or faster cloth the main difficulty is delivering an accurate stroke at such high speed. Focus on allowing for the effects of english and speed and aim accordingly.

If the cloth is slow and sandpapery it may be impossible to drive the cue ball all the way to the end rail for a Last Pocket shot on the 8–ball. Nevertheless, this is a good position route for shots into pocket **X** in regular 8–ball even if the cloth is too slow to get to cushion **A** for a Last Pocket shot.

Last Pocket #8

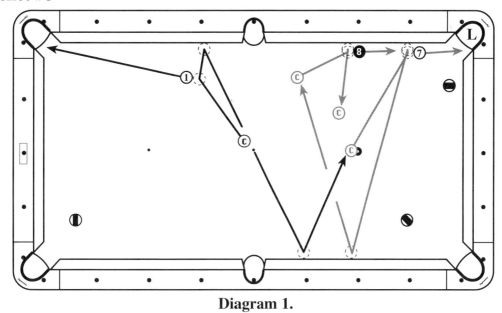

Diagram 1.

Diagram 1: Recognizing finishing sequences like the 1–, 7–, 8–ball is an invaluable skill.

Fitting good last balls into an end game pattern wins in Last Pocket.

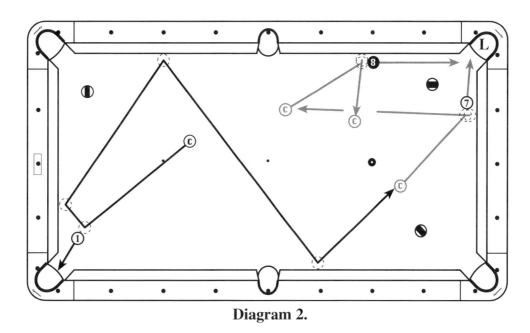

Diagram 2.

Diagram 2: Save critical out sequences until the right time because without them the game becomes impossibly difficult.

Shooting a good last ball out of turn is a major unforced error because there is no excuse for spoiling good opportunities like these.

Last Pocket # 9

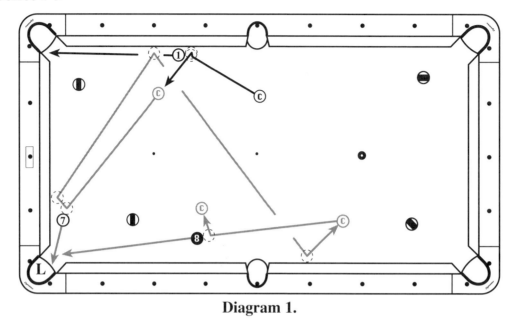

Diagram 1.

Diagram 1: Identifying out sequences is the key to victory in Last Pocket 8–Ball.

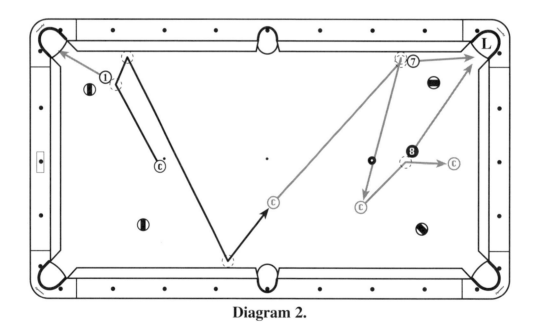

Diagram 2.

Diagram 2: Notice that most of these position plays are based on *1–2–3 System* shots.

Last Pocket #10

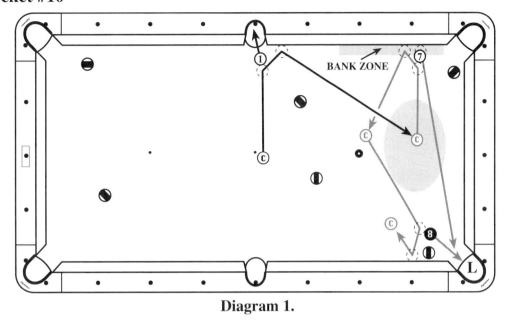

Diagram 1.

Diagram 1: Here are some Last Pocket bank sequences that come up now and then.

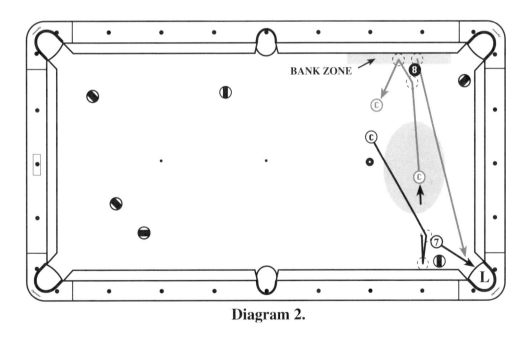

Diagram 2.

Diagram 2: As long as the shooter gets a square angle on the bank ball this should be a 90%+ shot.

I'd go for this pattern any time the position shown for the 8–ball is possible. No decent shooter should bypass this sequence because little banks like these are almost as certain as straight in shots.

Of course, you have to invest a little time learning the nuances of spin and speed that control these bank angles.

Last Pocket # 11

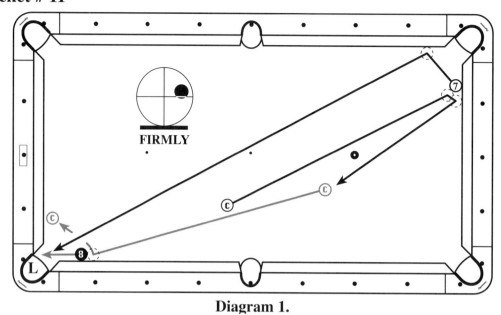

Diagram 1.

Diagram 1: One of the appealing features of Last Pocket 8–Ball is that players are often forced to attempt interesting shots like the two–rail bank above. If you are a One Pocket player this percentage shot should be familiar. You can clock these shots by observing where the object ball hits the second cushion on successful attempts. Forming an accurate mental image of the shot is essential for good results.

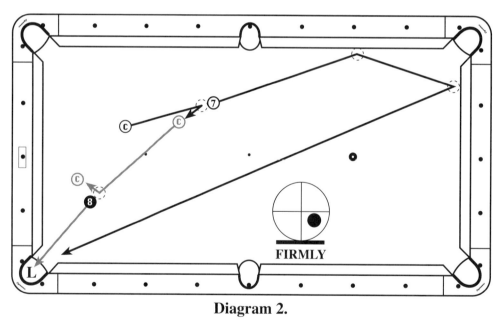

Diagram 2.

Diagram 2: Here's another One Pocket bank that may come up. Using right–hand english stiffens the rebound angle off the second cushion making this bank possible.

These are not high percentage shots for most players, but when there's no choice you might as well have a go at a two–railer. If you make the shot you win and at the very least you should leave the 7–ball in the vicinity of pocket **L** to create a potential Last Pocket finish.

Last Pocket #12

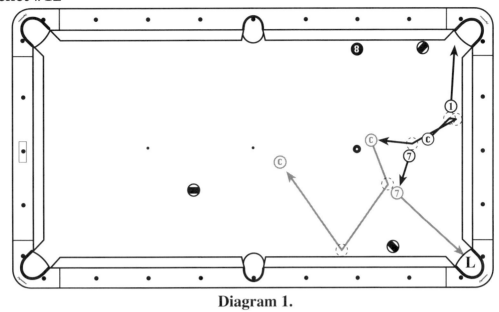

Diagram 1.

Diagram 1: Getting a Last Pocket out sequence sometimes requires skill and imagination, but what else is there?

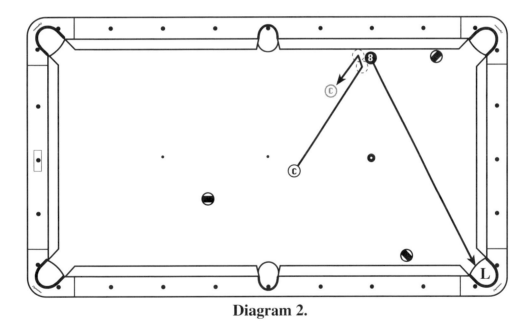

Diagram 2.

Diagram 2: Good bankers have an edge in Last Pocket 8–Ball

Last Pocket #13

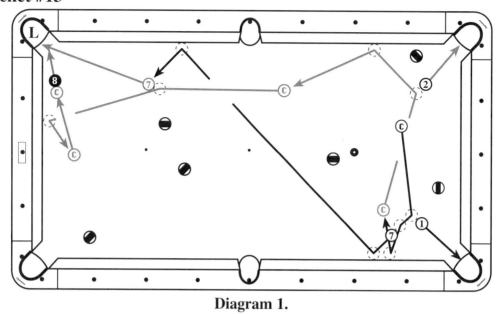

Diagram 1.

Diagram 1: Many times you must rearrange the furniture to get out in Last Pocket 8–Ball.

The play here is to drive the 7–ball down toward the 8–ball to create a Last Pocket sequence.

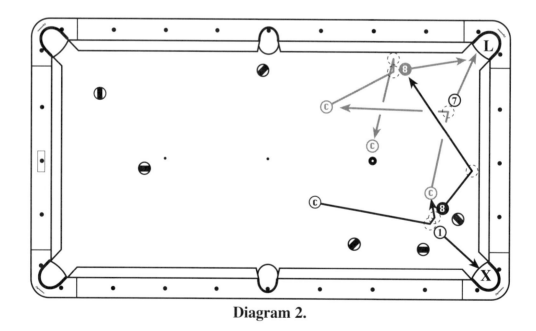

Diagram 2.

Diagram 2: The stripes crowding the 1–ball and the 8–ball prevent a Last Pocket sequence into pocket **X**, so moving the 8–ball cross table is necessary for a Last Pocket finish.

Last Pocket #14

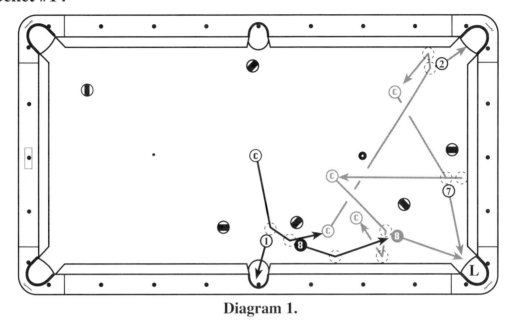

Diagram 1.

Diagram 1: Sending the 8–ball closer to corner **L** creates a Last Pocket ending.

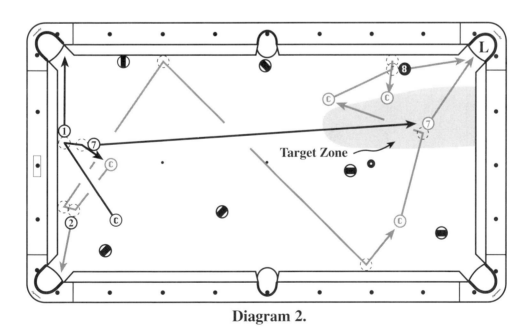

Diagram 2.

Diagram 2: Driving an object ball nearly the length of the table is usually a bad idea, but Last Pocket often demands such desperate and dangerous measures.

Attempts to create Last Pocket sequences by moving balls should be done as early in the rack as possible while there are supporting balls available to fit into a pattern.

Last Pocket #15

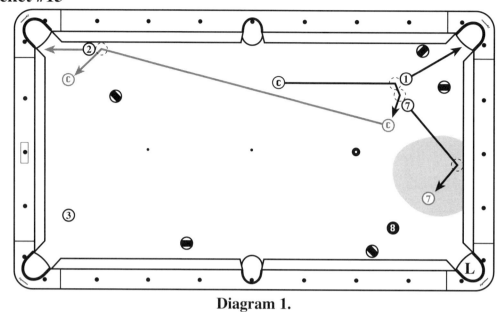

Diagram 1.

Diagram 1: When you have the opportunity to nudge a ball into a good Last Pocket position take it.

As long as the 7–ball lands on the Last Pocket side of the table without getting tied up with the 8–ball this should be a winning move.

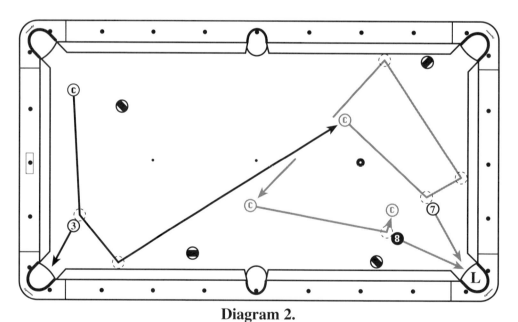

Diagram 2.

Diagram 2: This is a winner because there are at least four simple ways to make a good Last Pocket shot off the 7–ball depending on exactly where the cue ball lands.

The main thing is to remember is that the Last Pocket sequence takes precedence over all other concerns in this game.

The only hope to win after making a serious mistake with the last ball is for your opponent to *give* the game back.

Last Pocket # 16

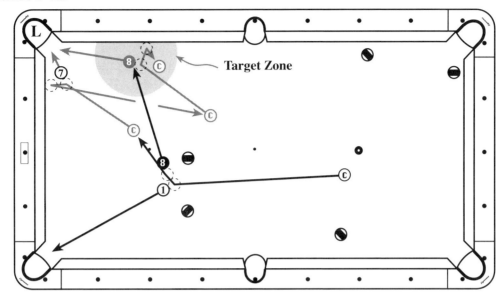

Diagram 1: When there is no last ball to 8–ball sequence available you must create one. Driving the 8–ball in front of pocket **L** makes the 7–ball a good last ball shot.

Focus on landing the 8–ball in the **Target Zone** so you do not tie up the 7–ball.

Last Pocket sequences often create a surprisingly easy end game flow in regular 8–ball.

Last Pocket has the wonderful effect of riveting a player's attention on figuring good patterns. Being forced to think ahead and choose shots carefully improves performance in regular 8–ball where simpler problems are involved.

It goes without saying that missing the last ball or the eight ball has dire consequences because your intentions are clearly seen and your plans will be easy to thwart.

In Last Pocket the last three or four balls in your group and the 8–ball should be made at the same time whenever possible. Going for a run when the end game sequence is not clear will beat you.

Last Pocket #17

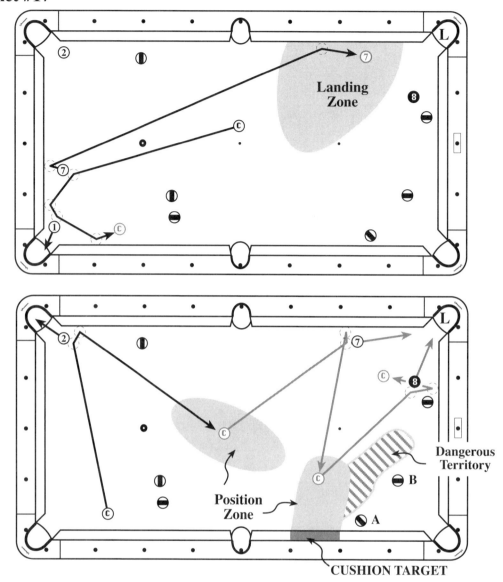

At first glance solids doesn't have a Last Pocket sequence, but creative thinking makes this position a winner. Just bank the 7–ball into the **Landing Zone** while making the 1–ball with a carom and you have a good Last Pocket finish available.

Take care to avoid snarling up the Last Pocket Sequence to the 8–ball and do *not* to make the 7–ball or your Last Pocket pattern will evaporate.

Once the 7–ball is positioned in the **Landing Zone** solids has an easy victory.

One of the things I really like about Last Pocket is the necessity to come up with clever moves and insightful shot patterns.

Here's a tip on pattern play. Even though making the 8–ball would be simple in the hatched area, I never give a thought to playing the position that way because over the years I've been tied up by balls like **Stripes A** and **B** a zillion times when I ignored the risk. The **Position Zone** is smaller, but risk–free. Using the *1-2-3 System* makes it easy to hit the **Cushion Target** between the second and third diamonds where there's no danger of getting tied up.

Last Pocket #18

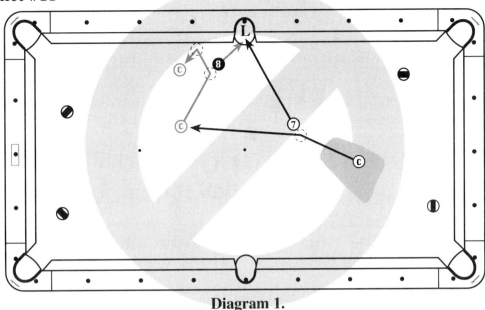

Diagram 1.

Diagram 1: It's no secret among Last Pocket players that the side pockets are the least desirable choice for a Last Pocket. First off, the pattern for a side is almost always more difficult than for a corner. Second, if you miss a side the eight can be played safe in half the table. Three, it is often impossible to avoid driving the eight to an unplayable location when it cannot be made in a side.

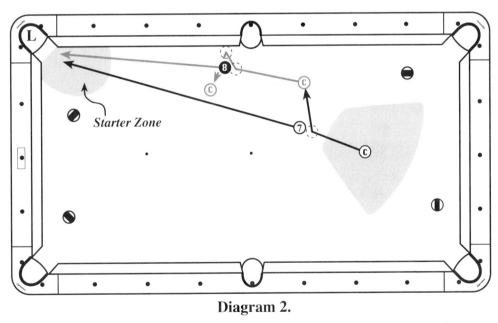

Diagram 2.

Diagram 2: The position area for a corner finish is usually bigger than for a side and if you miss a corner shot there's some chance you'll get a subsequent play at the ball while a side pocket miss usually means no more good shots at the 8–ball.

The side pocket lesson becomes crystal clear after one or two frustrating episodes where you cannot get out in a side even though the opposition repeatedly misses. All the opposition needs to do is leave the cue ball at one end or the other of the table and the 8–ball is virtually unplayable in a side.

Anytime you chose a side for a Last Pocket you must be absolutely sure to complete the game on the first try because against a fair player that's the only good shot you'll ever get.

WIN $50

CONTRIBUTE A SHOT TO A FUTURE EDITION OF
The Eight Ball Bible

If you have discovered a felony sentence safety, a great shot, a deadly shot-safety or a winning maneuver submit the shot(s) or the pattern for use in a future edition of **The Eight Ball Bible**.

If you have a cautionary shot that usually goes wrong that will also be considered.

If your shot is selected for use you will receive $50, credit for the idea in the text and a free copy of the updated book.

Send Submissions to:

8–BALL EXPRESS — Submissions
316 CALIFORNIA AVE #529
RENO, NV
89509

If similar shots are submitted the first entry will be paid.

To be considered, shots must be repeatable at least 10% of the time. If a precise ball path is required measure the contact points, angles etc used in your diagrams.

All shots will be tested before acceptance.

Performance Diary

Many players find it helpful to keep a graphic record of their progress and thinking about the game.

Make copies of the tables on the next page for mapping out shots and patterns that cause trouble. Often a diagram makes clear what is difficult to see during play.

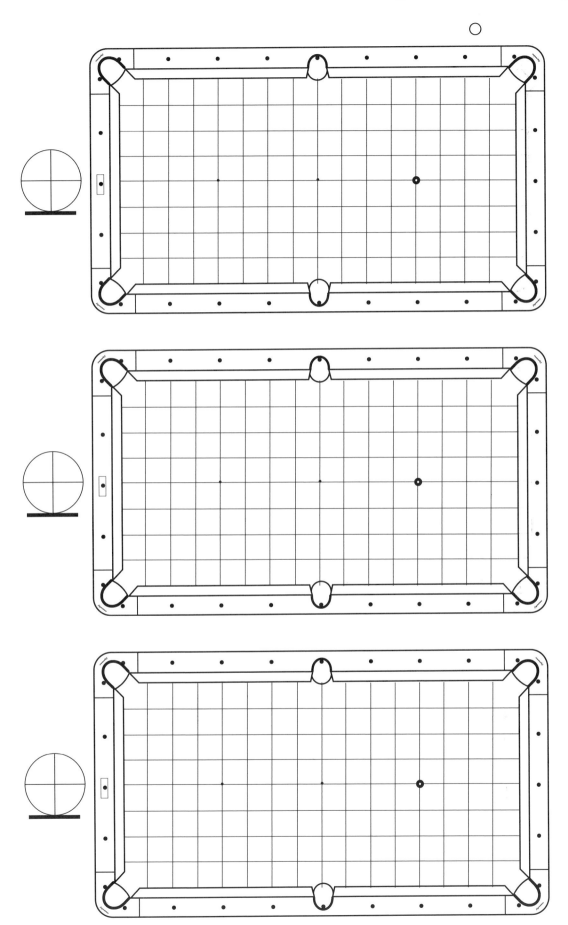

277
3138

100%
SATISFACTION GUARANTEED

If you are displeased with **THE EIGHT BALL BIBLE** for any reason return the book for full refund of purchase price + S & H and return postage.[1]

When returning a damaged copy for replacement write **REPLACEMENT** on the mailing label. Refunds should likewise be marked **REFUND**.

Books must be returned within 30 days for refund or replacement.

Return to:

> **8–BALL BIBLE**
> **1230 MARKET #643**
> **SAN FRANCISCO, CA**
> **94102**

[1]Return postage reimbursed at Flat Rate Envelope (EP14F) rate — $3.85 — EP14F Flat Rate Envelopes available free at US Post Offices.

NEW ORDERS

THE EIGHT BALL BIBLE
$29.95 + $4.00 S & H

PHONE — **1-877-Do8-BALL** (toll free)
(1-877-368-2255)

ONLINE — **www.8-BallBIBLE.com**

MAIL — **8-BALL BIBLE**
316 CALIFORNIA AVE #529
SEND **RENO, NV**
CHECK **89509-1650**
OR
MONEY ORDER